ll
SEPTEMBER

RELIGIOUS PERSPECTIVES ON THE CAUSES
AND CONSEQUENCES

RELATED TITLES PUBLISHED BY ONEWORLD

The Call of the Minaret, Kenneth Cragg, ISBN 1–85168–210–4
Christianity and Other Religions: Selected Readings, Edited by John Hick and Brian Hebblethwaite, ISBN 1–85168–279–1
A Concise Encyclopedia of Islam, Gordon D. Newby, ISBN 1–85168–295–3
Ethics in the World Religions, Edited by Joseph Runzo and Nancy M. Martin, ISBN 1–85168–247–3
Interfaith Theology: A Reader, Edited by Dan Cohn-Sherbok, ISBN 1–85168–276–7
Inter-religious Dialogue: A Short Introduction, Martin Forward, ISBN 1–85168–275–9
Islam: A Short Introduction, Abdulkader Tayob, ISBN 1–85168–192–2
Islam and the West, Norman Daniel, ISBN 1–85168–129–9
Muslims and Christians Face to Face, Kate Zebiri, ISBN 1–85168–133–7
The Palestine–Israeli Conflict: A Beginner's Guide, Dan Cohn-Sherbok and Dawoud El-Alami, ISBN 1–85168–261–9
What Muslims Believe, John Bowker, ISBN 1–85168–169–8

11
SEPTEMBER

RELIGIOUS PERSPECTIVES ON THE CAUSES
AND CONSEQUENCES

Edited by
Ian Markham and Ibrahim M. Abu-Rabi'

ONEWORLD
OXFORD

SEPTEMBER 11: RELIGIOUS PERSPECTIVES ON THE CAUSES
AND CONSEQUENCES

Oneworld Publications
(Sales and Editorial)
185 Banbury Road
Oxford OX2 7AR
England
http://www.oneworld-publications.com

ISBN 1–85168–308–9

Cover design by Design Deluxe
Typeset by Saxon Graphics Ltd, Derby, UK
Printed and bound in Britain by Bell & Bain Ltd, Glasgow

CONTENTS

Part III BROADER ISSUES

CONTRIBUTORS

IBRAHIM M. ABU-RABI' is co-Director of the Duncan Black Macdonald Center for the Study of Islam and Christian–Muslim Relations at Hartford Seminary and Professor of Islamic Studies and Christian–Muslim Relations. He is Senior Editor of the journal *Muslim World* published by Hartford Seminary. Dr. Abu-Rabi' earned his Ph.D. from Temple University in Islamic Studies (1987), two M.A. degrees, one from Temple University in Religious Studies, and the other from the University of Cincinnati in Political Science (1982). Born in Nazareth, Israel, and now a U.S. citizen, Dr. Abu-Rabi' has made research trips to Turkey, India, Hong Kong, Portugal, and elsewhere. He is a leading Islamic specialist in Islamic Revivalism and his books include: *Secularization and Its Discontents: The Recent Debate in the Arab World; Islam at the Crossroads: On the Life and Thought of Bediuzzaman Said Nursi (2002)*; and *Intellectual Origins of Islamic Resurgence in the Modern Arab World* (1996).

EFRAIN AGOSTO is Director of *El Programa de Ministerios Hispanos* at Hartford Seminary and Professor of New Testament. He is a graduate of Gordon-Conwell Theological Seminary and completed his Ph.D. in New Testament Studies from Boston University. Dr. Agosto teaches, researches, and writes on the Pauline Epistles, especially the leadership and ministry of Paul and others in these communities. He is writing *Leadership in the New Testament*. He serves on the Selection Committee and as a Mentor for the Hispanic Theological Initiative, a scholarship and mentoring effort to develop Latino and Latina doctoral candidates in religion and theology.

JACK W. AMMERMAN is the Librarian and Director of Educational Technology at Hartford Seminary. He holds a M.Div. from Southern Baptist Theological Seminary, a M.Ln. from Emory University and a D.Min. from Princeton Theological Seminary. He is an ordained minister in the Baptist Church. He has written widely on educational issues and technology.

NANCY T. AMMERMAN is Professor of Sociology of Religion at Hartford Seminary's Hartford Institute for Religion Research. She holds a Ph.D. from Yale University's Department of Sociology (1983) and an M.A. from the University of Louisville's Department of Sociology. Her undergraduate degree from Southwest Baptist University in Bolivar, Missouri (1972), was in American History and Sociology. Her early work focused on conservative religious movements and her publications include: *Bible Believers: Fundamentalists in the Modern World* (1987) and *Baptist Battles: Social Change and Religious Conflict in the Southern Baptist Convention* (1990). She has contributed chapters to several books on fundamentalism and edited the section on Christian movements for the volume *Accounting for Fundamentalisms*, part of The Fundamentalism Project of the American Academy of Arts and Sciences. Over the last decade, her focus has been on the role of congregations in U.S. religious and social life, with her 1997 book, *Congregation and Community*, focusing on religious responses to urban social change. She is currently examining the organizational networks that link congregations to persons, communities, and the world beyond.

KELTON COBB is Professor of Theology and Ethics and Seminary Academic Advisor at Hartford Seminary. He received his M.Div. from Princeton Theological Seminary (1983–1985) and Ph.D. in Theology and Ethics at the University of Iowa (1986–1994). Dr. Cobb works in the areas of systematic theology, environmental ethics, comparative ethics, public theology, theology and anthropology, and theology of culture.

CARL S. DUDLEY is Professor of Church and Community at Hartford Seminary's Hartford Institute for Religion Research. He is a graduate of Cornell University and Union Theological Seminary (New York), with a Doctor of Ministry from McCormick Theological Seminary. He served as a pastor in First Presbyterian Church of Buffalo, N.Y. and Berea Presbyterian Church in St. Louis, Missouri. He is nationally known for his work in mobilizing local churches for community ministries, and for supporting such causes as peace, civil rights, and housing reform. In 2000 he received the 2000 Higher Education Honors Award from the General Assembly of the Presbyterian Church, U.S., for lifetime professional contribution. His most recent publications include: *Congregations In Transition: A Guide for Analyzing, Assessing, and Adapting in Changing Communities* (with Nancy Ammerman); *Effective Small Churches in the 21st Century: Carrying Faith Into The Future*; and *Community Ministries: Proven Steps and New Challenges in Faith-Based Initiatives.*

JUDY FENTRESS-WILLIAMS is Director of the Black Ministries Program at Hartford Seminary and Professor of Hebrew Scriptures. She is a graduate of Yale University (1999), where she earned her Ph.D. in Religious Studies. Other scholastic achievements include a M.Div. from Yale University and an A.B. in English from Princeton University. She was the recipient of the John A. Wade Prize for great originality in expository preaching (1988–1990), a Dissertation Fellowship from Yale University (1993–1994) and the Henry Axelrod Fellowship (1992–1993).

HEIDI GEHMAN is a Ph.D. student at the University of Chicago Divinity School and is writing a dissertation entitled "Conscience and the Valuing Self: Iris Murdoch and H. Richard Niebuhr on the Formation of Moral Character." She holds a M.Div. from Princeton Theological Seminary (1994) and currently teaches as an Adjunct Professor at Hartford Seminary. She has published a number of book reviews in the *Journal of Religion* and is the recipient of numerous academic awards, including the Senior Prize in Theology from Princeton Theological Seminary in 1994 and the University of Chicago's Century Fellowship for the years 1995/96–1997/98.

HEIDI HADSELL is President of Hartford Seminary and Professor of Social Ethics. A graduate of the University of California (Berkeley) (B.A.), Union Theological Seminary (New York) (M.A.), and the University of Southern California (Ph.D. in Social Ethics), Dr. Hadsell has taught at: the University of Santa Catarina, Brazil; McCormick Theological Seminary (where she was also dean); and the Ecumenical Institute of the World Council of Churches, Switzerland (where she was also director). Her academic work has focused on globalization, environmental change (in Brazil in particular), and ecumenism, including leadership in the World Alliance of Reformed Churches.

IAN S. MARKHAM is Dean of Hartford Seminary and Professor of Theology and Ethics. He has degrees from the Universities of London, Cambridge

(M.Litt.), and Exeter (Ph.D.). He is the author of several books including *Plurality and Christian Ethics* (1994) and *Truth and the Reality of God* (1999). He is an active participant in the Interfaith Foundation. In 1996 Dr. Markham was the Frank Woods Fellow at Trinity College, Melbourne, and in 2000 he was the Claggett Fellow attached to Washington National Cathedral. He is a Visiting Professor at Liverpool Hope University College in the United Kingdom.

INGRID MATTSON is Professor of Islamic Studies and Christian–Muslim Relations at Hartford Seminary and Associate Editor of the *Muslim World* journal published by the Seminary. Her educational achievements include a Ph.D. (1999) from the University of Chicago in Islamic Studies and a B.A. (Honors, 1987) from the University of Waterloo in Philosophy and Fine Arts. Dr. Mattson researches Islamic law and history in classical Arabic texts. She was elected Vice President of the Islamic Society of North America in 2001 and serves on the Board of Advisors for the Nawawi Foundation of Chicago, IL, and the American Muslim Council in Washington, DC.

MIRIAM THERESE WINTER, a Medical Mission Sister, is Director of the Women's Leadership Institute at Hartford Seminary and Professor of Liturgy, Worship, and Spirituality. She has composed and produced fifteen CD/cassette collections (including the gold record album *Joy is Like the Rain; Hymns Re-Imagined* and *Spirit Song*) and is author of a dozen books, including: *Out of the Depths: The Story of Ludmila Javorova, Ordained Roman Catholic Priest; The Singer and the Song: An Autobiography of the Spirit; The Chronicles of Noah and Her Sisters: Genesis and Exodus According to Women; The Gospel According to Mary: A New Testament for Women;* and, *WomanWord: Women of the New Testament.* She also wrote, with Adair Lummis and Alison Stokes, *Defecting in Place: Women Claiming Responsibility for Their Own Spiritual Lives.*

ACKNOWLEDGEMENTS

The editors would like to thank Novin Doostdar of Oneworld for the support that he has given to the project, Yvonne Bowen-Mack for overseeing the project, and the benefactors, corporators, trustees, staff, students, and friends of Hartford Seminary who create the environment that enables us to discuss these questions with each other.

Finally, we acknowledge with sadness the many victims of September 11 and its aftermath; we continue to pray for the devastated lives of their families and friends.

INTRODUCTION

"Today, fellow citizens, our way of life, our very freedom came under attack in a series of deliberate and deadly terrorist acts. The victims were in airplanes or in their offices: secretaries, businessmen and women, military and federal workers, moms and dads, friends and neighbors. Thousands of lives were suddenly ended by evil, despicable acts of terror."
President George Bush

"I beg God to sustain you and the American people in this hour of suffering and trial."
Pope John Paul II

"This mass terrorism is the new evil in our world today. It is perpetrated by fanatics who are utterly indifferent to the sanctity of human life."
Prime Minister Tony Blair

"We are completely shocked. It's unbelievable."
Yasser Arafat

"I prayed for all the families and for all the people who died. But I'm afraid. If our sadness turns into violence, we're going to turn out just like those bad people in the airplanes."
Shirley Wepherhold (8-year-old girl lighting a candle in Union Square)

"Mohammed. Oh God! He is so decent, so shy and tender."
The father of Mohammed Atta, a hijacker

"My family and I still wrestle with what has happened, but are comforted with the knowledge that a sovereign God is in control and that 'God is not a God of disorder, but of peace.'" (I Corinthians 14: 33)
Lisa Beamer, wife of Todd Beamer who died on Flight 93

Coping in our modern world often is a matter of understanding complexity and the unthinkable. We seek clarity and simplicity, and are innately optimistic. Today, however, the modern world has assaulted our optimism to a point where we struggle to understand, or to cope. We have mechanisms that inflict destruction, and passion to use them, which are new to the world. Our response to such destruction often involves courses of action that are marked by moral ambiguity.

September 11, 2001 illustrates the complexity of coping that confronts us. We must come to terms with the "skill" required to embark on the destruction of the World Trade Center in New York, the thousands of devastated lives, and the gargantuan task of responding appropriately. The temptation when confronted with such complexity is to resort to silence. Silence, at least, ensures that we avoid the platitudinous or fatuous. Yet silence also ensures that we do not start to grapple with the complexity. It makes it less likely that our subsequent actions will be considered and reflective. So it is, with some nervousness and trepidation, that the faculty of Hartford Seminary invites you to join a conversation about who we are and what is happening in our society after September 11.

When approaching complexity, we do so with humility and with a strong commitment to pluralism. This book promises no answers. Instead as you turn the pages, you are joining us on a journey to understand the events of September 11 and the aftermath. We come from different places to our task. One editor is a Christian; the other is a Muslim. Worshippers in different Christian denominations, as well as Muslims, are represented in these pages. Understanding the complexity surrounding September 11 requires us to understand the views of the Other. Many of the differences between contributors are painful and significant, but we all believe that it is important that we learn to engage with these painful disagreements. This book will invite you to hear those disagreements and participate in them.

We also are all theologians. We are utterly persuaded that at the heart of "understanding" is theology. Theology touches everything. As Christians and

Muslims, we share a belief in a God who created and sustains everything that is. Many have asked where God was as the airplanes were flown into the World Trade Center and the Pentagon. Many have wondered about "true Islam" and how those who committed these acts could claim to be acting in the name of Allah. From all this arises the imperative to commit to dialogue and find constructive ways in which the strengths of our faith traditions might be used to alleviate the destructive tendencies of the traditions. There is much work for those of us who belong to religious traditions to persuade our fellow travelers of appropriate ways to join in dialogue in the modern world. And our religious traditions can enable us to consider the whole cluster of ethical questions that have arisen. Is the war just? How do we balance human rights and the need for security?

We do not promise to reflect on all your questions, but we do promise to make a beginning.

The opening chapter written by Heidi Gehman locates the fact of the tragedy and identifies some of the primary questions provoked by it. Gehman takes us back to H. Richard Niebuhr and his call for appropriate "reflection" in the context of war. Setting the scene for the tone of much that follows, Gehman raises the different questions and the difficult perspectives that need to be taken into consideration when thinking about September 11.

We then move to the first section of the book called the "Cultural and Social Context". Ibrahim M. Abu-Rabi' provides a masterful survey of the Muslim world. He provides an important mapping article that helps us understand relations between the Muslim world and the West, identifying three major factors that have shaped the Muslim world: modernization, nationalism, and Islamic revivalism. Much of his chapter is descriptive, although as with all description there are significant implications.

We then move to the American context. Nancy T. Ammerman suggests that the United States' response to September 11 illustrates the existence of social capital in America. She takes on the gloomier prognosis of Robert Putnam and others, who argue that American individualism has eroded social capital and demonstrates, decisively, that the reaction to September 11 shows a more positive view. In the same venue, Carl S. Dudley examines the devastating impact of September 11 upon welfare, philanthropy, and faith-based community ministries in the United States, suggesting several ways for congregations to adapt constructively to changed and challenging conditions.

The second section deals with the task of theological reflection. Ingrid Mattson sets the tone for Muslims. In addition to unequivocally condemning the terrorism, she also reflects upon the need for Islamic leaders who are grounded in the faith of Islam and willing to encourage both America to live up to the highest ethical ideals of justice and also Muslims to be equally willing to face up to injustice within their own community. She is calling for leadership grounded in faith.

Miriam Therese Winter reflects on the combination of patriotism and spirituality in a post-September 11 world. Located firmly in the New Physics (that demonstrates our fundamental interconnectedness), she argues that many of our reactions were spiritual. Her hope is that there is an emerging American spirituality that is constructed on such concepts as "spontaneity", "generosity", "hospitality", "compassion", "courage", "community", "adaptability", and perhaps most surprisingly "patriotism."

Kelton Cobb is a Christian theologian who confronts the violent strands that are found not only in Christianity, but also in Islam and Judaism. He suggests that contemporary Jewish attitudes to the non-Jew in Israel/Palestine and Islamic fears of a Zionist conspiracy feed on deeper underlying myths that are grounded in Scripture. He argues that admitting the extent of the problem is the first step to finding ways to ameliorate it.

The responsibility of theologians in advancing inter-religious relations in a post-September 11 world is taken up in the next two chapters from specialists in biblical studies. Efrain Agosto suggests that Christians should go back to Jesus and Paul. He finds in the ministry of Jesus and that of Paul a strong commitment to the marginalized and an insistence that we must work with others. Perhaps most significantly, Agosto argues that Jesus and Paul call for "humility" in our dealings with others and urges us to avoid the temptations of a violent response that can often obscure a fundamental hubris.

In a similar vein, Judy Fentress-Williams identifies a distinctively biblical argument for "dialogue." It is an argument that should appeal to both Christians and Jews. For, argues Fentress-Williams, embedded in the structure of the Hebrew Bible narratives is a commitment to different viewpoints in conversation. Given that explicit commitments to "pluralism" and "dialogue" are not found in the Hebrew Bible and Christian scriptures, it is striking that the use of biblical criticism creates a resource that is so important. Both Agosto and Fentress-Williams have begun the task of helping the faith traditions (in this case Christian) to find resources, within their own traditions, for a positive attitude to the other.

Ian Markham takes up the theme of "dialogue" in his essay. He argues that September 11 illustrates the need to move from "surface" dialogue, which involves a polite interchange, to the "science" of dialogue, which involves a more rigorous examination of world perspective, cultural presupposition, and the various explanations for disagreement. He suggests that if you look at reactions to September 11 in the United States most fall into one of four positions: the first is the mainstream American interpretation – a struggle between democratic pluralism and totalitarian Islamism; the second is a pro-Jewish interpretation that stresses the parallels between September 11 for America and the continuing problem of terrorism within Israel; the third is a pro-Arab interpretation that concedes that nothing justifies September 11 but says that the context that evoked such anger needs to be taken into account; and the fourth is the fundamentalist, religious interpretation.

In the third section, "Broader Issues," we start exploring the broader issues. At moments like this, the issue of the collection of data is especially important. We are already aware that our recollection of that vivid sense of shock is being displaced by the more mundane worries about the demise of big companies and the looming recession. Jack Ammerman provides a strong argument that there is an obligation on libraries to start "collecting ephemera," otherwise such moments are not documented accurately. Even though the task of selecting appropriately is difficult, it is essential to try. Heidi Hadsell explores the particular problem of terrorism and civil rights. Mindful that many other parts of the world have not managed to get this balance, Hadsell provides a warning that it is important that Americans do not make the same mistake.

It is perhaps necessary to stress that no one of us represents Hartford Seminary. Each contributor is simply expressing his or her own views. We are all very aware of the differences among ourselves, but these are differences that we believe are important to articulate and explore together. We are inviting you to get annoyed with some contributions, agree, perhaps, with others, but most important of all, participate in taking seriously the issues that are so important as we learn to live in a world changed by September 11.

Ibrahim M. Abu-Rabi' and Ian Markham
Editors

I

SEPTEMBER 11:
THE TERRORIST ATTACK ON AMERICA

Heidi Gehman

THE DAY OF TERROR

The morning of September 11, 2001, was at first only unusual because of the exceptional brilliance of late summer. The clear weather held for days, as this nation and the world looked on uncomprehendingly at the unfolding devastation of terrorist attacks on the two towers of the World Trade Center in New York City, the Pentagon in Virginia, and the crash of a hijacked jet in southwestern Pennsylvania. The coordination of the attacks and the ensuing destruction and loss of life as well as the method of the attacks were unfathomable that day, and so they remain. Here is what we know.

The first news reports simply stated that an airplane had hit one of the World Trade Towers, and the building had a gaping, burning hole in it. It was 8:48 a.m. on a Tuesday morning. Soon it became clear that it was a fairly large jet that had crashed into 1 World Trade Center, also called the south tower, and all TV stations then had their cameras trained on the towers. The panic in the building coupled with the confusion outside and in the second building, where some heard an announcement not to evacuate, soon became a general panic at 9:03 a.m. As a second plane flew over the city and into the second tower, there was an exploding of glass and fire out the other side. The clear image of the plane hitting the north tower of the World Trade Center, caught from various angles on camera, is imprinted on all of our minds.

In Sarasota, Florida, President Bush was speaking to an elementary school when he heard news of the first crash. He continued with his program, but on hearing of the second airplane, Bush made a brief statement condemning terrorism at 9:15 a.m. He was then spirited away by the Secret Service. The rest of us continued to stare at television screens or listen to radios, trying to understand what could be going on.

The horror of the situation was very clear to those in New York who were trying to escape or trying to help. Firefighters and police swarmed to the scene. Those in the twin towers and surrounding buildings had to decide what to do, and how to do it. People on the streets watched small objects plummet from the building, which they slowly realized to be bodies, either jumping or falling, some on fire. In the days following September 11, harrowing details emerged about what precisely was going on at this time – cellular 'phone conversations to loved ones, scrambles down smoke-filled hallways and flights of stairs, snap decisions that saved or lost lives. And there was more to come.

At around 9:45 a.m., a third aircraft that had been on a course toward the White House turned and smashed into the Pentagon, the home of the National Military Command Center and symbol of American military might. News of this was just getting out when, at 9:58 a.m. the most devastating aspect of the attacks unfolded. The north tower, the second one hit, began to collapse, as the floors exploded in glass and smoke, and fell one by one until the entire building collapsed in on itself as a torrent of debris and smoke billowed up and out from the site. Ash and dust coated people who were able to run ahead of the falling building and obscured lower Manhattan. It was an unbelievable sight of destruction that, even more than the sight of the second airplane, brought the reality and magnitude of this attack home. In less than two hours after the first plane struck, both 110-storey buildings were gone and Americans realized that the U.S. was not invulnerable to devastating terrorist attacks.

As the dust cloud from the collapse of the first tower billowed out from New York, and the slow clearing revealed that the entire tower was gone, news of a fourth airplane crashing in Pennsylvania at 10:10 a.m. came across the airwaves and added to the panic thought that this was just the beginning. The collapse of the entire second tower in New York at 10:28 a.m. marked the end of the immediate effect of the attacks, but more than three months later Americans had still to lose the feeling of imminent danger and to recover a sense of security. This marks the loss of the usual way of life in America as so many commented on in the days following September 11.

Physical destruction, injury and loss of life, and loss of a way of life are three of many dramatic effects of the terrorist attacks in the U.S. and in the world. In the rest of this chapter, I will briefly sketch these effects and reflect upon the moral, religious, and political questions we are left to struggle with post-September 11.

THE FALLOUT

The method of using commercial airliners as weapons was both carefully coordinated and highly effective in causing the maximum physical destruction imaginable. The four aircraft departed within one hour of each other, all bound for California from the East Coast. American Airlines Flight 11 left Boston for Los Angeles and crashed into 1 World Trade Center. United Airlines Flight 175 left Boston for Los Angeles and hit the second tower of the World Trade Center. American Airlines Flight 77 flew out of Washington's Dulles Airport bound for Los Angeles and hit the Pentagon. United Airlines Flight 93 was flying from Newark, NJ to San Francisco and crashed in Pennsylvania. Two of the airplanes were Boeing 767s and two were Boeing 757s. All had a small number of passengers and a large amount of fuel for the cross-country flight. It was the intense heat of thousands of gallons of burning jet fuel that caused the collapse of the twin towers in New York, according to construction experts.[1] The collapse of the World Trade Towers and the resultant fires caused untold damage to surrounding buildings as well. By early evening, 5 and 7 World Trade Center, two smaller buildings in the complex, also had collapsed.

At the Pentagon, the jet smashed into the west side of the building, which had recently undergone renovations. The aircraft hit between the first and second floors of the five-storey building and penetrated the first three of five concentric rings of the building. Blast resistant windows and other protective features in the building's construction helped, but a portion of the building collapsed shortly after the crash.

Flight 93 crashed in a field in Pennsylvania, its target unknown. Like the others, the full-throttle speed at which it crashed left few large pieces of the plane intact. There was no damage to the surroundings other than the crater left by the plane's impact.

The total death toll from the attacks on September 11, including those still missing and presumed dead was 3,117 as of January 9, 2002, and this does not include the nineteen hijackers. At the World Trade Center, original estimates hovered between 5,000–6,000 a few days after the attack, but that figure has dropped steadily, and on January 9 the *New York Times* reported the total to be

2,893, including 147 on the two airplanes.[2] The total number includes victims from sixty-two countries. New York firefighters suffered a devastating loss of 343 of their comrades who had rushed into the buildings and up the flights of stairs to rescue survivors on the burning floors of the towers. At the Pentagon, the death toll stands at 184, fifty-nine of them on Flight 77. Forty people were on the flight that crashed in Pennsylvania.

Apart from the physical destruction and the loss of life, the horror of which continues to haunt us, the attacks had a reverberating effect on other aspects of life. Air travel, the lifeblood of movement in the United States, was halted completely at 9:40 a.m. on September 11 by the Federal Aviation Administration, the first time ever in commercial air travel. All flights in the air were instructed to land as soon as possible, and incoming flights were diverted to Canada. On September 12, only the diverted flights were allowed to continue their voyage. Frightened people began canceling their flight reservations. More than three months later, with new security measures in place, airlines were still struggling to achieve profitability with fewer flights. Occasional security breaches continue to cause airport shutdowns and huge financial losses. In November, the airport security act made baggage screeners federal employees and required that they be American citizens. The *New York Times* reported on December 12, 2001, that one quarter of 28,000 U.S. baggage screeners were not U.S. citizens. Whether purging these experienced immigrants from the system will make airports more secure remains to be seen.

Bomb threats and evacuation of buildings occurred in New York and around the country in the days following the attacks and this further shook people's sense of security. A case of anthrax reported in Florida on October 5 (at first thought to be the result of contamination from the environment) turned out to be the first in a string of cases. Hoaxes and threats of anthrax had public health officials panicking. It is still unclear whether the anthrax, sent in letters to Senator Tom Daschle, Senator Patrick Leahy, Tom Brokaw at the National Broadcasting Corporation, and to the *New York Post*, was a second wave of terrorism from the perpetrators of September 11, or from some other source. The *New York Times* reported on November 17 that a senior federal law enforcement official said it was believed that a domestic terrorist was responsible. The spores in all instances have been of a similar type and the same type of anthrax that is made at U.S. facilities. Five people died as a result of anthrax infections.

For these and other reasons, the already faltering U.S. economy suffered from the post-September 11 fallout. The economy, subsequently, met the technical definition of a recession, giving rise to the possibility of a worldwide recession. Fear and caution among consumers and businesses as a result of the attacks are at least part of the problem. Some newsmakers have referred to the current economic situation as "Osama's recession."

Before turning to the role of Osama bin Laden and his al-Qaeda network in the September 11 attacks, I want to sketch what people mean when they speak about the American way of life, and whether September 11 has changed it. It was not just people's vulnerability that was highlighted by the attacks, but the fact that the very freedoms of the U.S. open society were exploited, in order to attack civilians, by anonymous attackers with no clear demands. This is typical of modern-day terrorism, but the magnitude and success of the attack on American soil astounded all but a few. The result has been both the proclamation that this will not change the U.S. way of life – with its freedoms and privacy, and security – and the passage of laws that take some of those freedoms away.

The uniqueness of the American way of life can be described, in part, by the conjunction of a free and open society, where privacy and individual rights hold a high place, and the safety enjoyed in the midst of such openness and freedom. It is this balanced combination that will be difficult to maintain in light of September 11. In the days following the attacks, news commentators and others suggested that the American way of life was changed forever by the events. On the evening of September 11, President Bush described the attacks by saying that "our way of life, our very freedom, came under attack."³ At the same time, President Bush and other public officials took a view in line with comments made by former Secretary of State George P. Shultz, who said, "We're not going to allow these terrible people to change our way of life."⁴

As Heidi Hadsell documents there are legitimate concerns about various changes: the presidential order to allow for secret military prosecution of foreign suspects involved in terrorism; the passage of new laws that ban foreign baggage screeners; the monitoring of conversations between suspected terrorists and their lawyers; and the secret detention of non-citizens who are viewed as a threat to national security. According to a *New York Times*/CBS News Poll reported in the *New York Times* on December 12, while many people support these changes, and in particular support the curtailment of freedoms for suspected terrorists and foreigners, they also are worried about the possibility of their own civil liberties being infringed.⁵ This suggests that the American way of life has changed. Citizens are willing to forgo some of their civil liberties, and especially those of foreigners and suspects, in order to feel safe. It may or may not be a fair trade-off, but it is a trade-off. Whether this change in the balance between freedom and security is permanent depends in part on whether there are further attacks, and whether the current change brings about the desired effect – additional safety without glaring or unfair breaches of civil liberties.

This brings us to the final major aspect of the September 11 attacks: the terrorists. Who were they? Why did they do it? How are Americans responding? On the day of the attacks, experts in terrorism pointed to Osama bin Laden, a militant Muslim operating from Afghanistan, where he has been since he was expelled from Saudi Arabia in 1996. The fact that the attacks were highly coordinated and skilled, along with a recent history of similar attacks on American targets, indicated that bin Laden and his al-Qaeda network could be responsible. The ruling Taliban of Afghanistan denied that bin Laden could have carried out such an attack, and there were various suggestions that Israel, American white supremacists, or people from some other country were responsible. In the ensuing investigation, the profile of the hijackers who were all of Arab decent, some with known connection to bin Laden, surprised investigators. The typical stereotype profile of young, indoctrinated zealots with little to lose did not fit these terrorists. Rather, they were older men, educated, and middle class, and some were married with children. Although it is not clear whether all the hijackers realized that they were on a "suicide" mission, it is clear that some decided that they were prepared to sacrifice their lives for the cause.

From the beginning, President Bush vowed to find the culprits and bring them to justice. In his speech on the evening of September 11 he said that the United States would "make no distinction between the terrorists who committed these acts and those who harbor them." The U.S. would "go forward to defend freedom and all that is good and just in our world." The following day, he adopted the language of war. In the war on terror, President Bush proclaimed, you are either "for us or against us," it is a battle of good against evil, and America would rally the world. Indeed, a leading French scholar on international affairs stated, "we are all New Yorkers."[6]

Reaction around the world included the condemnation of terrorism and expressions of solidarity from countries such as Cuba, China, Iran, and Libya. At the same time, state television in Iraq claimed that the U.S. deserved what it got, and in the West Bank people were shown to be cheering and shooting off guns. More shockingly, Jerry Falwell and Pat Robertson, both representatives of American Christian fundamentalism, agreed that the United States deserved the attack because of a failure to quash the views of "abortionists," feminists, gays, and the American Civil Liberties Union (ACLU), among others. From their perspective, God allowed the attack to happen because of the U.S.'s national sins.

The U.S. demands to hand over bin Laden were met with refusal by the Taliban of Afghanistan. They threatened retaliation in kind against any attack on their soil. With broad international support, the U.S. began military action against Afghanistan, the Taliban, and Osama bin Laden and al-Qaeda on October 7. A bombing campaign began, followed by operations by ground troops, the fall of the Taliban in every major city in Afghanistan, and the routing of al-Qaeda forces in the mountain hideout of Tora Bora. A President who claimed not to be a nation-builder has now involved himself in the reconstitution of the Afghan government and peacekeeping plans for the region. The war on terror is far from over – Osama bin Laden and many of his top advisors remain at liberty and the same is true for many Taliban leaders. Despite the growing evidence against bin Laden, including a video tape released by the White House on December 13 in which he happily states that the number of casualties surpassed his wildest dreams and that he did not expect both towers to collapse completely, some Muslims still refuse to believe that he is responsible and suggest that he has been framed.

Where does this leave us? The questions are: who did this, why did they do it, what is the appropriate response? It seems that we know who did it and we are responding with a war on terrorism. In fact, the question of why the terrorists attacked innocent citizens has been raised but not addressed in this essay, any more than it has in much of the public discussion over the events. Why is the United States the target of attack? Jerry Falwell's answer to this was roundly condemned. Was it simply the work of insane criminals filled with hate? Was it religious fanaticism? Was the attack aimed at the open society and pluralism of the U.S., which tends to "dilute purity"? Does the hatred stem from U.S. foreign policy in the Middle East? Are capitalism and globalization the problem? From the perspective of Christian ethics, the question of why this act was committed is, I think, the first moral and religious problem that should be addressed. It is, perhaps, unfortunate that America and her allies have chosen to respond first, and think seriously about the causes later.

THE MORAL, RELIGIOUS, AND POLITICAL ISSUES

As is often the case, in the course of describing what has happened we have already stated, explicitly or implicitly, many of the moral and religious issues. Many of these, along with deeper analysis of the September 11 aftermath, will be discussed at greater length in the chapters which follow, but I offer a simple overview of some of the many immediate moral questions directly related to the attacks.

First, why did this happen, or to put it another way, what is going on? To state it this way is to agree with the theologian H. Richard Niebuhr, who along with others understands moral life to be one of responsibility and responsiveness, that prior to deciding what to do, how to respond, we must ask the question, "What is going on?"[7] This is the primary moral question because a fitting, moral response depends on a fitting, moral interpretation of the events and the context in which one responds. With respect to the response to the September 11 tragedy, this means understanding not only the *how* and *who* of what took place, but also the *why*. Perhaps the current unfolding response of the United States is the proper response – and maybe the only possible response – to this situation, perhaps not. But it seems to me that we have failed to show this one way or another by the lack of reflection, understanding, and dialogue regarding the reasons behind such acts.

Still following Niebuhr, it seems that a clear view of what is going on in such a terrible act of war and the suffering inflicted on the innocent requires repentance, "a total revolution of our minds and hearts."[8] For Niebuhr, repentance includes a willingness to accept some responsibility for a world in which human beings can feel justified in such an act. This is in no way to say that September 11 is justifiable by any stretch of the imagination, or that we have somehow reaped what we deserve, but simply to say that the hatred and anger that motivated it have many sources, and perhaps we need to be willing to recognize our culpability for some of them. In other words, I am drawing a distinction between the immediate act of September 11, which is to be unequivocally condemned, and the context of the action, the conditions which allow terrorism to seem for some a legitimate, or the only possible, response. The U.S. is not responsible for September 11, but may be responsible for some of the conditions that provided the context for it and we should try to identify and correct those conditions.[9] There are other parties who have allowed the conditions for terrorism to flourish, and they, too, should carry out this same kind of analysis.

In an ethics of responsibility, we are partly responsible for others' responses to us. Are there other avenues of action, in conjunction with or other than war, by which we can seek to prevent further terrorist acts and the murder of civilians? Is there something that can be done to stem the hatred evident in such acts? Should there be a questioning of American foreign policy and America's role in the international economy and globalization? Is the current response causing further suffering for the innocent? This kind of questioning, or self-analysis, opens up the possibility that war can be a time for redemption, a time for us to repair what has gone wrong and work toward healing.

This attitude of humility and responsibility has played little role in the stated goals of the U.S. reaction to and retaliation for September 11. The government acts in order to rid the world of evil, "to defend all that is good and just in our world." The moral language of the Bush administration relies on a pure dichotomy between good and evil, and commands the world to see the situation in those Manichean terms. In response to such a horrific act, the language of good versus evil may be appropriate, but it is too easy and too irresponsible to answer the question, "What is going on?" in this way. That the Bush administration referred to the military campaign as a "crusade" and initially named it "Infinite Justice" shows a further lack of religious understanding, not to say moral humility. A moral judgment must be made condemning the acts of September 11. So too must a moral judgment be made regarding our response to it.

Following the general moral question of what is going on, many other more specific moral, political, and religious issues emerge which further complicate and help to explain what is going on. These include the relationship between the Islamic world and the West; the U.S. role in Israel and the Middle East conflict; the notions of freedom fighters and just revolution; war without a defined enemy; civil liberties and security; inter-religious dialogue and understanding religious commitment; the relationship between religious purity and violence; the question of theodicy; and the feminist perspective on "What is going on?" This is not an exhaustive list, but represents what I take to be the most pertinent issues, which now demand our attention.

To fully understand what is going on here, a better appreciation of the relationship between the Islamic world and the West is necessary. Many Muslims feel that their own governments are controlled or at least influenced by U.S. foreign policy in a way that is unfriendly to their freedom to practice their religion. Osama bin Laden's campaign to paint the United States as anti-Muslim seems to be working. It is a political necessity for the U.S. to sort out propaganda from truth here, and to change foreign policy if it does infringe the rights of Muslims. The responsibility of the leaders of Muslim countries, both political and religious, also needs to be examined.

Another significant political issue that has caused resentment amongst Muslims towards the U.S. is the relationship of the U.S. with the State of Israel, and the seeming lack of concern for the Palestinians. A number of chapters in this book explore this. Ibrahim Abu-Rabi' provides a historical survey; Ian Markham and Kelton Cobb touch on the relationship of the West with Israel. The conflict in this area of the world is so deep and complex that I will not say more than that the U.S. must seek to understand its role, both real and perceived, and to be sensitive to the moral and political concerns of both sides.

September 11 is a clear example for most of us of a totally unacceptable method of resistance. But what, now, is a just revolution or a positive definition of a freedom fighter? The issue of what constitutes a legitimate or moral mode of resistance to a political or moral power must be clearly defined or we risk losing these valuable means of challenging overweening authority.

Also problematic is that we are confronted with a war in which there is no country or state as a clear-cut enemy. Who, in fact, is the enemy, and how can we involve ourselves in a war with such an elusive and scattered enemy? The "War on Terrorism" seems as if it stands on morally unquestionable ground because of the unequivocal condemnation we feel for the tragedy, death, and destruction inflicted on innocent civilians. But the difficulty of applying international law, or "just war" criteria, to a war on terror is a new moral problem we must face. There are no clear guidelines for such a war. This also raises a similar question for the pacifists. Does the moral decision to avoid violence and war as a political solution continue to make sense in light of the kind of attack of September 11? How does the pacifist's moral reasoning apply in this war?

Turning to an issue of domestic policy, the balance in America between civil liberties and security is now also a moral, political, and religious issue. Should we allow civil liberties to be curbed by Presidential order in this time of crisis, or should it be a more open process? Should the government have greater power to infiltrate religious groups without clear cause? Is it fair to place greater scrutiny on those of Arab descent without any other warrant? There are no easy answers and the new measures already in place to help the war on terrorism will be likely to result in the unfair treatment of innocent people. Is this a price we are willing to pay for security?

Questions more specifically religious in nature demand our attention. The effort to understand different religions and the power of religious commitment has been happening on informal, personal, and communal levels since the attacks. Mosques have opened their doors to those seeking to understand Islam and the role it may have played. People are listening to the argument that Islam does not support such violence, and are going further to understand what Islam is about. Books on Islam have been extremely popular. There has been more interfaith dialogue and ecumenical services have taken place with greater intensity since September 11. The openness and inclusivity in American society for a diversity of faiths even in the wake of such a religiously motivated and terrible act is impressive. Perhaps this will lead to the effort to understand the role of religions in political and international affairs on a deeper level. More specific questions such as the relationship between faith and politics, the issue of religious freedom, and the possibility for inter-religious dialogue arise here. These issues apply both internally to the U.S. and to its relationships with other countries.

Religious communities have their own new dilemmas. One of them is how to deal with the possibility of violence that may arise in any community that seeks moral and religious purity. As Efrain Agosto notes the role of religious leadership here is crucial. Religious leaders, scholars, and lay people should speak out against acts and words that distort a tradition. This has been done frequently in the condemnation of the terrorist attacks, as well as by Christians who strongly disagree with Jerry Falwell's interpretation of events, but more must be done, both in admitting that such violence and hatred can grow out of legitimate aspects of religious traditions, and in providing arguments from within those same traditions that delegitimate violence. The line between good and evil does not lie between different religions, peoples, or nations, but within every tradition, faith, and community.

Religious leaders must help their constituents to reflect on the more theological question of theodicy – the existence of evil in a world created and ruled by a good God. How could God allow the acts of September 11? This event is not the only one that raises the question of theodicy, but perhaps it will make Americans more sensitive to the suffering of others around the world. The question of theodicy is often a faith-making or faith-breaking question, and religious leaders should help believers to think it through.

The final issue I raise is the feminist perspective on this event. Like the others, this perspective has moral, political, and theological aspects. We must reflect on the fact that, although it is primarily men who are in the direct line of fire in a war, it is often women and children who suffer most in such a conflict. Further, we have to question our sudden concern for the plight of Afghani women, which received little attention from the U.S. government until it needed to portray its military action as right, good, and just. Where was our just concern for these women a few months ago? If we want to rally against misogyny and sexism, perhaps war is not the best method of attack.

There is also the theological question of the status of women in Islam which I leave to the scholars of Islam, but we must bear in mind that the mythology of any religion must be critiqued for the way it guides the treatment of women.

These are a few of the most obvious dilemmas, very briefly sketched, with which we must now be prepared to deal. There are many others. The terrorist attacks of September 11 have shaken the U.S. more than any event since the bombing of Pearl Harbor. As the many acts of heroism during and after the attacks showed, Americans have the moral, religious, and political resources with which to respond. The richness of the democratic tradition, the balance of powers in the government, the free expression of dissent, and the continuing search for religious truth and value in this life will help in the response to this national tragedy.

NOTES

1. "A Day of Terror: The Buildings," *New York Times*, Wednesday, September 12, 2001.
2. "A Nation Challenged: Dead and Missing," *New York Times*, January 9, 2002.
3. "A Day of Terror," *New York Times*, September 12, 2001.
4. "Abroad at Home; A Different World," in Ibid.
5. "A Nation Challenged: Attitudes," *New York Times*, December 12, 2001.
6. "After the Attacks: News Analysis," *New York Times*, September 14, 2001.
7. H. Richard Niebuhr, *The Responsible Self: An Essay in Christian Moral Philosophy* (San Francisco: Harper & Row Publishers, 1963), 60.
8. H. Richard Niebuhr, "War as Crucifixion," *Christian Century*, 60 (April 28, 1943), 515.
9. Sometimes, the context of an action does justify the action. In this case, I suggest that the context does not justify the action, but should nonetheless be considered in our response. Thanks to Ian Markham for helping me to clarify this point.

PART I

THE CULTURAL AND
SOCIAL CONTEXT

2

A POST-SEPTEMBER 11 CRITICAL ASSESSMENT

OF MODERN ISLAMIC HISTORY

Ibrahim M. Abu-Rabi'

"Secularism came to us on the back of a tank, and it has remained under its protection ever since."
Exiled Tunisian Islamist leader Rashid al-Ghannoushi.[1]

INTRODUCTION

The tragic events of September 11, 2001 have raised in the minds of many in the West a number of questions about the connection between the sacred and violence in Islam, and some Western commentators have gone as far as to claim that violence is built into the Qur'an.[2] The main argument of this chapter is that explaining the attacks on the United States in light of "a Qur'anic rationale for violence" dismisses the socio-historical and political context in the modern Muslim world that gave rise to such a terrible act in contemporary human history. Instead of focusing on a "theology of violence," this chapter seeks to shed critical light on the main political, social, and religious dynamics of the modern Muslim world, which have evolved against a complex backdrop of colonization, national independence, and the exhaustion of the nationalist project in many an Arab and Muslim country. To come to grips with the tragedy of September 11, 2001, and the reasons behind the attacks on the United States, one also must delve into the Western impact on the modern Muslim world. Furthermore, one must underline the fact that Americanization, although a relatively new historical phenomenon, has been a leading ideology in the world, particularly since the collapse of the Soviet system in the late 1980s.

In addition to focusing on the role of modernization, nationalism, and religious revivalism in the modern and contemporary Muslim world, this chapter will highlight social and educational changes in Muslim countries, with special reference to Saudi Arabia, home to the two holiest cities in the Muslim world and bin Laden's native country. It is one of the main arguments of this chapter that the Muslim world needs to foster a pluralistic and democratic environment that should be open to a multiplicity of voices, such as nationalism, Islamic revivalism, and secular modernization. It is only by creating such an environment that the Muslim world may reduce the role of the army in society and help create a new secular and religious leadership that is engaged with the challenges and problems of its society.

MODERN HISTORICAL DEVELOPMENTS

The history of the Western world since the fourteenth century, at least, has been inextricably connected with that of the Muslim world. The reconstitution of Europe in the early modern era took place against the background of the hegemony of the Muslim world in North Africa, the Middle East, and Eastern Europe.[3] For example, the fifteenth century witnessed three major events that had an immeasurable impact on the history of Muslim–Western relations: the first was the Ottoman conquest of Constantinople in 1453; the second, the expulsion of the Muslims from Spain; and the third was the unintended European discovery of the new world through the efforts of Columbus.

It is quite difficult to understand the modern formation of Europe apart from these events, which, combined with internal changes in Europe (such as the Reformation), have had a lasting impact on the history of the modern Third World. We often use the terms Reformation, Industrial Revolution, Enlightenment, and Capitalism to refer to specific post-fifteenth century economic, philosophical or religious events, which catapulted Europe to a truly global scale of economic, military, and political activity. The growth of capitalism in European societies in the seventeenth and eighteenth centuries had a far reaching impact on the economic environment of the world, which prompted Europe to colonize many Third World countries in search of cheap resources. European expansion reached its zenith in the nineteenth century, when every erstwhile power in Europe was looking for a colony. Even the smaller European powers were involved in this. Benedict Anderson catches the historical mood of Europe succinctly by arguing that "mottled European imperialism," spanning a period of five centuries, became the norm, "The Portuguese and Spaniards arrived in the late feudal sixteenth century, the Dutch in the mercantilist seventeenth, the British in the enlightened eighteenth, the French in the industrialized nineteenth, and the Americans in the motorized twentieth."[4]

One can locate the genesis of the modern Muslim world in the early modern period of the fifteenth and sixteenth centuries, when three world empires were in the making: 1) The Ottoman Empire based in Turkey; 2) The Safavid Empire based in Persia; and 3) The Mughal Empire based in India. All three of these empires were complex manifestations of the Islamic entity. Far from being a simple religious phenomenon in the above contexts, Islam was highly complex and profoundly intertwined with the economic, political, and cultural realities of these empires. Compared to the early Islamic period of the seventh century, Islam in the early modern period was no longer the pristine simple world of the Prophet and his disciples. All three were multi-religious, multi-ethnic, and multi-glot empires, which understood globalization in their own terms. These empires, however did take Islam as their starting point.

These political and religious formations in the Muslim world began to weaken by the beginning of the nineteenth century for two important reasons: first, the stagnation of central authority and its failure to modernize society before the rise of Europe, and second the expansion of European powers in the Muslim world, as the result of immense internal developments within Europe. The Western colonization of many parts of the Muslim world in the nineteenth century was a reflection of inner Muslim stagnation and the triumph of European models of society and economy. The Muslim world was confused, baffled, and anxious. The Muslim intelligentsia reflected this in many of their writings and speeches in exile, and in political struggles.

The Muslim world's response to the challenges of colonization was multi-faceted. It sought to revive or reconstruct the religious, social, political, and economic institutions of the modern Muslim world. On the whole, three different movements channeled this response: *modernization, nationalism,* and *religious revivalism.*

The European challenge to the Ottoman Empire in the nineteenth century helped awaken the central authority from its slumber and encouraged it to launch an ambitious program of modernization called the *Tanzimat,* which began in the early nineteenth century. The Empire responded by adopting *Tanzimat,* a wholesale modernization of Ottoman society from the top down. The Ottoman political and military elite were aware of the necessity of taking drastic "modernization measures" if they wished to keep the Empire afloat. Most leading Ottoman bureaucrats and the intelligentsia, including the religious intelligentsia, were firmly behind modernization. The ulama [Muslim religious leaders] supported modernization in the hope that "the welfare of the *umma*" would be safeguarded.[5] Although the different nineteenth-century Ottoman Sultans put their weight behind the *Tanzimat*, the process did not prevent the collapse of the Empire by the end of the First World War. Before the Empire unraveled, however, a new breed of secular Ottoman intelligentsia arose, a small group of which saw the salvation of the state in adopting Westernization. They viewed this as the only solution to the backwardness of the state. The discourse of this community of people centered on a new understanding of nationalism, secularism, and progress.

Nationalism, therefore, represents the second tier of the nineteenth-century Muslim response to the predicament of the Muslim world and the Western challenge. Nationalism, in Anderson's celebrated phrase, "is an imagined political community – and imagined as both inherently limited and sovereign."[6] Nationalism is a limited imagining of the nation, much more limited, let us say, than Christendom or the Muslim *umma*. Nationalism did not have to defend a stagnant past, although very often it resorted to inventing its own past in order to give a certain measure of authenticity to its actions. The nationalist movement in the Muslim world led the nation in a struggle against colonialism, which paved the way to creating several nation-states in the Muslim world. As a matter of course, nationalist leaders of the Muslim world did not use religious themes in their speeches or slogans. Such personalities as Ahmed Sukarno in Indonesia, Kemal Atatürk in Turkey, Muhammad 'Ali Jinnah in Pakistan, and Jamal 'Abd al-Nasser in Egypt represent this trend. Being highly charismatic, these founding figures fought for the political independence of their nations from the West while being, at the same time, envious of Western scientific and political achievements. Although they fought political domination by the West, they opted to model their societies according to the Western philosophy of life.

It is interesting to examine the conditions in which Third World nationalisms arose. So much literature has appeared on the social or philosophical origins of European nationalism, but very little addresses the origins in the Muslim world. Overall, nationalism in the Muslim world fought very hard for liberation from imperialism in two important domains: the spiritual and the institutional. On the spiritual level, as Partha Chatterjee ably shows, nationalism seeks to ensure its sovereignty on the personality of the nation, its past, and cultural identity. On the institutional level, it seeks to establish the nationalist state by learning from Western science and institution building.[7]

The rise of nationalism in India is particularly interesting. Most of the Indian intelligentsia of the nineteenth century, regardless of their religious affiliation, were united on an ambitious nationalist program of ridding the country of British domination.[8] Any cursory reading of the career of the Indian Congress from the latter part of the nineteenth century until the 1947 Partition will undoubtedly reflect this preoccupation. However, under pressure from the British and because of certain religious and economic conditions, some Indian Muslims began to contemplate a separate state from the Muslims of India, which became Pakistan after Partition.

Since Partition, there has been some confusion about the true identity of Pakistan. Was Pakistan created for the Muslims of India or was it created as an Islamic state?[9] The careers of the founders of Pakistan and the movement behind the establishment of the country have reflected this uncertainty.[10] What is certain is that only a portion of Indian Muslims were interested in migrating to Pakistan after Partition, and initially, the Jamaʿat al-Islami, founded by Abu al- ʿAla al-Mawdudi in 1941, stood against Partition on the grounds that the future Islamic state would be limited to Pakistan only.[11] The Pakistani movement was spearheaded by the Muslim 'salariat class' of North India, a class that was "the product of the colonial transformation of Indian social structure in the nineteenth century and it comprised those who had received an education that would equip them for employment in the expanding colonial state apparatus as scribes and functionaries."[12] This class did not represent the interests of the majority of the Muslim peasants in rural India or those of the Muslims in South India. This helps explain why the majority of Muslims in the South and in the rural areas did not migrate to Pakistan after Partition. The creation of Pakistan, however, did not solve the problems of Muslims in India. In 1971, Pakistan lost East Pakistan, and Bangladesh was established in the name of Bengali nationalism.

The third major response to the challenge of European colonization was Islamic revivalism. At the outset, it is crucial to differentiate among four major groups or classes of revivalism in the modern Muslim world: 1) pre-colonial; 2) colonial; 3) post-colonial; and 4) post-nation-state. The Wahabiyyah of Saudi Arabia is a pre-colonial Islamic movement, which was created in reaction to internal Muslim decadence. It sought to revive Islamic practices in light of a strict adherence to Islamic law and theology. To do so, the charismatic Muhammad ibn ʿAbd al-Wahab allied himself with the Saudi family, which led to the creation of the modern Saudi state.

Of the second form of colonial Islamic revivalism, examples are the Muhammadiyyah and Nahdatu ul-Ulama organizations in Indonesia, established in the first half of the twentieth century.[13] One might also add the Muslim Brotherhood of Egypt and the Jama'at al-Islami of India. These were mass-oriented social and religious movements committed to ambitious programs such as the reform of Islamic education or the control of political authority in preparation for implementing the Shari'ah in the larger Islamic society.

With the onset of the nation-state in the Muslim world in the middle of the twentieth century and the supervision of the religious institution by the state, coupled with the failure of the nation-state on many fronts, post-colonial forms of Islamic revivalism came into being, some of which reflected extremist interpretations of religion and resorted to violence to achieve their objectives. The Egyptian Jihad of the 1970s and 1980s is a case in point.

The Taliban stands to be one of the major Islamist movements which arose at the time of disintegration of the nation-state in Afghanistan. The Taliban emerged in response to the failure of the secular nation-state to build a new civil society and also to the failure of the urban Islamist movement in Afghanistan to arrest the further disintegration of the state, especially in the wake of the withdrawal of Soviet forces in the late 1980s.[14] The Taliban movement was formed in the context of the chaos in the country in the 1990s, especially after the "Americans had turned their backs on the ruins of Afghanistan."[15]

It is clear that the most significant post-nation-state Islamist movements, that is, the Egyptian Jihad, the bin Laden movement, which must be examined against the wider context of Saudi Arabia in the 1970s and 1980s, and the Taliban, appeared at major historical junctures in contemporary Islamic history, precisely when secularism and the nation-state became exhausted, and when new possibilities of establishing a novel Islamist order seemed to arise.

Although Saudi Arabia bases its constitution on the Qur'an, a vigorous Islamist movement that sought to topple the Saudi regime appeared in the country in the late 1970s. To the minds of many Islamist intellectuals, the wedding between the Wahabiyyah movement and the Saudi state, beginning at the end of the eighteenth century, was no longer viable in the tumultuous years of the twentieth century. Islamist activism in the Gulf, and especially in Saudi Arabia in the latter part of the twentieth century, is very interesting, for it opposed not just the state but also the Muslim clergy who provided a rationale for the existence of the state. Although leading to the modernization of Saudi society, the oil boom of the 1970s and 1980s created a fissure between the young generation of the Saudi religious intelligentsia and the state. Even before the Iraqi invasion of Kuwait in the summer of 1990, young Saudi Islamists began to criticize the ruling family and its Western allies, especially the United States. The Iraqi invasion of Kuwait and its aftermath heightened the tension between Islamists and the state. Because of the unlimited oil resources, the modern Saudi nation-state under the leadership of the royal family was able to launch a very ambitious modernization program in the 1970s, which created a brand new class of Saudi modernizers who opted to Westernize their society. The Saudi royal family, however, created a form of modernization without any indigenous component, and without parallel democratic institutions to guarantee political participation in society. Although the royal family enlisted the support of the major ulama in its modernization program, the younger ulama, especially from the Hijaz area, were uncomfortable with the fast pace of modernization and its inevitable impact on, what they perceived as, "orthodox Islam." I think that the bin Laden phenomenon was the product of this tension between Saudi modernization and Islamic values.

As a military and political phenomenon, the Taliban is a post-colonial movement, as well. Undoubtedly, the theological background of the Taliban, which goes back to the introduction of Islam in South Asia,[16] points to the status of the Taliban in traditional Afghan society. The rise of the Taliban to military and political prominence must be linked to the active engagement of the Pakistani state in the internal affairs of Afghanistan and the support given by the Pakistani army to the Taliban after the different bands of Mujahideen failed to reach an agreement on the future of Afghanistan.[17]

The Taliban movement was born in the great vacuum created in Afghanistan in the wake of the withdrawal of Soviet troops and the failure of different factions of Mujahideen to agree on power sharing. The Taliban emerged in a fractured traditional society that was betrayed by both its urban modernizing and religious elites. As a theological movement, the Taliban was the last resort of an exhausted nation trying to restore stability and stop bloodshed and chaos. In that sense, the Taliban stress in their historical narrative that their main objectives were: first, to end violence and chaos in the country; second, to stop any form of foreign intervention; and, third, to restore the dignity to the common people, the masses, refugees, and women. In the chaos engulfing Afghanistan after the withdrawal of the Soviets

ordinary people raised their voices to ask the ulama to face up to the challenges and provide leadership. Out of that sense of deep suffering resulting
from a long period of violence in modern Afghan history, the Taliban took a
drastic step, which is not Islamic in my view, to order all women to stay at
home, so foregoing their education and opportunities of employment.
According to Taliban, "the Islamic State decided to pay the salaries of these
women at their homes, so that they could stay home and take care of their
families and children. The purpose of this policy is to help revive the Afghan
family and household, as the foundation of the Afghan society, a foundation
that was intentionally destroyed by the communist regime." The Taliban
movement is the only one in modern Afghanistan that succeeded in mobilizing violence to control violence in society and to create a new social and
political order based both on the fear of God and the possibility of a fresh
outbreak of violence. They were able to create "a primitive egalitarian
society" suspicious not just of Communism, capitalism, and the West, but of
the city and the urban Afghan intelligentsia that was, in their view, responsible for borrowing foreign ideas which destroyed the traditional bases of
Afghan society.

The Taliban movement, the Egyptian Jihad, and the bin Laden movement
were all born in desperate circumstances of social dislocation. Supporters
were the prey of an ambitious state modernization program, such as that of
Saudi Arabia in the 1970s, and the absence of democratic institutions in their
home countries. What the movements have in common is not just the goal,
which is to restore the orthodox discourse of Islam, as understood by them,
but also a background of social and military violence. Neither the Egyptian
Jihad and the bin Laden movement, nor other Islamist movements in the
contemporary Arab and Muslim world, have been absorbed by the mainstream ideology of the state. They have not been permitted to exercise
freedom of expression in a democratic environment. As long as conditions of
dislocation, injustice, and lack of democratic freedoms continue in the
Muslim world, an extremist interpretation of Islam will be the norm.

EDUCATION IN THE MUSLIM WORLD: MODERN OR
TRADITIONAL?

Almost every Muslim country had to accept a degree of modernization in
the past century. Both the colonial state and the nation-state supported
modernization. Some Muslim countries, such as Indonesia, Pakistan, and
Egypt sought to modernize and nationalize their educational institutions after

independence by making education free to all. In some Muslim countries, however, religious education has not been modernized sufficiently to reflect the enormous changes wrought in society after independence. In some instances, the military and political leaders gave active support to traditional educational institutions in order to maintain the *status quo*. This has been true in South Asia after independence. It is the argument of this section that a pluralistic educational environment is needed in the Muslim world, and that the state should encourage traditional Muslim institutions to be open to new ideas in their curricula.

In one of his outstanding chapters on the link between the growth of civilization and the cultivation of scientific research in all fields of knowledge, Ibn Khaldun, the Arab historian of the fourteenth century, argues that the scientific mind is the product of a sedentary civilization. However, if a civilization experiences an absence of group feeling [*'asabiyyah*], scientific research tends to deteriorate. This is what happened in Muslim Spain in the twelfth and thirteenth centuries to the extent that the classical Islamic science of jurisprudence became "an empty institution among them [Spaniard Muslims], a mere shadow of its real self."[18] Ibn Khaldun was primarily concerned about a scientific discourse in philosophy, history, and the traditional sciences as a means of keeping Muslim culture dynamic and alive. In addition, he was concerned about enhancing the role of the intelligentsia in society. For this kind of scientific culture, endowments and years of study are needed. Sedentary life provides the context for such scientific pursuits.

Ibn Khaldun's proposition of creating a scientific discourse in the Muslim world is on the whole still valid in contemporary Arab or Muslim contexts. It is true that scientific knowledge has proliferated greatly since the fourteenth century and that the Muslim world has long ceased to be the center of civilization. Ibn Khaldun's remarks help us to understand the position of the "traditional Islamic sciences" in the modern educational systems of Arab and Muslim nation-states in the twentieth century. One may agree with Ibn Khaldun that the practitioners of the traditional sciences are "dull or at any rate did not try not to be dull." Various reasons account for this.

The theoretical treatment of Islam in either Western or Islamic literature has been conspicuously meager. At best, Islam is an object of ideological disagreement between different authors, and has proven to be the Achilles heel of modern theoretical reflection. Perhaps a scientific definition of Islam is an impossibility. In a controversial little book on "The Modernization of Modern Islamic Thought," ʿAbd al-Majid al-Charfi of Tunisia advocates the need to distinguish between "Islamic thought" and Islam. Islamic thought refers to all branches of Muslim sciences developing in the formative phases, such as Qur'anic exegesis, Hadith studies, Kalam, Fiqh, and Sufism.[19] Islam, to his mind, refers to the sacred. The former is subject to change, while the latter is not.[20] I think that this type of distinction is very useful, although in the final analysis, unsatisfactory. In speaking of Islam, it is significant to point out the following ideas: first, Islam has become a philosophical/theological/ideological problematic in modern Arab and Muslim thought. Some speak of elite Islam (that is, official Islam), while others speak of popular Islam (that is, oppositional Islam). Both positions agree, however, that Islam can be either a passive or revolutionary force in society. Others go even further in arguing that the concept of Islam as "revelation" is untenable, and that Islam is what people make of it. It can be "used" as a movement of progress or as a means to justify social and economic disparities in society.[21] In other words, according to this position, Islam cannot be distinguished by a "sacred core." Practically speaking, Islam has been amenable to more than one definition.[22]

Second, on the theological plane, Islam can acquire an open-ended meaning extending from a belief in one God to a theological connection with all revelations preceding it; on the other hand, it can have as simple a definition as the submission to one God. In other words, one can examine the theological nature of Islam from the perspective of the history of religions, especially from Judaism and Christianity. Or one can see Islam from an inclusive theological viewpoint, the oneness of God.

Third, the text (*nass*) has been at the center of Muslim culture.[23] According to the majority opinion of Muslim jurists, both the Qur'an and Hadith form the textual base of Islam, which furnish the main foundations of Islamic theology. Therefore, it may be valid to argue that since the inception of Islam, a dialectical relationship has existed between text and (human) history, and text and human thought. In other words, Muslim history and thought have been the products of a complex interchange between the "human" and the "divine"; or between the religious text and socio-economic and political factors.

Fourth, one might present Islam as a comprehensive anthropological fact, as Rochdy Alili notes in a recent work.[24] It is true that Islam has a normative core. However, in its historical evolution, Islam has given birth to a complex cultural, social, literary, philosophical, and political tradition that still informs the worldview of Muslim people. Islam has become interested in issues of political and social power and organization. It is important to note that the various intellectual and political movements have interpreted this tradition differently. In that sense, tradition can be either a passive or revolutionary force.

One may say that both Islamic thought and Islamic history, two major dimensions concomitant with the theological essence of Islam, have given rise to a complex plethora of religious and ideological attitudes and forces that have taken the Qur'an and the Sunnah as their starting point. Perhaps, here it would be useful to remind ourselves of the multiplicity of meanings the term Islam carries: Islam as text and theology; Islam as human thought; Islam as history; and Islam as one or several institutions. It is with all these different levels of Islam in mind that I raise the issue of the Islamic problematic.

Why do the political elite in the contemporary Muslim world, unlike the founding fathers of Muslim states, pay so much attention to "Islam" in their official pronouncements? What is the relationship between official culture and the Muslim intelligentsia in the Muslim world? Undoubtedly, Islam took on a revolutionary character in the colonial age, as seen in the careers of 'Abd al-Qadir al-Jaza'iri and Shaykh al-Sanussi in North Africa. However, the Muslim world in the colonial era lacked the necessary power to arrest the gradual Westernization of Muslim societies. Before Europe intervened in the Muslim world, Muslim society was, more or less, governed by the ideology of Islam, which was interpreted by a traditional class of learned men. European intervention created dichotomies in all walks of life, including culture and education.

In one important sense, the introduction of European educational and technological systems made the traditional Muslim branches of learning, especially ones that lacked scientific focus, quite obsolete and relegated the traditional Muslim intelligentsia to a secondary status. This drastic change in the system of education did not take place because of any inherent superiority of Western education (over Islamic education), but was mainly the result of the complex power structure embarked upon by the colonial West in order to secure its interests in the Arab/Muslim world.[25] The introduction of Western norms of education in India, for example, created a new class of Muslim (as well as Hindu) intelligentsia, which began to use a new language relevant to the problems of Indian society in the nineteenth century. One example is the creation of the Anglo-Muhammadan College, which became Aligarah Muslim University, by Ahmad Khan in India at the end of the nineteenth century.[26]

With the rise of the nation-state, traditional religious education gained an important edge in society and the traditional religious intelligentsia became, more or less, a prominent class in the new state. Very often, the tiny and afflu-ent political elite in the Muslim world worked very hard after independence to reconstitute religious classes in society as a means of enhancing their *status quo*. One fundamental means of reconstituting this class was through education. The new power given to the religious intelligentsia in society created dichotomies, though, between two different educational systems within the new nation-state, one Western-oriented and the other Islamic. In Pakistan, for example, the religious intelligentsia gained tremendous power under the regime of Zia al-Haq, the military ruler of the country from 1977 to 1988. The Dini Madaris, the theological schools of the country that follow an obsolete curriculum of education, became the focus of the state's interest, especially after Zia al-Haq resorted to his dubious program of Islamization. The Dini Madaris survived the colonial era and they have played a significant role in the educational policies of the new nation-state. The leading ulama are usually recruited from such schools, and they gave Zia al-Haq his rationale for Islamization in the 1980s.[27] In addition, these Madaris, especially in the 1980s, at the height of the Soviet intervention in Afghanistan, provided many student-fighters for the different Mujahideen in Afghanistan.[28] Space does not permit a detailed discussion of the attempts of the modern Pakistani state to subordinate the traditional educational system to the modern one; however, it suffices to mention that the control of the different *awqaf* (endowments) by the state and the creation of the Ministry of Religious Affairs augmented the power of the official traditional intelligentsia, who, since independence, have given an Islamic voice to the secular elite of Pakistani society.

Against the above, it is important to investigate as closely as possible the philosophy of education in the modern Muslim world, especially in relation to traditional Islamic education. Perhaps one might reach conclusions similar to those of Ibn Khaldun's on the state of Muslim education in the thirteenth and fourteenth centuries or those of Shaykh 'Abdul Rahman Jabarti in nineteenth-century Egypt. Muslims, by and large, preferred memorization to scientific disputation and study.[29]

Islamic education gained prominence in many Muslim nation-states because of the need of the ruling elite for a group of traditional educated intellectuals to defend the *status quo*. In the greater Muslim world, official ideology defended a reified notion of Islam as a means of spreading false consciousness. Very often, official ideology dismisses critical or revolutionary articulations of Islam. The official position on Islam is most obvious in Arab and Muslim academia, where in departments of theology the notion of "production of knowledge" is considered repugnant and "memorization" of classical texts is held in high esteem. "Knowledge" and power are intertwined. Furthermore, the absence of a theoretical treatment of Islam in the Muslim world can be detected in the curricular construction of the field of Islamic Studies in leading Muslim universities, such as the Azhar University in Egypt, the Imam ibn ʿAbd al-Wahab University in Saudi Arabia, and Dar al-Hadith al-Hassaniyah in Morocco, and the thousands of traditional madrasas in South Asia, most notably in India, Pakistan, and Afghanistan. Because of the centrality and sensitivity of the subject of Islam, the state has directly intervened in constructing Islamic studies in a way that does not threaten its interests or weaken its hold on official Muslim clergy. The modern construction by the state of Islamic or Shariʿah studies has been done in a way to ensure the neutrality of religion in social and political matters. With the blessings of petro-dollars, the ulama in leading Saudi universities spend their time debating a dead classical culture that revolves around a closed field, Arabic rhetoric and grammar. The state has reduced these shaykhs to mere consumers of its imported products, thanks to the international need for Arab petroleum. A trouble-seeking shaykh faces a grim future, stripped of his honorary degrees and thrown in a dungeon while being denied the blessings of the state's modernization.[30] The Algerian thinker Malek Bennabi comments on the same phenomenon without, however, adducing the necessary conclusions from his remarks. He says that, "In the independent Muslim institutions, the syllabi and methods of instruction also seem to defy time; the principles have remained the same since the Christian Middle Ages."[31] It is clear that these methods of instruction and the knowledge associated with them collapsed the moment they encountered a superior capitalist civilization in the nineteenth century. The Muslim ruling elite were quick to reconstruct the field of Islamic Studies in the name of authenticity, and without any critical perspective, in order to have the blessings of the religious elite.

In this regard, one must agree with the contention of Muhammad Arkoun, that "the history of Islam as a school of thought, as a culture, as a system of trans-social and trans-historical beliefs and norms is still written, taught and used as an ideology of legitimization."[32] This is why the Ministries of Education in many Muslim and Arab countries have complemented the work of the Ministries of Religious Affairs in that only a limited and very controlled reading or interpretation of Islam has been permitted.[33] In the mind of the official guardians of Islamic Studies in the Muslim world (that is, the power elite), Islam has ceased to be an intellectual problem and they believe it is high time it ceases to be a question of power, as well.[34] The core of the field revolves around Shariʿah and Fiqh studies that have been, very often, emptied of any critical or political content, or relevance to the present situation. A clear-cut distinction has been made between the "theological" and the "political" or the "theological" and the "social," with the former being understood as rites, symbols, and historical texts only. Furthermore, the perspective of the social sciences or critical philosophy is regrettably absent. The field of modern Shari'ah studies in the Muslim world has remained closed off to the most advanced human contributions in critical philosophy and social science. It does not see the need of employing such concepts as class, social structure, criticism, and modernity in its philosophical worldview. Rationalism, which was celebrated in classical Islamic thought as the handmaid of theology and metaphysics, has been reduced to a narrow technical enterprise confined, as it were, to the fields of Arabic grammar and jurisprudence. Contemporary scholasticism, with the help of foreign currency generated from the production of oil, has waged the most successful "silent revolution" in the Arab world. It has created a fissure between "thought" and reality, between "Islam" and reality.

The secular educational systems in many Muslim countries did not fare better than the traditional. I. H. Qureshi, former Minister of Education of Pakistan, vehemently criticizes the secular educated elite in Pakistan by saying that, "Our secular educated elite is the most spineless, the most unscrupulous and the most mercenary in the world. What has gone during this quarter of a century that has eaten into the vitals of our society and the grit of its leaders except the continuation of a faulty, aimless, and diseased system of education that has bred no social virtues, no depth of feeling, no sense of responsibility – nothing except selfishness, corruption and cowardly lack of initiative and courage?"[35]

On the other hand, graduates of the traditional system of education spend the best years of their lives memorizing ancient religious texts without having the understanding or the courage to link or reflect on the themes of these texts in the contexts of modern challenges.[36] Many Shari'ah graduates, who are lucky indeed to find a job in their field of specialization, are instructed not to tackle the real social and economic problems that face the average Muslim individual on a daily basis. Shari'ah education in the Arab and Muslim world has been constructed ideologically to maintain, and not question, the *status quo*. It has become a shell without much substance. The end of the Cold War, which may have liberated the field of the humanities and social sciences in the West from narrow dogmatic confines, does not seem to have affected the field of Shari'ah studies in the Arab world. On the contrary, the end of the Cold War unleashed the power of the authoritarian state to attack any other interpretation of Islam as unacceptable and irrational.[37]

This strange state of affairs has created a backward class of Muslim intelligentsia in Muslim societies who are well versed in the Islamic text, but who do not necessarily know how to examine the text critically in relation to their surrounding social and political conditions. This state-controlled intelligentsia revels at discussing the most minute theological questions, or raising a battle cry about questions that died hundreds of years ago, as long as they have no bearing on present social and cultural conditions. This intelligentsia is oblivious to the crises besetting its societies; it simply ignores the existence of such crises. It is more interested in "authenticity" than in real-life problems. In his analysis of the genesis of Pakistan, Hamza Alavi argues that a large number of the ulama in Pakistani society have gone through the Dars-e Nizami, "a syllabus that was laid down in medieval India and has hardly changed. Generally they [the ulama] have little knowledge of the world they live in, nor even of the world of Islam except for myths and legends. They inhabit little temples of their own uncomprehending and enclosed minds in which they intone slogans, petrified words and dogmas. Affairs of state and society are, generally, beyond their narrowed vision. There are only a few amongst them who have had the benefit of some tolerable education and who, in their own ways, try to follow current affairs."[38]

The above analysis cannot be complete, however, if mention is not made of the fact that a small number of traditionally educated intelligentsia have opposed Arab and Muslim regimes and have paid for their opposition either in terms of exile or imprisonment.[39] This might explain in part the use of the Sacred Text as an ideological weapon in the hands of the state against those who may venture to criticize the state and its supporters.[40] Furthermore, the depoliticization and pacification of Islamic Studies may explain one interesting fact in the history of contemporary Muslim revival in the Muslim world: some of the leading activists of Islamic resurgence on campuses do not come from Shari'ah or arts colleges but from science colleges. Often, the arts colleges are the preserve of leftist students, whereas science colleges are dominated by Islamists. This explains why, in spite of the millions of dollars spent on "modernizing" this field of study, Islamic Studies in the Arab world has produced only a handful of internationally known scholars.[41]

The multiple sources of education in the Muslim world have created different types of intelligentsia with different worldviews, but what underlies these worldviews is the fact that memorization is the rule of the day in all types of education.[42] The Egyptian thinker Rifʿat al-Saʿid thinks that memorization is the basis of education in government, private, and Azharite schools in

Egypt, which encourages the creation of a textual-based culture, distinguished at the core by literalism and radicalism.[43]

The absence of social science or critical philosophy perspectives from the field of Shari'ah studies can be illustrated by the fact that most students who acquire a government scholarship to pursue their graduate education abroad, especially from the Gulf states, study only the hard sciences or business administration, supposedly value-free or criticism-free subjects. In my many years in the United States (almost twenty years now), I have never encountered a single student from the Gulf pursuing a graduate degree in political science, philosophy, or history. Closing the door to any type of critical perspective has been the underpinning of the field of Religious Studies (especially Islamic Studies) and made it quite irrelevant. This fact has made it quite difficult in many Arab countries to encourage the growth of a scientific tradition, developed mainly in the West, to study the complex interplay between religion and society in the modern Arab world. The discipline of the sociology of religion is looked upon as a *bid'ah*, or innovation, that does not convey the real essence of Islam. Just like the study of the modern Arab state systems, the sociology of religion is a necessity in the Arab world.

This begs the question, once again, of both cultural change and the nature of official culture in the contemporary Muslim world. Undoubtedly, the modernization drive in the Arab world since 1945 created, on the whole, a much more literate culture than existed a century ago. In that sense, cultural change has been an inevitable process, and one can employ various methods of assessing the extent of cultural change in a society over a certain period of time. One such method is perhaps the number of books or/and newspapers published in a country and the contents of such publications. However, the quality of what gets conveyed through the mass media is suspect. One must agree with Raymond Williams' brilliant observation that means of communication are themselves means of production.[44] That is to say, that as with any means of production, means of communication are owned by a few individuals in the Muslim world, and a host of skilled and non-skilled laborers are employed to support those individuals. In addition, since the mid-1970s, the Gulf bourgeoisie has taken advantage of the globalization of the mass media. A number of television stations and publications offer programs to their audiences in the Arab world from selected European capitals without necessarily being at odds with the official culture of the Arab ruling elite. The globalization of official ideology, supported by the influx of oil money, is a major characteristic of contemporary Arab culture. With the help of the most advanced capitalist technologies, official culture presents itself globally as the only credible voice in the contemporary Arab world.

It is crucial to elaborate on the question of the globalization of official Arab ideology in relation to the entire Muslim world, which looks at the Arab world, and especially at a country like Saudi Arabia, as the locus of "authentic Islam." The traditional madrasa system in many Muslim countries, such as in Afghanistan, Pakistan, Malaysia, and Indonesia, or in a non-Muslim country such as India, is a replica of the old madrasa system that dominated the Arab world on the eve of the Western intervention. This system uses Arabic as the main language of instruction, in addition to using the Qur'an, Hadith, and other classical manuals in Fiqh and Arabic grammar. Global "official Arab ideology," especially the conservative ideology of the Gulf, finds a great audience among the teachers and graduates of these traditional madrasas, even if no financial donations are made to such institutions. The preservation of such a mentality does not help promote healthy cultural change enabling young Muslim or Arab students to accommodate the enormous changes engendered by recent globalization or even to understand the nature of globalization itself.

As I have argued above, one must understand the absence of critical vision in most of the educational systems in the Arab world, especially in conservative Arab states, as closely linked to the complex process of modernization launched by the Arab political elite after independence. The influx of oil money in the Gulf states made the technical process of modernization a much easier task than in most Arab states. One must, however, emphasise that the modernization program, however creative it is, did not entail from the beginning any substantial change in the political fortunes of the ruling elite or families. Putting aside the valid argument that international capitalism, which uses democracy as a cover in its home countries, has never been worried about the implementation of democracy in the Arab world, except in those countries that turn against the West, democratic forces in the Arab world have a hard time trying to push their discourse in public. Arab regimes have hijacked democracy, without apology.[45]

CONTEMPORARY ELITE AND RELIGIOUS REVIVALISM IN THE ARAB WORLD

On the whole, the ruling elite in the contemporary Muslim world (in the past four decades) is not interested in democratizing societies for fear of losing its grip on power. Pakistan has gone through four military coups since its foundation in 1947, the last of which brought General Musharraf to power in November 1999. In May 1998, Indonesia, the largest Muslim country in the world, went through a popular uprising to oust Suharto's dictatorial regime. Yet, the process of democracy is far from complete. In most of the Arab world, the shock of the 1967 defeat by the Israelis, coupled with the failure of the modernization project of the nation-state, resulted in several forms of response to the issue of secularization and religion. In this section, I will focus on the post-1967 Arab world by examining the relationship between religion and society, which is the key, to my mind, in shedding light on the rise of Islamism in the Arab world in the late twentieth century. Once again, I reiterate that the Muslim world must foster a democratic and pluralistic environment open to the participation of Islamist and non-Islamist forces and trends.

The starting point of this analysis is the 1967 Arab defeat by Israel, a crucial event in the history of the contemporary Arab world. Although defeat did not lead to drastic political changes in the Arab world it has influenced the creation of new social, religious, and intellectual movements. Several responses to the defeat have appeared. The first and most poignant was the response of the modernizing elite that led the Arab world into defeat. As seen above, the political modernizing elite was heir to a long tradition of modernization that began in the Arab world before the advent of official colonialism. On the whole, it was an elite that was not devout in private but which exploited religious symbols in public. It employed both Western rationalism and Muslim religious symbols in order to keep itself in power. This is true even in the case of the tribal state in the Gulf, which has exploited the tribal element in order to modernize society. Out of its disarray after defeat, the political elite resorted to camouflaging its losses with religious symbols and ideas. To this elite, religion is not a matter of piety but a means to achieve political and social ends. Because of its unwillingness to give up power and concede defeat, this modernizing elite betrayed its grandiose modernization scheme by simply resorting to Islamic symbols, in a dishonest manner. The same happened, as is well known, after the Iraqi defeat in the second Gulf war. This use of religion as an instrument for politics, is quite serious in traditional societies that value religious life.

The second major response to defeat was that of the "secular" intellectual elite of all shades and colors. This intellectual elite was of three major orientations: 1) Arab nationalist, such as Qustantine Zurayk;[46] 2) critical Marxist, represented by such thinkers as Adonis,[47] Ghali Shukri,[48] Abdallah Laroui,[49] al-Afif al-Akhdar;[50] Sadiq Jalal al-'Azm,[51] Tayyib Tizine,[52] and Halim Barakat;[53]

and 3) liberal or Enlightenment (*tanwiri*), represented by such people as Zaki Najib Mahmud,[54] Jabir 'Asfur,[55] and Fouad Zakariyya.[56] The critique of this class of intelligentsia centered on the premise that the Arab state lost the 1967 war because both the Arab state and masses were not modern enough or that their level of modernization was not on a par with that of the Zionists. The Lebanese thinker Hassan Sa'b best represents this trend when he argues that the Arab–Israeli conflict is civilizational, centered around technological competence. The Arab world faced defeat because of its failure to achieve technological and scientific superiority over "the Israeli settlers."[57] This Arab group was a loosely organized collection of public thinkers, many of whom were philosophers in the academic sense and who assumed teaching positions in the most distinguished Arab universities, especially in Beirut, Cairo, Damascus, and Rabat.

These thinkers showed bitter disappointment with defeat and in the reasons behind it. Some blamed the small national bourgeoisie for leading the Arab world into defeat because of its class position or inexperience in the world of politics. They considered religion, and mainly Islam, as a major hurdle to the development of Arab society. The extreme of this trend goes as far as to associate everything Islamic with the destruction of civil society. This is clear in the writings of Faraj Fuda[58] and many Algerian and Tunisian thinkers, who rushed to congratulate the state for purging Islamic elements from society. Hijacking the election from FIS in Algeria in 1992 was seen as the intervention of the army to salvage civil society from the hands of the Islamists.[59] In their loose way, they were united in an ambitious program which was, and is, not just to modernize Arab society but also to rid it from the entire question of religion. This response attacked traditional ways of life and the mental/theological structures behind them, and called for a radical transformation of Arab society. These thinkers believe the only way for the Arab state to achieve victory is through complete submission to secularization and modernization, that is, no authority must exist over human reason. Religion and religious symbols must be completely banished from the public sphere.

The philosophical writings of this group of Arab critics, especially those produced by the Marxist subset, are a brilliant exercise in comprehensive and piercing social, political, and cultural criticism, a vocalized anguish of many hidden feelings about predicaments and challenges, and a painful expression of the state of affairs of contemporary Arab history.[60]

Out of the last response, a new and interesting one emerges: the conversion of a good number of influential Arab intellectuals from critical Marxism and nationalism to Islam. As far as I know, this response has not been analyzed in detail in article or book form, although it is referred to here and there.[61] This response reflected a collective plea on the part of Arab society to first be anchored in Islamic authenticity and specificity and then to learn from the universality of ideas. This wave of thinkers completely lost faith in the political elite, and resorted to the Qur'an as their main solace against an unstable world. Some of these thinkers are: 'Adil Hussain, Tariq al-Bishri,[62] and Muhammad 'Imarah[63] all from Egypt, Rashid al-Ghannoushi from Tunisia,[64] and Munir Shafiq[65] from Palestine. As a result of their theoretical sophistication, these thinkers converged to create a new rational Islamic discourse that was not tainted with the superstition of the petroleum-nurtured Muslim clerics from the Gulf. Their discourse was marked by its honest and direct approach.

The discourse that evolved shouldered the responsibility of betraying the complicity of the Arab political elite with the colonialist project, both Western and Israeli, and its hidden designs for the Arab world, especially in the so-called peace era between Israel and some Arab countries. For example, Rashid al-Ghannoushi argues that what underlies this complicity is violence, that of the state and Westernization, "Violence is at the heart of the relationship between the dependent [Arab] state and its citizens. Inarguably, Westernization is the most poignant and damaging form of violence perpetrated by the state; it is cutting off society from its roots and worldview so that the so-called modernity could be imposed. In fact, this modernity allows the West to exercise its dictatorship on our people with the help of the modernizing elite, so much so that this modernization or Westernization becomes the real antithesis of democracy from all angles."[66] Besides criticizing the state, this discourse has brought back to the fore the question of Palestine as the most central question facing the contemporary Arab world. Is this a reactionary approach representing the Arab right or the interests of the petroleum rich countries? No, rather, it is a new approach born in the throes of defeat and in the hope that only a civilizational Islamic approach can salvage the Arab world and humanity at large from the ills of modernity and from the firing power of NATO.

Islamic revivalism (or Islamism) represents the fourth response. One must draw a line between the response of the organized Islamic movement or movements and that of the masses. There is a difference between what has been termed "political Islam" and the Islamic religious phenomenon. The latter is a much larger notion and practice than the former. It denotes a living Islamic tradition that has survived against many odds in the modern world.

One must agree with Ghali Shukri's insightful analysis that the Arab masses practice "Islam" in their daily praxis without theological or legal complications. The collective memory of the masses is based on a simple and pristine Islam, which is based on tolerance and acceptance.[67] In academic and journalistic literature, it has become a cliché to speak of "political Islam" or "fundamentalist Islam" or "radical Islam" in a pejorative sense.[68] These terms do not accurately describe the discourse of organized Islamic movements, a discourse that is not incongruent with the main legal and theological principles of Islam.[69] This response, and its various offshoots, is the only one that offers a real political alternative to the crisis of the ruling Arab political elite. The immediate response of this trend (a large number of whose adherents were in prison, barred from being part of the political process or were in exile either in the Gulf states or in the West), was the response of the twice-defeated person phenomenon: once by Western civilization and the second by the Arab states. Therefore, the discourse of the doubly defeated took the position that God destined defeat because of the ungodliness of the Arab regimes and their preference of secularism over Islam. With the progress of years, newly organized Islamist responses have emerged in different Arab countries, especially in Sudan, Tunisia, Algeria, and Morocco. All argue that religion must furnish the ideological bases of the new state. They call for the formation of a new state.

The second dimension of this response was that of the masses, including a large number of the middle classes that were adversely affected by the modernization of the state. One must remember that a major social and political cleavage still exists between the "masses" and the "modernized elite." Most of the masses still live either in the countryside or in countryside-like neighborhoods in the cities. It is true that a sizable number of children of the masses went to schools of the nation-state, but not many were absorbed after graduation by the state and its institutions. This phenomenon is apparent in most Arab and Muslim countries, especially in Tunisia, Algeria, Morocco, Egypt, Indonesia, and Pakistan. It is doubtful that the recent process of privatization begun in earnest in many Arab countries under the impact of globalization and the IMF will do much to remedy this situation. Jabiri sees the reasons for this in the West's successful attempts to suffocate the growth of the national Arab bourgeoisie, and its continuing refusal to support democratization and liberalization in the Arab world.[70]

There was a large-scale process of revival that was not necessarily political, but which revolved around the formation of a new collective identity that follows the broad guidelines of Islamic principles.[71] The modernizing elite was far less preoccupied with "institutional Islam" than with a mass-oriented Islamic movement. The bet of the modernizing elite before 1967 was that large doses of state modernization would be enough to reduce, if not amputate, religious symbols from the public sphere. The 1967 defeat proved them wrong. Large sections of the masses, including the most educated, began to rediscover a new meaning of religiosity and to reaffirm the notion that traditional ways of behavior would provide a sense of identity and belonging in the context of modernization that had gone amok. The bourgeoisie in most Arab countries felt betrayed and a good number began to discover the ways of Islam.[72] The mass response to defeat, which even the state tried to exploit, became manifest not just in the increase in public attendance of prayers or the increased number of pilgrims to Saudi Arabia every year, but also in the increase of Islamic literature people read, and other such tangible efforts.

The mass Islamic response to defeat was justified by several factors that seem to be unchanging in modern Arab political and social life: first, the failure of the modernization program of the nation-state that emerged onto the scene after the recession of colonialism. The 1967 defeat wrecked the grandiose claims of the Arab states, including those that do not share borders with Israel. In several Arab countries, modernization created dualism: two countries within one; one is urban and advanced and the other is rural and backward. In addition, mass education which was adopted by a number of Arab nation-states did not deliver the poor from their misery but made them thoroughly aware of the conditions of their misery and the economic and political reasons responsible for these conditions. Another reaction was the accumulation of more power in the hands of a few, even after defeat and failure of the modernization project, and the loss of public freedoms. Harold Laski's observation about the loss of political freedom aptly describes the situation of the Arab world today, "If in any state there is a body of men who possess unlimited power, those over whom they rule can never be free."[73] The history of freedom in the Arab world after 1967 is sad. Besides incurring the wrath of Islamist forces, the expansion of the power of the political elite has led to a deep resentment on the part of the masses not seen in the Arab world since the days of colonialism. Third, the decline of democratic freedoms of all sorts and the acute crisis of civil society has led to the stifling of the potential that had been won through education. No new leadership seems to be in sight, except perhaps that of the military. The crisis of society deepens day by day. Fourth, the state, in its attempt to silence dissent and camouflage the real problems in society, unleashes the power of technology, that is the mass media, by encouraging a shallow artistic environment where songs reflect only the trivial side of official Arab culture.

In North Africa, most notably in Morocco, Algeria, and Tunisia, the modernization "mind" of the state exhausted its possibilities, as well. The 1967 defeat did not have the same impact on North Africa as it did on the Arab countries in the Middle East, but similar policies of nation-building and modernization had been underway since these countries achieved independence (Algeria in 1962). The long history of French colonization in North Africa and the bitter struggle for freedom left these countries in economic shambles. The flight of the poor from the countryside to the cities, the enormous difficulties facing these nascent countries and population growth were major challenges to new regimes. The answer of the modernizing elite, in emerging from the shadow of colonialism, was to try to impose modernization on poor and backward societies.

The Bourguiba regime in Tunisia was perhaps the most radical Arab system to imitate Kemal Atatürk's Turkish model in secularization and nation-building.[74] The state imposed secularism on all aspects of society with the dual purpose of diminishing the power of religion in the social and cultural spheres and creating a new identity congruous with the demands of modernity. The religious institutions, especially the ancient Zaituna University, were marginalized and the separation of state and religion was effected.[75] One major characteristic of the state's imposition of secularization was to ensure its "hegemony over the social *imaginaire* of people or their collective memory."[76] Here, the secularization process in Bourguiba's Tunisia included an important aim: to create subtle new mechanisms of identity-formation through the state apparatuses, especially the party, mass media, schools, and the charisma of the leader.

The process of dominating the "social *imaginaire*" of the people faltered in the early 1970s with the rise of a new and educated generation of young Tunisians who rebelled against the modernization program of the state. The same was true of other countries in North Africa. In the words of 'Abd al-Hamid Ibrahimi, the contemporary state in North Africa, after several decades of independence, finds itself dependent on the West and carrying a huge foreign debt. In addition, its citizens find that the margins of democracy have receded.[77] The modernized state could not absorb their potential and many felt that Islam would provide them with an answer.[78] In other words, the Islamic response in Tunisia was a manifestation of a deep resistance to the modernization policies of Bourguiba, which was seen and experienced by a large number of people as a policy of full cultural and linguistic subjugation to the West and a loss of the national-religious identity of the nation.[79]

The example of Algeria is also akin to that of Tunisia. Post-independence Algeria took major strides to modernize society. The Algerian intelligentsia, however, as the most conscious group in society, has experienced a "loss of hegemony" since independence, as Ali El-Kenz puts it, because of the excessive control of the army, the Westernization of the Arab collective identity of the country, and the derailment of the economic program of reform in the 1980s. Because of this neglect by state and society, the "intellectuals took refuge in the silence of the embassies and factories."[80] In short, the contemporary state in North Africa has imposed its rationalist vision of modernization on a traditional society that was still recovering from the long years of colonialism. The modernization vision of the state has been complicated by the facts of heavy concentration of power in a few hands, a growing population, internal and foreign immigration, and failed economic development.

CONCLUSION

The Muslim world at present exhibits complex social, ethnic, and cultural formations that have been influenced in the modern period by three major factors: modernization, nationalism, and Islamic revivalism. These three tendencies have had a legitimate presence in the Muslim world since the end of the nineteenth century. Each of these three movements vied to achieve independence from colonialism and reconstruct the Arab and Muslim personality. Nationalism was a leading force in the Muslim world in the 1950s and the 1960s. International and domestic factors meant that the nationalist project of modernization remained incomplete or, as in the case of Saudi Arabia, the ruling elite adopted a fast and ambitious modernization program. In both cases, Islamic revivalism, even the most moderate, was suppressed and very often its representatives were banned from taking part in normal political life.

Political authoritarianism is widespread in the Muslim world. Three major reasons help explain this phenomenon: first, the failure of the nationalist movement (which inherited the state after the collapse of colonialism) to foster democratic forms of government; second, the increasing meddling of the army in politics; and, third, the support given to authoritarian regimes by many Western powers. One way of enhancing democracy in the Muslim world is to allow the three major currents (nationalism, modernization, and Islamic revivalism) to shoulder the responsibility of building a new civil society.

Whether we are discussing Indonesia, Malaysia, Pakistan, or Algeria, a plurality of voices must be heard.

In some Muslim countries, such as Pakistan and Afghanistan, traditional Islamic education survived through independence without any major change in the medieval curriculum. In Saudi Arabia, a traditional educational system was resurrected in the 1960s and 1970s. The result has been the creation of two different, and sometimes antagonistic, kinds of intelligentsia that have nothing to do with each other. Although it is important to build a pluralistic society in the Muslim world, it is high time to bridge the gaps between the traditional and modern intelligentsia.

NOTES

1. Rashid al-Ghannoushi, *On Secularism and Civil Society* [Arabic] (London: al-Markaz al-Magharibi li'l Buhuth, 1999), 175.
2. See for instance Andrew Sullivan, "This is a Religious War." *New York Times Magazine*, October 7, 2001.
3. "The process of Christian *reconquista* in the Iberian peninsula was a forerunner – in its chronological context of the great oceanic discoveries which the Spanish and Portuguese explorers were to initiate in the fifteenth century. These quickened the pace of seaborne trade and at the same time delivered a mortal blow not only to Muslim supremacy in the western Indian ocean but also to the introspectiveness of India and China." K. N. Chaudhuri, *Trade and Civilization in the Indian Ocean: An Economic History from the Rise of Islam to 1750* (Cambridge: Cambridge University Press, 1985), 9.
4. Benedict Anderson, *The Spectre of Comparisons: Nationalism, Southeast Asia and the World* (London: Verso, 1998), 5.
5. "Leading ulema not only sanctioned and supported the innovations initiated by the Sultans and their military and civil advisors, both Ottoman and European. Some of them also played a major role in conceiving, suggesting, and planning reforms on European lines." Uriel Heyd, "The Ottoman Ulema and Westernization in the Time of Selim III and Mahmud II." In Albert Hourani, Philip Khoury and Mary Wilson, eds., *The Modern Middle East: A Reader* (Berkeley: University of California Press, 1993), 30.
6. Benedict Anderson, *Imagined Communities* (London: Verso, 1991), 6.
7. Chatterjee argues that "anticolonial nationalism creates its own domain of sovereignty within the colonial society well before it begins its political battle with the imperial power. It does this by dividing the world of social institutions and practices into two domains – the material and the spiritual. The material is the domain of the "outside," of the economy and state-craft, of science and technology, a world where the West had proved its superiority and the East had

succumbed. In this domain, then, Western superiority had to be acknowledged and its accomplishments carefully studied and replicated. The spiritual, on the other hand, is an "inner" domain bearing the "essential" marks of cultural identity. The greater one's success in imitating Western skills in the material domain, therefore, the greater the need to preserve the distinctness of one's spiritual culture. This formula is, I think, a fundamental feature of anticolonial nationalisms in Asia and Africa." Partha Chatterjee, *The Nation and Its Fragments: Colonial and Postcolonial Histories* in *The Partha Chatterjee Omnibus* (New Delhi: Oxford University Press, 1999), 6.

8. Some leading Muslim thinkers, notably Sayyid Ahmad Khan, were pro-British. According to M. J. Akbar, "This disciple of the British [Ahmad Khan] became hero to the elite of a community which had lost its pride and confidence after a century of stagnation; whose leaders had degenerated from emperors to caricatures; whose poetry had collapsed from philosophy to self-deprecation or lament; whose vision was so debilitated that when asked to surrender self-respect in return for bread, it happily did so. For a pat on the back and a knighthood, Sayyid Ahmad Khan happily denounced the bravery of those numerous Muslims who fought the British in the wars of 1857. Inevitably, he could not resist becoming a bit of a caricature himself, wearing English clothes after his knighthood in 1888 and acquiring a knife and fork for his table. *But he still did his writing still sitting on the floor.*" M. J. Akbar, *Nehru: The Making of India* (London: Viking, 1988), 16–17.

9. This question is at the heart of many studies of modern Pakistan. See Akbar Ahmed, *Jinnah, Pakistan and Islamic Identity: The Search for Saladin* (London: Routledge, 1997); Tariq Ali, *Can Pakistan Survive? The Death of a State* (London: Penguin, 1983), and Lawrence Ziring, *Pakistan in the Twentieth Century: A Political History* (Karachi: Oxford University Press, 1997).

10. See Jean-Luc Racine, "Pakistan: Quel islam pour quelle nation? *Le Monde Diplomatique*, December 2001, 12–13.

11. Mushirul Hasan, *Legacy of a Divided Nation: India's Muslims since Independence* (Boulder: Westview Press, 1997), 69.

12. Hamza Alavi, "Pakistan and Islam: Ethnicity and Ideology." In Fred Halliday and Hamza Alavi, eds., *State and Ideology in the Middle East and Pakistan* (New York: Monthly Review Press, 1998), 68.

13. On the Muhammadiyyah, consult the major study by Deliar Noer, *The Modernist Muslim Movement in Indonesia, 1900–1942* (Kuala Lumpur: Oxford University Press, 1973); see also George Kahin, *Nationalism and Revolution in Indonesia* (Ithaca: Cornell University Press, 1952) and Robert Hefner, *Civil Society: Muslims and Democratization in Indonesia* (Princeton: Princeton University Press, 2000).

14. See M. Hassan Kakar, *Afghanistan: The Soviet Invasion and the Afghan Response, 1979–1982* (Berkeley: University of California Press, 1995).

15. John K. Cooley, *Unholy Wars: Afghanistan, America and International Terrorism* (London: Pluto Press, 2000), 7.

16. On the introduction of Islam to South Asia between the seventh and fifteenth centuries, consult André Wink, *Al-Hind: The Making of the Indo-Islamic World*, 2 vols (New Delhi: Oxford University Press, 1996).

17. On the rise of the Taliban to power, see Anthony Davis, "How the Taliban became a Military Power." In William Maley, ed., *Fundamentalism Reborn: Afghanistan and the Taliban* (New York: New York University Press, 1998), 43–71. See also Kamal Matinuddin, *The Taliban Phenomenon: Afghanistan 1994–1997* (Karachi: Oxford University Press, 1999), Larry P. Goodson, *Afghanistan's Endless War: State Failure, Regional Politics, and the Rise of the Taliban* (Seattle: University of Washington Press, 2001), and Ahmed Rashid, *Taliban: Militant Islam, Oil and Fundamentalism in South Asia* (New Haven: Yale University Press, 2001).

18. Ibn Khaldun, *The Muqaddimah: An Introduction to History*, vol. II (New York: Pantheon Books, 1958), 430: "The Institution of scientific instruction has disappeared among the inhabitants of Spain. Their former concern with the sciences is gone, because Muslim civilization in Spain has been decreasing for hundreds of years. The only scholarly discipline remaining there is Arabic philology and literature, to which the Spanish Muslims restrict themselves. Jurisprudence is an empty institution among them and a mere shadow of its real self."

19. Ibn Khaldun calls these the "traditional, conventional sciences. There is no place for intellect in them, save that the intellect may be used in connection with them to relate problems of detail with basic principles." *Ibid.*, 436.

20. 'Abd al-Majid al-Charfi, *Tahdith al-fikr al-islami* (Casablanca: Nashr al-Fennek, 1998), 7–16.

21. Fouad Zakariya, *al-Sahwah al-islamiyyah fi mizan al-'aql* (Cairo: Dar al-Fikr li'l Dirasat wa'l Nashr wa'l Tawzi', 1989), 9.

22. For a theoretical argument on the issue of Islam in Orientalist and Marxist scholarship, see Rema Hammami and Martina Rieker, "Feminist Orientalism and Orientalist Marxism." *New Left Review*, 170, July–August 1988, 93–106.

23. Nasr Hamid Abu Zayd, *Mafhum al-nass: dirasa fi 'ulum al-qur'an* (Casablanca: al-Markaz al-Thaqafi al-'Arabi, 1988).

24. Rochdy Alili, *Qu'est-ce que l'islam?* (Paris: La Découverte, 1996).

25. See Sa'd al-Din Ibrahim, "al-Mufakkir wa'l amir: tajsir al-fajwah bayana sani'i al-qarar wa'l mufakirrin al-'arab." In al-Tahir Labib, *al-Intellijensia al-'arabiyyah* (Tunis: al-Dar al-'Arabiyyah li'l Kitab, n.d.), 213–45.

26. "To have been an Aligarah man, I have over and over again found, a passport to the respect and confidence of both Englishmen and Indians." Sir Auckland Colvin as quoted by Khaliq Ahmad Nizami, *History of the Aligarah Muslim University* (New Delhi: Idarah-I Adabiyat-I Delli, 1995), xii.

27. Jamal Malik, *Colonialization of Islam: Dissolution of Traditional Institutions in Pakistan* (New Delhi: Manohar, 1996), 130.

28. "Quite a few young minds were brainwashed by these religious groups [in the Dini Madaris] into carrying forward the messianic spirit of Islam into others parts of the world. Their dogmatic approach and intolerance of others' points of view often produced fanatics who were recruited for trans-territorial missions." Matinuddin, *The Taliban Phenomenon*, 13.

29. "Some students spend most of their lives attending scholarly sessions. Still, one finds them silent. They do not talk and do not discuss matters. More than is necessary, they are concerned with memorization. Thus, they do not obtain much of a habit in the practice of science and scientific instruction. Some of them think that they have obtained the habit. But when they enter into a discussion or disputation, or do some teaching, their scientific habit is found to be defective. The only reason for their deficiency is lack of instruction, together with the break in the tradition of scientific instruction that affects them. Apart from that, their memorized knowledge may be more extensive than that of other scholars, because they are so much concerned with memorizing. They think that scientific habit is identical with memorized knowledge. But that is not so." Ibn Khaldun, *The Muqaddimah; II*, 429–30.

30. "Le clerc écarte depuis longtemps, le liberal déchu depuis peu, se rabattent, dans l'État nationale, sur le champ favori des études littéraires et c'est au nom de ces études que se hisse le drapeau de la culture nationale. La culture dont il s'agit est la culture classique profane, celle de l'Arabe, littérature au sens restrictif du terme et dont les composants sont la poèsie, la prose artistique, les manuels d'etiquette et le savoir-vivre." Abdallah Laroui, *L'idéologie arabe contemporaine* (Paris: Maspero, 1970), 85.

31. Malek Bennabi, *Islam in History and Society*, tr. Asma Rashid (Islamabad: Islamic Research Institute, 1988), 27.

32. Muhammed Arkoun, "History as an Ideology of Legitimation: A Comparative Approach in Islamic and European Contexts." In Gema M. Munoz, ed., *Islam, Modernism, and the West* (London: I. B. Tauris, 1999), 27.

33. In many Muslim countries, no preacher is allowed to mount the pulpit before his *khutbah* is approved by the Ministry of Religious Affairs.

34. I am indebted in the phrasing of this statement to L. Kolakowski, *Main Currents of Marxism*, vol. III (Oxford: Oxford University Press, 1978), 465. In speaking of post-1968 communism in East Europe, Kolakowski notes that communism "ceased being an intellectual problem and became merely a question of power." *Ibid.*

35. Ishtiaq Husain Qureshi, *Education in Pakistan* (Karachi: Ma'aref, 1975), 119 [quoted by Fazlur Rahman in *Islam and Modernity: Transformation of an Intellectual Tradition* (Chicago: University of Chicago Press, 1982), 111. According to the renowned Pakistani critic Iqbal Ahmad, higher education in Pakistan has almost collapsed. There are multiple reasons for that. The first relates to the ques-

tion of language; the second to the failure of the modern state to introduce an alternative system of education to the colonial; and the third concerns the different functions of education under both colonial and nationalist regimes. See David Barsamian, *Iqbal Ahmad: Confronting Empire* (Cambridge: South End Press, 2000), 19.

36. We must not underestimate the large number of women who graduate from Shari'ah colleges in Muslim universities.

37. On the end of the Cold War and the social sciences in Europe, see Ignacio Ramonet, "Nouvel ordre, rébellions, nationalismes: Un monde à reconstruire." *Le Monde Diplomatique*, May 1992, 1.

38. Hamza Alavi, "Pakistan and Islam: Ethnicity and Ideology." In Halliday and Alavi, eds., *State and Ideology*, 81.

39. Talal Asad, *Genealogies of Religion: Discipline and Reasons of Power in Christianity and Islam* (Baltimore: Johns Hopkins Press, 1993).

40. See Fouad Zakariyya, "al-Falsafah wa'l din fi'l mujtama' al-'arabi al-mu'asir." In Markaz Dirasat al-Wihdah al-'Arabiyyah, *al-Falsafah fi'l watan al-'arabi al-mu'asir* (Beirut: Markaz Dirasat al-Wihdah al-'Arabiyyah, 1985), 43–69.

41. In a visit to Srinagar, Kashmir, in the summer of 1998, I was invited to give a talk in Arabic at Ahl al-Hadith College, a Wahhabi-financed Islamic school with 500 students. I was surprised to learn that all the students at that school, none of whom left Kashmir, spoke fluent Arabic. On Ahl al-Hadith in the South Asia, see Bashir Ahmad Khan, "The Ahl-i-Hadith: A Socio-Religious Reform Movement in Kashmir." *The Muslim World*, 90 (1&2), Spring 2000; 133–157.

42. In his discussion of the rise of the Islamic movement in the Sudan, al-Haj Warraq speaks about the political exploitation of Sufi brotherhoods by the Numayri regime in the 1970s and 1980s and the rise of Islamic radicalism. In the first instance, some Sufi leaders in the Sudan cooperated with the regime in exchange for financial remuneration and political prestige, and in the second, Islamism found a big support among some university students of rural and poor back-grounds, who lacked any critical sense of education, "The reason for the rising influence of the Islamist trends amongst the students is to be explained by the nature of the dominant educational systems in the country. Curricula and methods of teaching depend to a large extent on rote memorization, which kills in the student the desire for free enquiry and open dialogue." Al-Haj Warraq, "Sina'at al-wahm: al-asbab al-ijtima'iyyah li dhahirat al-hawas al-dini fi'l sudan." In *Qadayah Fikriyyah*, vol. VIII, 1989, 217.

43. Rif'at al-Sa'id, "al-Islam al-siyasi: mina al-tatarruf ila mazind mina al-tatarruf." In *Ibid.*, 19.

44. See Raymond Williams, "Means of Communication as Means of Production." In his *Problems in Materialism and Culture: Selected Essays* (London: Verso, 1997), 50–63.

45. Islamists have begun to take the issue of democracy seriously. In the view of Khurshid Ahmad, a leading Pakistani Islamist thinker, "Islam and the Muslim Umma brook no sympathy for arbitrary and authoritarian rule. Whatever arbitrary power reigns is more a product of colonization and Westernization, and not of Muslim ideals, history or contemporary aspirations ... Whatever despotic or arbitrary rule exists in the Muslim lands is part of an alien and imposed tradition, against which the forces of Islamic resurgence are struggling." Khurshid Ahmad, "Islam and Democracy: Some Conceptual and Contemporary Dimensions." *The Muslim World*, 90 (1&2), Spring 2000, 19.

46. See Q. Zurayk, *al-Mualafat al-kamilah li'l doktor Qustantine Zurayk*, 4 vols (Beirut: Markaz Dirasat al-Wihdah al-'Arabiyyah, 1995).

47. See Adonis ['Ali Ahmad Sa'id], "Reflections on the Manifestations of Intellectual Backwardness in Arab Society." In *CEMAM Reports* (Beirut: St. Joseph University, 1974), and *al-Thabit wa'l mutahawwil*, 3 vols (Beirut: Dar al-'Awdah, 1983).

48. See mainly Ghali Shukri, *al-Nahdah wa'l suqut fi'l fikr al-misri al-hadith* (Beirut: Dar al-Tal'iah, 1982), and *Mudhakarat thaqafah tahtadir* (Cairo: al-Hay'ah al-Misriyyah al-'Ammah, 1995).

49. Laroui, *L'idéologie arabe contemporaine*, and *The Crisis of the Arab Intelligentsia: Traditionalism or Historicism?* (Berkeley: University of California Press, 1976).

50. Al-'Afif al-Akhdar, "Min naqd al-sama' ila naqd al-ard". In F. Lenin, *Nusus hawla al-mawqif mina al-din*, tr. Muhammad al-Kabbe (Beirut: Dar al-Tali'ah, 1972).

51. Sadiq Jalal al-'Azm, *Naqd al-fikr al-dini* (Beirut: Dar al-Tali'ah, 1969); *al-Naqd al-dhati ba'da al-hazimah* (Beirut: Dar al-Tali'ah, 1969), and "Sur l'islam, la laïcité et l'Occident." *Le Monde Diplomatique*, September 1999, 16–7.

52. Tayyib Tizini, "Nahwa 'ilmaniyyah takun madkhalan li mashru' 'arabi nahdawi jadid." *Al-Tariq*, 55 (6), 1996, 4–6.

53. Halim Barakat, *The Arab World: Society, Culture, and Change* (Berkeley: University of California Press, 1993).

54. Zaki Najib Mahmud, *Tajdid al-fikr al-'arabi* (Cairo: Dar al-Shuruq, 1978).

55. Jabir 'Asfur, *Hawamish 'ala daftar al-tanwir* (Cairo: Dar Su'ad al-Sabah, 1994), 13. 'Asfur argues, along the famous line of Hisham Sharabi, that patriarchal thought and structure permeate contemporary Arab societies. Neo-patriarchy in Arab society has marshalled both physical and mental powers to safeguard its interests. The result has been a new type of irrationalism, which is supported by unlimited amounts of funds and the official mass media.

56. Fouad Zakariyya, "al-'Ilmaniyyah darurah hadariyyah." *Ibid*.

57. Quoted by Ghali Shukri in *Diktatoriyat al-takhalluf al-'arabi* (Cairo: al-Hay'ah al-Misriyyah al-'Ammah li'l Kitab, 1994), 43.

58. See the moving account of the recent civil war in Algeria in Nuri al-Jarrah, *al-firdaws al-dami: wahid wa thalathin yawman fi'l jaza'ir* [*The Bleeding Paradise: 31 Days in Algeria*] (London: Riad al-Rayyes Books, 2000).

59. François Burgat, ed., *L'Islamisme au Maghreb: La Voix du sud* (Paris: Karthala, 1988).

60. See the writings of Sadik Jalal al-'Azm, Adonis, Abdallah Laroui, and Yasin al-Hafiz.

61. See Ghali Shukri, "Misr: firdaws khayru al-umam." In *Qadayah Fikriyyah*, vols 13–14, 1989 and Yusra Mustafa, "Azmat al-muthaqaf al-'aqlani." In Mahmud Amin al-'Alim, *Qadayah Fikriyyah, al-Fikr al-'Arabi 'ala masharif al-qarn al-wahid wa'l 'ishrun* (Cairo: Dar Qadayah Fikriyyah, 1995), 219–228.

62. See Tareq al-Bishri, *al-Hiwar al-islami al-'ilmani* (Cairo: Dar al-Shuruq, 1996).

63. Muhammad 'Imarah, *al-Dawlah al-islamiyyah bayna al-'ilmaniyyah wa'l sultah al-madaniyyah* (Cairo: Dar al-Shuruq, 1988).

64. In his preface to his major book on public freedoms in Islam, al-Ghannoushi says, "I present this book to the city Damascus that witnessed my second birth with the help of the unknown soldier, the pharmacist Muhammad Amin al-Mujtahid." Rashid al-Ghannoushi, *al-Huriyyat al-'ammah fi'l dawlah al-islamiyya*h (Markaz Dirasat al-Wihdah al-'Arabiyyah, 1993), 5.

65. See Munir Shafiq, *Fi al-hadathah wa'l khitab al-hadathi* (Casablanca: al-Markaz al-Thaqafi al-'Arabi, 1999).

66. al-Ghannoushi, *al-Huriyyat al-'ammah*; 310.

67. Shukri, *Diktatoriat al-takhalluf*, 114.

68. See Nazih Ayubi, *Political Islam* (London: Routledge, 1994).

69. Fahmi Huwaydi, *al-Maqalat al-mahdhura*h (Cairo: Dar al-Shuruq, 1998), 17.

70. Muhammad 'Abid al-Jabiri, "al-Mujtama' al-madani: tasa'ulat wa afaq." In 'Abdallah Hammoudi, *Wa'y al-Mujtama' bi dhatihi: 'an al-mujtama' al-madani fi'l maghrib al-'arabi* (Casablanca: Dar Tubqal, 1998), 43.

71. 'Ali al-Kenz, "al-Islam wa'l hawiyyah: Mulahadhat li'l bahth." In Markaz Dirasat al-Wihdah al-'Arabiyyah, *al-Din fi'l mujtama' al-'arabi* (Beirut: Markaz Dirasat al-Wihdah al-'Arabiyyah, 1990), 105.

72. See Ramzi Zaki, *Wada'an li'l tabaqah al-mutawasitah* (Cairo: Dar al-Mustaqbal al-'Arabi, 1998).

73. Harold J. Laski, *Liberty in the Modern State* (Harmondsworth: Penguin Books, 1938), 49. Laski further notes that, "Liberty always demands a limitation of political authority, and it is never attained unless the rulers of the state can, where necessary, be called to account." *Ibid.*, 50.

74. See L. Carl Brown, *Tunisia: The Politics of Modernization* (New York: Praeger, 1964).

75. 'Abd al-Hamid al-Ibrahimi, *al-Maghreb al-'arabi fi muftaraq al-turuq fi dhil al-tahawwulat al-duwaliyyah* (Beirut: Markaz Dirasat al-Wihdah al-'Arabiyyah, 1996), 112–13.

76. Abdelwahab Bouhdiba, "Place et fonction de l'imaginaire dans la société arabo-musulmane." In *Culture et société* (Tunis: Université de Tunis, 1978), 45, and

Munassif Wannas, "al-Din wa'l dawla fi Tunis: 1956–1987." In Markaz Dirasat al-Wihdah al-'Arabiyyah, *al-Din fi'l mujtama' al-'arabi* (Beirut: Markaz Dirasat al-Wihdah al-'Arabiyyah, 1990), 475.

77. Ibrahimi, *al-Maghreb al-'Arabi, ibid.*, 461. See also, 'Abd al-Hamid Ibrahimi, *Stratégie de développement pour l'Algérie* (Paris: Economica, 1991).

78. Abdelkader Zghal, "Le retour de sacré et la nouvelle demande idéologique de jeunes scolarises: Le cas de la Tunisie." *Le Maghreb Musulman*, 1979.

79. Abdelkader Zghal, "al-Istratijiyya al-jadidah li harakat al-itijah al-islami: munawara an al-ta'bir 'an al-thaqafah al-siyasiyyah al-tunisiyyah." In Markaz Dirasat al-Wihdah al-'Arabiyyah, *al-Din fi'l mujtama' al-'arabi* (Beirut: Markaz Dirasat al-Wihdah al-'Arabiyyah, 1990), 341.

80. Ali El-Kenz, *Algerian Reflections on Arab Crises*, tr. Robert W. Stooky (Texas: University of Texas Press, 1991), 26.

3

GRIEVING TOGETHER: SEPTEMBER 11 AS A MEASURE OF SOCIAL CAPITAL IN THE U.S.

Nancy T. Ammerman

In his 1995 article and subsequent book, Robert Putnam famously lamented that Americans are spending too much time "bowling alone," that our individualized leisure pursuits are but one measure of the degree to which our store of "social capital" has been depleted.[1] Putnam convincingly argues that social capital is good for us. We are healthier, happier, and have more robust democracies when we spend time with our fellow citizens in face-to-face voluntary organizations and when we exchange favors with neighbors we know by name. But households whose members work more hours, watch more TV, and commute longer distances are less likely to engage in such civic activities. Those changes and others have created major challenges for U.S. society, challenges that our current store of social institutions seem to Putnam and others ill-equipped to meet. The Elks, Kiwanis, and Shriners of an earlier era have declined precipitously, with no other community organization apparently available to take their place.

What about religion? Putnam is not convinced that religious organizations are immune from the dangerous slide he sees. Even though attendance and membership have not dropped at anything like the rate observed in other organizations, the most "civic" religious groups (mainline Protestants) have experienced real losses, while less "civic" groups (evangelicals) have increased in numbers. Putnam and others worry that these evangelical groups will not provide the sorts of public benefits we need.[2] They excel at "bonding" social capital, but not at "bridging." According to these observers, evangelical groups help their own members to feel accepted and cared for, but are less concerned with the sorts of "public" activities that bring diverse groups together around common concerns.

The tragedies of September 11 offer a window on this argument. In the aftermath of that horrific day, U.S. society was in dire need of both bridging and bonding. Thrown into a state of chaos, with enormous immediate and long-term social and economic needs, Americans will have to reach deeply into their store of social capital to continue to thrive. Facing unknown enemies, reeling from personal and institutional losses, recovery will require real investments of whatever social capital might be at hand. Do they have what it will take? Has the store of social capital been so depleted that there are no reserves with which to meet this challenge?

In this chapter I will address those questions by looking at the role of congregations and other religious organizations. I will begin by acknowledging the challenges that have indeed transformed religious institutions over the last generation, creating networks of "loose connections" out of the parish-based loyalties of earlier times. I will then lay out the critical social-capital-building roles that are still played by congregations and look at how they have responded to the challenges of September 11. Throughout, I will argue that existing U.S. institutions have demonstrated a latent capacity that may have surprised those who took them to be near death. In addition, I will argue that we have seen a remarkable capacity for the creation of new religious social institutions – from shrines to vigils – that extend the ability of existing organizations to create and nurture the social capital that is needed.

CREATING SOCIAL CAPITAL IN A POST-1960S WORLD

Much of the worry about civil society in the U.S. has centered around the cultural shifts that began as the Baby Boom generation came of age and gradually replaced its more settled and loyal parents in the population. An older generation who invested in clubs and civic groups over a lifetime are being replaced by volunteers who sign up for specific and limited tasks. Newer generations are less eager to do whatever the organization needs to have done than to accomplish a task that uniquely expresses their own gifts and commitments.[3] But it is not just that the nature of voluntary engagement has changed. As Robert Wuthnow points out, all of our institutions are now more "porous".[4] Our jobs and neighborhoods, even our families, are less permanent and certainly less taken-for-granted. The kinds of connections that characterized earlier times are simply less common today. Like Wuthnow, I would argue that the issue is change, not decline; but there is no denying that these changes have posed serious challenges for many existing U.S. institutions, including congregations.

In our mobile, fragmented, and presumably secular society, any assumption that congregations occupy a place of privilege or establishment-induced loyalty is impossible. They cannot count on a position at the center of town or the prestige and connections of their members or the loyalty and stability of multiple generations to fill the pews. While American disestablishment has always meant that citizens were free to choose how and whether to be religious, since the 1960s increasing levels of education and mobility have dislodged familial commitments and made religious choice a real fact of life.[5] Indeed, religious commitment is not even simply a matter of choosing a single church or synagogue or mosque. Rather it is often a matter of choosing a variety of religious groups – some inside a single congregation and others scattered among all the many places where we do our living.[6] Congregations, like all the rest of our connections, are less a matter of lifelong loyalty and more a matter of contingent commitments. In Wuthnow's words, our spiritual lives are now more a matter of "seeking" than of "dwelling."[7] Our commitments are no less vital for their contingency, but for institutions accustomed to family-like loyalty this new reality is requiring serious adjustment. Creating and nurturing communities of faith in today's world is not easy. But precisely because of the disestablishment and fragmentation of that world, they are all the more critical.

THE EVERYDAY WORK OF CONGREGATIONS: CAPACITIES FOR CRISIS RESPONSE

For much of the last decade I have been engaged in the study of congregations, observing and interviewing and surveying people in communities across the country and in every sort of religious tradition.[8] They range from tiny to enormous and from declining to thriving, from old and venerable to new and fragile. Some are visible and active in their communities, while others seem to lurk in the background. Some seem ready to meet any new challenge, while many seem bewildered by the changes surrounding them. In short, there are real differences in the degree to which they seem to have the capacity to contribute to the social capital of their communities. Whatever we may say about congregations in general will clearly not be true of each congregation in particular. Nevertheless, taken together, the 300,000 or more congregations in the U.S. form a significant institutional network on which we depend in ways we do not always recognize, but which the events of 2001 have made more apparent. Just how do congregations contribute to the well-being of their communities?

Congregations as social service hubs

Congregations provide direct and tangible benefits to their members and communities – food, clothing, shelter, education, counseling, medical assistance, and more. As Carl Dudley points out in chapter four in this volume, when people seemingly have nowhere else to turn, they turn to churches and synagogues and mosques. In recent years, a number of studies have attempted to quantify the social service contributions of congregations. A University of Pennsylvania study looked at 111 congregations that occupy historic buildings in cities around the country. It was estimated that these 111 average contributing the equivalent of $145,000 per year in services to persons outside their own membership.[9] The recent National Congregations Survey, using the most nearly-representative sample of congregations we have ever had, found that 57 percent of all congregations are involved in social service activity, either through their own programs or by supporting others.[10]

At least as important as counting the contributions is simply noting that this pattern of care is lodged in an institutionalized set of cultural expectations. U.S. culture sees helping the needy as a religious virtue and expects religious organizations to be engaged in service activities. That same cultural definition makes it likely that people in need will seek out congregations as sources of help, but it also makes congregations a likely vehicle for the volunteer energies of those who want to serve. Even people who are not members may join in a congregation's tutoring program or help out at the shelter once a week. A *New York Times* editorial two months after the attack noted that "people in New York have been eager to do something – *anything* – to help." The editors offered a long list of suggestions, among them the "churches, synagogues and mosques in every borough in need of reliable help with their community programs."[11] Congregations create what Wuthnow calls "helping roles."[12] They construct opportunities for doing good that allow for a bounded exercise of compassion – one that is recognized as legitimate and honorable, but one that allows us to do good without being absorbed by the effort. Congregations are able to expend social capital in service to the community because they are recognized as legitimate places for investment by people with social capital to spend. Congregations are a critical strand in the social fabric because U.S. society retains this cultural expectation linking religious organizations and community service.

The strength of these U.S. cultural expectations can be found in their effects on groups that are new to this society. While this sort of community engagement remains most common among traditional Protestants, Catholics, and Jews, it is also becoming part of the emerging traditions of American Hindus, Buddhists, Muslims, and others. At the Jamhiyatut Tahaawon Islamic Center in the Bronx, for instance, routine activities include a blood drive, a food pantry, and outreach that links members with city social services.[13] And in cities across the country, our own research found Hindu, Muslim, Buddhist, and Ba'hai congregations becoming a part of the network of care in their communities.[14] Similarly, as Dudley notes, the Faith Communities Today study found mosques to be as active in basic social service ministries as were other congregations around the country.[15]

Mobilizing their own resources and the volunteer resources of others, then, congregations routinely provide food, clothing, and shelter; but they also provide community groups with meeting space and transportation, bulletin boards and public address systems, copying machines and paper. The diverse material resources of congregations provide an infrastructure for caring, an infrastructure often made most visible in times of crisis. In the days after the 1992 uprising in south central Los Angeles, for instance, the normal flow of food into the area was seriously disrupted. Supermarkets had been burned and looted, but the churches were still standing, and nascent distribution systems swung into action. Everyone from the Episcopal diocese to The Salvation Army to Catholic Charities activated their food and clothing networks, and soon eighteen-wheelers were arriving at church doors, and neighborhoods were getting food. As researcher John Orr and his associates note, "Inventories were already in place. Volunteers were already recruited. The distribution mechanism had already been charted. The distribution sites were already identified – religious institutions, located on almost every square mile of the affected area."[16]

We have seen this all over again since September 11. When people needed a place to gather, organize, and care for each other, congregations were already there. Perhaps most visible of the responding congregations has been St. Paul's Chapel, just one block from the former World Trade Center site. Miraculously unscathed, the building was quickly opened as a place of refuge for the relief workers. Soon, "it was overflowing with supplies. Pillows were in the pews so workers could take naps. A handwritten sign attached to a music stand near the entrance said, 'Counselor available. Please ask.'"[17] St. Paul's Chapel has provided "hundreds of hungry, tired, dirty, and often stressed-out rescue workers with everything from coffee and meals to eye drops, clean underwear, and a place to catch a little sleep." Father Lyndon Harris, the church's pastor, noted, "That first week after the disaster, … we had a really fluid staff of volunteers working at the chapel, making calls for all sorts of donations. We had all kinds of people walking in, offering us their services on behalf of the rescue workers, everything from massage therapists to grief counselors to podiatrists."[18] Its beautiful historic building was readily recognized as sacred and trusted space. Its infrastructure and connections brought volunteers and donations to the site. Its staff stepped in to coordinate and encourage. In a time of extraordinary need, this congregation – like many others – did what it already knew how to do.

What is also clear, however, is that a great deal of what congregations do in the community is not done alone. Far more common than programs run by single congregations are patterns of service provision that involve a complex network of organizational partnerships – connections that include everything from informal coalitions among churches to formal programs run with government backing to support for religious and secular nonprofit agencies locally and around the world. At St. Paul's Chapel, in fact, it was a sister church and a nearby seminary that helped to get the ball rolling. Seamen's Church, located in the nearby South Street Seaport organized the first relief efforts and coordinated the activity of scores of volunteers recruited by Manhattan's General Theological Seminary.[19]

Across all the congregations we surveyed in our most recent study, there are, on average, six partnerships through which outreach work is done.[20] This is over and above whatever connections a congregation may have through its own denomination and beyond what it may do on its own. This pattern is virtually a universal for Mainline Protestant congregations, but the norm is nearly as strong in the other Christian and Jewish traditions as well, even if overall levels of activity are lower.[21] Only among the most sectarian groups (Mormons and Jehovah's Witnesses, for instance) is it common to find congregations that have no connections outside their own religious world. Partnerships between congregations and other community organizations have simply been institutionalized as an expected pattern in most of American religion.

Just what kinds of commitment do such partnerships entail? Rarely does a partnership involve a whole congregation on an on-going and intense basis.

But rarely is it something about which the group knows or cares little. Nearly two-thirds of all congregations, for instance, have at least one outside organization that uses space in their buildings (either donated outright or made available at minimal cost). On average, in fact, there are two such organizations for every congregation. If nothing else, congregations are valuable to their communities because they provide meeting space and other facilities to support the work of organizations beyond their own membership.

But it is not just empty space; it is also person-power. Each congregation contributes, on average, volunteers to three organizations. That, of course, does not begin to count the number of groups in which individual members work, not as official representatives of their congregations, but at least in part because their congregation encourages such activity. In fact, 60 percent of the individual members we surveyed claim that they participate in community service organizations at least a few times a year, and 75 percent claim that they, at least occasionally, provide informal service to people in need.

This is not just about mobilizing volunteers. On average three organizations receive monetary contributions from each congregation, for an average of nearly $1400 per organization per year. And most churches supplement their monetary contributions to at least one organization with other material goods – food, clothing, furniture, Christmas gifts, and the like – collected by the members.

To at least some minimal degree nearly every congregation (91 percent) has some connection with an organization that allows it to serve people in need, even if it does not have the resources or inclination to provide help on its own. Congregations offer critical resources of money, space, personpower, and other support to a wide array of organizations engaged in providing for the well-being of communities. The work being supported is most often first-line assistance to people with critical physical and economic needs, but nearly as often congregations support work that is aimed at the enrichment of the community's educational, recreational, and cultural life. Through congregations people learn about others who share common needs and interests, often banding together in support groups, forming recreational and cultural organizations, and offering resources to a larger community. Politics, economic development, and issue advocacy are on the agenda as well, but they are not the primary ways in which most congregations seek to contribute to the well-being of their communities. It is routine networks of service and enrichment that sustain those communities, and it is congregations that are key nodes in that network.

The networks in which congregations participate reach, of course, beyond the immediate neighborhoods in which they are located. Most commonly they are metropolitan and county-wide, linking groups into cross-town relationships. They also stretch across the nation and around the world, and it was especially these larger networks that sprang into action following September 11. People far from New York and Washington found ways to be connected to people who needed their help. Among the most visible and trusted of the responders was The Salvation Army, a religious group with a long history of work where society's needs are most acute. This corps of evangelical believers regularly partners with contributors, volunteers, and other agencies from across the religious and secular spectrum. In November, 2001, they summarized their work this way:

> Out of the initial confusion of mountains of donated supplies and more volunteers than jobs has coalesced a finely-tuned relief operation. The Salvation Army is supporting the city's efforts and coordinating with other relief organizations to fill in any gaps in the delivery of services to those affected by the terrorist attacks. Around the clock, The Salvation Army is operating mobile canteens, hydration centers, supply centers, and providing grief counseling and hot meals to relief workers. Centers in New York City and New Jersey are offering immediate financial assistance to those with urgent needs, as well as assisting those who do not qualify for aid from other organizations. Existing Salvation Army corps community centers will be providing this type of assistance, making it easier to get help. The Salvation Army is developing long term programs to support the families of victims and others affected by the disaster which are estimated to operate for several years.[22]

Their existing network of centers and staff was ready to expand to accommodate the enormous influx of donations and volunteers that poured in from around the country. Another major clearing house for faith-based relief efforts was Church World Service (CWS), the humanitarian ministry of the National Council of Churches. Because they had blankets pre-positioned on Long Island, they were able to respond immediately to supply the relief centers that were being set up. Since then, they have concentrated on crisis and pastoral counseling, providing teams of trauma counselors who had previously worked in such places as Oklahoma City and Kosovo. They have also sponsored webcasts that have provided opportunities for people in the more dispersed communities to find resources for dealing with grief and trauma. And CWS also helped mobilize a team from the Church of the Brethren to provide child care and spiritual support for victims' children.[23]

Similarly many individual denominations mobilized their disaster relief teams to help. American Baptist Men sent crews of volunteers to the Trade Center area to help residents clean their apartments.[24] One local pastor who went with a crew from his church in Essex, Connecticut, reported that "these apartments received a direct hit. Most of them were initially covered in several inches of debris. The four-week effort cleaned over 400 apartments and involved over 3,000 volunteers".[25] The Convoy of Hope, an agency of the Assemblies of God, sent trucks full of aid, and the Assemblies' minister Denny Nissley set up the primary feeding program that served the recovery effort at the Pentagon.[26] Lutherans concentrated on shoring up the ministries of congregations throughout the New York metropolitan region that had lost members in the attacks. By November, their focus had turned to the impact of the coming holidays: to resources for children and adolescents, and to equipping pastors and lay leaders to deal with issues of grief and anger and injustice. Gil Furst, Director for Lutheran Disaster Response, said, "Once more I thank God for the privilege of connecting the outpouring of love from across the country to the desperate needs that continue to arise."[27] From Greek Orthodox to Presbyterian to Disciples of Christ, denominations used their networks of communication to let people know what was needed and their staff and expertise to coordinate efforts. Like the larger ecumenical and parachurch networks, they provided direct physical, financial, and emotional support to the families of victims and to the recovery crews.

These same networks were also mobilized to care for the people of Afghanistan. Many individual denominations began collecting money and supplies for people who had already suffered from decades of civil war and oppressive rule and now endured a new round of bombing and war. Church World Service and World Vision were among the most visible of the faith-based organizations channeling the resources of U.S. congregations into this larger arena. In addition to managing and brokering contributions from dozens of governmental and business sources, World Vision mobilized its own formidable network of individual and church donors. From contributions already in hand, they were able to send "five containers of relief supplies from [their] warehouse in Denver for distribution in Afghanistan. The supplies include blankets, cooking utensils, water containers, tents, plastic sheeting and emergency food rations and [would] be pre-positioned in Uzbekistan at the end of November."[28] Organizations like this will remain in place for the long period of recovery work and rebuilding, but their pre-existing infrastructure was critical in the immediate days and weeks of crisis response.

Congregations as community

Congregations, of course, are much more than simply links in the social service network. As critical as this "bridging" work is the work of "bonding". Congregations gather people together, providing a focal point of belonging, caring, and comfort for their own members and for strangers who may join them. In fact, congregations themselves recognize this internal community-building role as among the most important things they do. They provide "fellowship" activities and try to build a family-like atmosphere for their members. The point is that congregations take seriously the task of creating communal events and spaces where people meet, debate, celebrate, grieve, and know each other on a face-to-face basis.[29] They foster the "gathered happenings" out of which our stories are made.

Because they are, in Stephen Warner's words, "presumptively legitimate," congregations also provide places where our gathering implies something positive about our participation in the society as a whole.[30] Attendance at church or synagogue (and now mosque) signals our willingness to invest in the community and communicates our desire to be seen as good citizens.

These are also places where people take care of each other. They are a "first response" social service agency for their own members. They supply food and child-care, and job assistance, and in-home visits to the elderly, sick, and mourning. At the Bronx mosque one of the leaders reflected that "this is a center where problems can be known and solved, where weddings take place, where, if a person is tired, he can come to rest." Not surprisingly, the mosque is providing financial support for one of their members whose husband, a cook at Windows on the World, was lost on September 11.[31]

We should not ignore the degree to which these "extended family" or "village" style services sustain people in ways that might otherwise require external agency assistance. The congregation is a place of belonging that is bigger than the family itself and into which one does not have to be born, but a place where virtues of common good and public accountability can be learned and practiced in ways that benefit the society as a whole. A healthy society depends on there being places where relationships of trust are formed, where a sense of identity is nurtured. These relationships of trust are social capital in its most basic form. They facilitate communication and coordination of activities, and they provide basic well-being to their participants. Both individuals and society as a whole are healthier for the simple fact of belonging.

After September 11 many in the U.S. seemed to sense exactly this. To be well, they needed to gather, and many chose to gather in communities of faith. Especially in the days immediately after the attacks, wounded and grieving Americans wanted to be with others, to share feelings and stories, to touch and be touched, to declare their citizenship and belonging in some tangible way. When the first weekend after the attack arrived, attendance at services nationwide jumped by at least 15 percent, bringing nearly half the U.S. population into its sanctuaries.[32] Numbers of worshippers were up everywhere, but especially in the New York and Washington areas. The Roman Catholic Archdiocese of Newark reported attendance up 30 percent. Synagogues were "bursting at the seams" for the High Holidays that came soon after the attacks. Mosques were full of people attempting to comprehend the complicated effects of this tragedy in the Muslim community. Even Zen Centers were full.[33] These numbers may or may not be maintained. Probably they will not. The issue here is that in a time of need, U.S. congregations were there to provide the gathering spaces people needed.[34] Rabbi David Wolpe, spiritual leader at Sinai Temple in Los Angeles, said that at the first Friday night service after the attack, "the whole place just wept. We all put our arms around each other." At Willow Creek Community Church, near Chicago, a representative said, "We experienced big crowds, I believe, because people felt helpless ... They just had a hunger to get together as a church body."[35]

Gathering is one of the fundamental "social capital" tasks that congregations do everyday. Their presence is part of the glue that binds people together in such times of crisis. It remains to be seen how patterns of bonding are woven into the larger social fabric. Gathering with others who are recognized as "brothers and sisters" can sometimes lead to dangerous antagonism against those outside the religious family. Bonding can have a dark side. Since September 11 there have been attacks on mosques and harassment of individual Muslims, presumably by those whose sense of community and belonging allowed Muslims to be denied the benefits of participation and respect, but there have also been new interfaith connections and initiatives, with Christians and Jews organizing protection and care for vulnerable Muslims. As we will see below, these new forms of religious social organization provide means by which more insular forms of bonding can be overcome.

Congregations as sacred space

In the face of massive suffering and incomprehensible evil, simply gathering was important, but not enough. As Rabbi Wolpe noted, "There are some things that only a religious community can allow you to express."[36] Both our laments and our hopes needed a sacred hearing. As much as people know they can turn to congregations for material assistance and as a gathering place, they also know that congregations are primarily spiritual institutions. Indeed, the vast majority of congregations themselves are very clear that their primary task is a spiritual one – to provide opportunities for their members to worship, to help those members deepen their individual spiritual lives, and to provide religious education for their children.[37] We would fail to understand the fundamental nature of congregational life if we did not take seriously the religious character of their work.

We would also fail to understand them if we labeled their spiritual activities as otherworldly and therefore irrelevant in the here and now. As Peter Berger pointed out more than three decades ago, the root of the word "ecstacy" is "ex-stasis" or literally standing out of place.[38] The liminal space (as Victor Turner[39] would have called it) provided by worship can often provide both critical perspective and a sense of possibility that have real effects in how people then engage the world outside. Very few congregations utterly shun attempts to make the world a better place. Not all churches are "activist," in the usual sense of that word, but nearly all churches think that the spiritual work they do makes a real difference in this world.[40]

That spiritual work has taken as many forms as there are religious traditions in the U.S., and even within the most settled traditions, after September 11, leaders have reached for words and music and rituals that have stretched beyond the ordinary. Those that could quite literally opened their doors for anyone who needed a place to pray and to be reminded of the sacredness of life. Even when relief workers needed no food or supplies, they came to St. Paul's to pause and regain the spiritual energy to go on. At Judson Memorial Church, in Greenwich Village, the pastor watched with the crowds in Washington Square Park as the second airplane struck the World Trade Center. He immediately opened the church and invited people in to pray. Throughout the coming days, he also invited them to talk, listening to their grief and anger and their memories of those who died, gathering the people's experiences into the words he would voice when it came time to preach.[41]

Around the nation, clergy searched for the words to use that next weekend, with record crowds in their pews. Many reminded their hearers to beware of vengeance, to refuse to stereotype people with dark skins and unfamiliar religions, noting that every religion has its zealots who commit violence in the name of God. Others simply voiced the unanswerable questions about why evil exists. Many pointed to the stories of heroism and kindness as evidence that good has emerged out of this evil, pointing to the love communicated even by those who knew they were about to die. Some simply invited congregants to cry. And others pointed forward to the hope of rebuilding, but cautioned that human effort would not be enough. In some sanctuaries, the call was to envision a world in which just societies no longer breed terror.[42] Some wondered whether these were signs of the "end times." In whatever theological categories they had at hand, clergy played their role in helping citizens make sense of a crisis, giving it enough comprehensibility to allow life to go on.

Beyond their sermons, clergy were also challenged to deal with the myriad of other complications of life and death. Catholics and Jews faced the liturgical dilemma of how to have funerals in the absence of a body. Leaders of all faiths found themselves offering pastoral care for griefs they might never have faced before and in a volume unprecedented for most.[43] One of many touching and creative responses to these dilemmas came from Stern College for Women, located within blocks of the New York City morgue where remains of victims were brought. Orthodox Jewish commandments include the duty to keep watch over the dead, never leaving them alone from their passing until burial. "Sitting *shmira*" is normally done by Orthodox men, but on the Sabbath, the morgue is too far for the Orthodox men to walk, so the women of the college volunteered to take the weekend shifts, and the president of Yeshiva University agreed that this was a ritual exception worth making. One of the women, Judith Kaplan, "made up slow, sad tunes for each psalm and sings them in a clear soprano, sweet as birdsong ... By singing them, she is fully mindful. [She reflected,] 'Time completely stops ... Now I understand what it is to pray with your heart.'"[44] Both the living and the dead needed the blessing of religious leaders and religious traditions that could anchor and comfort them in the midst of chaos.

Religious responses were not just words. In the face of such tragedy, many of the most meaningful moments came through sight and sound. Sometimes it was the elusive but deep comfort of a familiar sanctuary, where memories of weddings and baptisms and generations of participation spoke of transcendent connections. Sometimes it was the silence of a sacred space, even an ancient burial ground, or the inspiration of sacred art, stained glass, or soaring steeples. And sometimes it was the sound of a bell. At noon on Friday the 14th, the U. S. President had declared a Day of Prayer and suggested that church bells be rung. As people paused on that day, in a world still disrupted and too quiet, bells rang out, reminding communities that their religious institutions were still there. Nowhere was that message more powerful than at Ground Zero itself. Most of the churches within earshot of the destruction were damaged, destroyed, or still closed. And at St. Paul's, there was still no electricity with which to activate the clapper for the bell, but two members were there at noon, walking through with city officials to inspect the building. Michael Borrero later recalled, "I saw an iron piece of metal and I picked it up and I crawled up to that bell and I beat the hell out of it!" Upon hearing the bell's peal, workers throughout the site stopped, removed their hard hats, and wept.[45]

Whether ringing a bell or conducting a funeral or asking and answering life's questions or voicing laments or creating quiet sacred space, religious institutions provide critical resources to U.S. society. Even the most secular society is humbled by the unanswerable questions posed by death and tragedy. As Grace Davie has pointed out, even seemingly secular European societies still turn to the churches when faced with death – not so much for doctrinal answers as for the opportunity for ritual mourning.[46] As human communities we meet the mystery of death with actions and words that connect us with each other, with long-held tradition, and with a sense of hope and transcendence. Our religious institutions hold in trust for us the space and the ritual knowledge that allows this to happen.

RELIGIOUS SOCIAL CAPITAL BEYOND CONGREGATIONAL WALLS

Apparent after September 11 is the degree to which people in the U.S. (and around the world) are capable of drawing creatively on existing ritual traditions to invent new forms of religious solidarity beyond existing institutions. In a culture already characterized by widespread spiritual questing,[47] this crisis brought questing people together in new ways. Interfaith prayer services, candlelight vigils, and spontaneous public shrines were three of the most common ways that strangers came together to express their griefs and their hopes.

While interfaith prayer services were not unknown before September 11, they have surely become more common and more visible since that day. As early as 4:00 p.m. on the 11th, our own Hartford Seminary opened its chapel to the community, inviting Christian, Jewish, and Muslim leaders to voice prayers that expressed both our profound sorrow and our confidence in God's mercy. The following Friday, most of the nation stopped to watch a nationally televised service from Washington's National Cathedral, a service shaped by its broad inclusion of diverse religious leaders, each speaking from his or her own tradition, but choosing words that acknowledged the many spiritual streams present in the building and beyond. Similarly, the memorial service at Yankee Stadium a little over a week later, and the service at Ground Zero on October 28, included Christian, Jewish, Muslim, Hindu, and Sikh prayers. Music included both "Ave Maria" and "Amazing Grace" and the more generic spirituality of "Let Us Love in Peace" and "Wind Beneath My Wings," with its reminder of the inspiration that comes from quiet heros.[48] In each of these settings, the U.S. has been publicly experimenting with ways to express its enormous religious diversity. Before September 11, few Christian congregations maintained any on-going interfaith connections, but since then, the number is surely rising.[49] Both in common work undertaken and in times of common worship, new forms of religious solidarity are emerging.

Other religious expressions are less clearly connected to any existing tradition. In "moments of silence" gathered throngs sense their connection to the sacred. And in lighting candles, people have drawn on the ancient wonder of fire's warmth and light to express what they have no words or other rituals to express. Around the world, especially on that Friday "Day of Prayer," candles were placed on porches and sidewalks, sometimes only one, sometimes hundreds. At 7:30 that evening, nearly every resident of my own religiously diverse block came out to light candles that remained burning on each front porch throughout the evening. When stars of the entertainment industry broadcast their telethon on September 21, they chose candles as their only stage setting. People who had no other religious connection or tradition drew on this one to mark their participation in something beyond themselves, something somehow eternal.

Public religious expression has gone far beyond these organized events. In recent years, spontaneous public shrines have become increasingly common, and this event was certainly no exception. Perhaps most poignant was the wall of "missing person" photos that was created near the Armory in New York City. At first simply a cry for help, this gallery of beloved faces made the shared loss visible. Similar "walls" of remembrance were created in some of the city's busiest locations – Grand Central Terminal, Pennsylvania Station, and the 42nd Street subway station.[50] More common – at firehouses and public squares, embassies, and the disaster sites themselves – were the assemblages of flowers, candles, and mementos that have become the material "vocabulary" of this modern grieving ritual.[51] Begun without official deliberation or fanfare, one bouquet invites another.

> [The shrines] are primitive and beautiful, at once messy and scattered ... Offerings are piled up against the walls. Colors are intense, almost candied. We see row upon row of variously sized and colored candles; decaying flowers from Korean delis; flags pointing askew; private messages publicly scrawled on different kinds of paper. Amid the profusion are photographs of lost comrades, often reverentially positioned.[52]

Each new contributor expresses her or his own attempt to come to grips with tragedy, bringing objects particularly appropriate to the event. This action helps the individual to "feel less helpless and powerless ... The shrines are a metaphoric threshold which represents the end of numbness and the beginning of the ability to take action," writes Sylvia Grider, who has studied such shrines in recent years.[53] She points out that shrines also become collectively recognized sacred ground to which pilgrimages are made and in which silence and reverence prevail. And when images are broadcast on television or sent via the internet, the shrine's power is felt much more broadly. The official memorials will follow, after the flowers and candles have faded, but in the immediate aftermath, we have learned new collective rituals that remind us we are not alone.

CONCLUSIONS

Not being alone is what social capital is all about. Pundits have been worried that we have forgotten how to work together, how to communicate with neighbor and stranger, how to trust one another. They have worried that our sustaining institutions have lost their power to hold society together. Most often those worries are based on data showing declines in membership and participation in various traditional voluntary organizations. The aftermath of September 11 demonstrates two key flaws in that approach. First, it fails to recognize the importance of latent capacity. Even when on-going participation has fallen, existing trusted social institutions retain a capacity to act. They stand ready when needed. Since September 11 we have seen that religious institutions in the U.S. remain trusted instruments for mobilizing assistance and volunteer action, as well as for gathering in solidarity with our fellow citizens. They retain an ability to help us make sense of and transcend the tragedies we have experienced. This latent capacity is not best measured by current levels in attendance, but by a baseline of institutional presence. The ability to maintain that base is clearly an open question for those concerned about social capital, but this crisis has demonstrated that we have not yet lost our necessary basic institutional capacity. In addition, stories of crisis response, told again and again, will continue to link congregations to the collective memory in the years to come.

The second key flaw in existing social capital arguments is a failure to take innovation into account. Even without a crisis, multitudes of new forms of religious gathering were present in U.S. society. From spiritual support groups to mega-churches and internet chat rooms, people who were not attending traditional churches and synagogues were not necessarily religious individualists. Interfaith worship represents a vitally important emerging new religious practice, but spontaneous vigils and shrines represent equally important public religious activities. In each case, people are experimenting with new ways to be together in sacred public space, and these experiments are becoming part of the religious social capital which will continue to be drawn upon.

The U.S. continues to need congregations and these new sacred gatherings as sources of belonging and compassion, mobilizing and serving. They are also needed to do the spiritual work of reminding all of the highest values and most transformative experiences that shape us. Sacred gatherings continue to hold up the highest of our virtues and the best in our morality, reminding us of our imperfections and calling us to better lives. Sacred gatherings are where people encounter a presence beyond themselves. In the ecstasy of rituals, the singing of hymns, the reading of sacred texts, critical perspectives are nurtured and solidarities are celebrated. People who have tapped into this spiritual strength see their own lives differently, and they can see the world differently, as well. It is in worship that sacred gatherings perform their most important social functions, sustaining the perspectives that come from outside the taken-for-granted everyday world. The crises of September 11 have shown that to be more true than ever.

NOTES

1. Robert D. Putnam, "Bowling Alone: America's Declining Social Capital," *Journal of Democracy* 6 (1), 1995; Robert D. Putnam, *Bowling Alone: The Collapse and Revival of American Community* (New York: Simon & Schuster, 2000).
2. Robert Wuthnow, "Mobilizing Civic Engagement: The Changing Impact of Religious Involvement," In eds., Theda Skocpol and Morris P. Fiorina, *Civic Engagement in American Democracy* (Washington, DC: Brookings Institution Press, 1999).
3. Joanna B. Gillespie, "Gender and Generations in Congregations." In ed., Catherine Prelinger, *Episcopal Women* (New York: Oxford University Press, 1993).
4. Robert Wuthnow, *Loose Connections: Joining Together in America's Fragmented Communities* (Cambridge, Mass.: Harvard University Press, 1998).
5. Robert Wuthnow, *The Restructuring of American Religion* (Princeton, N.J.: Princeton University Press, 1988).
6. Nancy Eiesland, *A Particular Place: Urban Restructuring and Religious Ecology* (New Brunswick, NJ: Rutgers University Press, 2000); Wade Clark Roof, *Spiritual Marketplace: Baby Boomers and the Remaking of American Religion* (Princeton, New Jersey: Princeton University Press, 1999).
7. Robert Wuthnow, *After Heaven: Spirituality in America since the 1950s* (Berkeley: University of California Press, 1998).
8. Nancy T. Ammerman, "Unpublished Findings from the 'Organizing Religious Work' Project," (Hartford Institute for Religion Research, 2000); Nancy Tatom Ammerman, *Congregation and Community* (New Brunswick, NJ: Rutgers University Press, 1997).
9. Ram A. Cnaan, "Social and Community Involvement" (University of Pennsylvania School of Social Work, 1997).
10. Mark Chaves, "Religious Congregations and Welfare Reform: Who Will Take Advantage of 'Charitable Choice'?," *American Sociological Review*, 64 (1999), 836–846.
11. "Harnessing the Spirit of Sept. 11," *New York Times*, November 5, 2001, A, 16.
12. Robert Wuthnow, *Acts of Compassion: Caring for Others and Helping Ourselves* (Princeton: Princeton University Press, 1991).
13. Daniel J. Wakin, "Bronx Mosque Provides a Place for Prayer, and More" [internet] (*New York Times* on the Web, November 16, 2001 [cited November 20, 2001]); available from http://www.nytimes.com/2001/11/16/nyregion.
14. Ammerman, "Unpublished Findings".
15. Carl S. Dudley, "Faith-Based Community Ministries in a 9–11 World," Chap. 4 in this vol.
16. John B. Orr et al., *Politics of the Spirit: Religion and Multiethnicity in Los Angeles* (Los Angeles: University of Southern California, 1994).

17. Daniel J. Wakin, "Attacks Spur a Surge of Interest in Religion: As Attendance at Services Rises, Clerics Hope for a General Moral Uplift," *New York Times*, September 30, 2001, 1A, 33.

18. Kathryn Soman, "St. Paul's Chapel in Wake of WTC Disaster: 'an Organic New Ministry Finds Us'" [internet] (St. Paul's Chapel News, 2001 [cited November 25, 2001]); available from http: //www.saintpaulschapel.org/news/alert[rule]91.html.

19. Ibid.

20. Nancy T. Ammerman, *Doing Good in American Communities: Congregations and Service Organizations Working Together* [internet] (Hartford Institute for Religion Research, March, 2000 [cited 2001]); available from http: //hirr.hartsem.edu/about/about[rule]orw[rule]cong-report.html.

21. The following summary is based on Nancy T. Ammerman, "Connecting Mainline Protestant Congregations with Public Life." In eds., Robert Wuthnow and John Evans, *Quietly Influential: The Public Role of Mainline Protestantism* (Berkeley, Cal.: University of California Press, 2002).

22. "The State of the Relief Effort" [internet] (The Salvation Army, November 7, 2001 [cited November 30, 2001]); available from http: //www.salvationarmy-usaeast.org/disaster.

23. "Fact Sheet – CWS Domestic Terrorism Recovery" [internet] (Church World Service, October 16, 2001 [cited November 20, 2001]); available from http: //www.churchworldservice.org/WTC/factsheet.htm.

24. "American Baptist Men Disaster Relief Teams Participate in New York City Clean-Up" [internet] (American Baptist News Service, October 22, 2001 [cited November 26, 2001]); available from http: //www.abc-usa.org/news/102201.htm.

25. Personal communication.

26. Dan Van Veen, "'How Can I Help?' Christ in Action Ministry Explains What Is Needed" [internet] (Assemblies of God News Service, September 21, 2001 [cited November 26, 2001]); available from http: //ag.org/top/news.

27. Gil Furst, "September 11 Attack: Report" [internet] (Evangelical Lutheran Church in America, November 16, 2001 [cited November 30, 2001]); available from http: //elca.org.dcs/disaster/sept11.html.

28. "World Vision Response: Making an Impact" (World Vision International, November 20, 2001 [cited November 20, 2001]); available from http://www.wvi.org/ home.shtml.

29. Ammerman, *Congregation and Community*; Penny Edgell Becker, *Congregations in Conflict: Cultural Models of Local Religious Life* (Cambridge: Cambridge University Press, 1999); R. Stephen Warner, "Changes in the Civic Role of Religion" In eds., Neil J. Smelser and Jeffrey C. Alexander, *Diversity and Its Discontents: Cultural Conflict and Common Ground in Contemporary American Society* (Princeton: Princeton University Press, 1999).

30. R. Stephen Warner, "The Place of the Congregation in the Contemporary American Religious Configuration." In eds., James Wind and James Lewis, *American Congregations: New Perspectives in the Study of Congregations* (Chicago: University of Chicago Press, 1994).

31. Wakin, "Bronx Mosque Provides a Place for Prayer, and More."

32. The Gallup Organization, "Gallup Poll Topics: Religion" [internet] 2001 [cited December 1, 2001]); available from http: //www.gallup.com/poll/indicators/indreligion.asp.

33. Wakin, "Attacks Spur a Surge of Interest in Religion."

34. Martin E. Marty makes a similar point in "America at Prayer," *Christian Century*, 118 (26), 2001.

35. Gustav Niebuhr, "At Houses of Worship, Feelings Are Shared and Comfort Is Sought in Greater Numbers," *New York Times*, September 17, 2001, A, 9.

36. Ibid.

37. Ammerman, "Unpublished Findings".

38. Peter L. Berger, *The Sacred Canopy* (Garden City, New York: Anchor Doubleday, 1969).

39. Victor Turner, *The Ritual Process* (Ithaca, New York: Cornell University Press, 1977).

40. Omar M. McRoberts, "Saving Four Corners" (unpublished dissertation, Harvard University, 2000).

41. Gustav Niebuhr, "Clergy of Many Faiths Answer Tragedy's Call," *New York Times*, September 15, 2001, B, 6.

42. Gustav Niebuhr, "After the Attacks: A Day of Worship; Excerpts from Sermons across the Nation," *New York Times*, September 17, 2001, A, 8.

43. Daniel J. Wakin, "Seeking Guideposts to Help in No-Man's Land," *New York Times*, November 18, 2001, 1B, 9.

44. Jane Gross, "Stretching a Jewish Vigil for the Sept. 11 Dead," *New York Times*, November 6, 2001, B, 1.

45. David W. Dunlap, "Near Ground Zero, Unbowed Spires," *New York Times*, September 30, 2001, Section 11, 1.

46. Grace Davie, *Religion in Modern Europe: A Memory Mutates* (Oxford: Oxford University Press, 2000).

47. Roof, *Spiritual Marketplace*.

48. Shaila K. Dewan, "Feelings of Loss and the Sound of Silence Greet Families at the Site," *New York Times*, October 29, 2001, B, 9; Robert D. McFadden, "In a Stadium of Heroes, Prayers for the Fallen and Solace for Those Left Behind," *New York Times*, September 24, 2001, B, 7.

49. Hartford Institute for Religion Research, "How Common Are Interfaith Ties among U.S. Congregations?" [internet] (2001 [cited November 29, 2001]); available from http: //www.hirr.hartsem.edu/research/quick[rule]question14.html.

50. Gustav Niebuhr, "Shrines Serve the Need for Healing in Public Spaces," *New York Times*, October 6, 2001, A, 12.

51. Sylvia Grider, "Preliminary Observations Regarding the Spontaneous Shrines Following the Terrorist Attacks of September 11, 2001" [internet] (*New Directions in Folklore*, October 5, 2001 [cited November 20 2001]); available from http://www.temple.edu/isllc/newfolk/shrines.html.

52. Mark Stevens, "Modern Ruins: How the Spontaneous Outpourings of 'Art' since the Disaster Have Brought a New (Old) Look to the City" (November 12, 2001 issue of *New York Magazine*) [internet] (Newyorkmetro.com, 11/20/01 2001 [cited November 20, 2001]); available from http://www.nymag.com.

53. Grider, "Preliminary Observations."

4

FAITH-BASED COMMUNITY MINISTRIES IN A 9.11 WORLD[1]

Carl S. Dudley

DIAL 911 IN AN EMERGENCY!

Nine-one-one has new meaning that has been burned into national consciousness following the terrorist attacks on the United States on September 11, 2001. "Emergency conditions" continue for people of the United States and in other countries throughout the world. Among its countless consequences, this event is a profoundly religious challenge that finds broad forms of expression from the most personal psyche to national policies and even international relations. This new consciousness increases the need for faith-based[2] social ministries for compassion and justice, while at the same time it changes significant elements of organizing and supporting these throughout the country.

Religious responses to the attack were immediate and widespread. Following the attack, impromptu religious shrines and worship events occurred in public places along with spontaneous, traditional liturgies in established sanctuaries.[3] News media provided religious images and interpretations, and even seasoned reporters presented theological reflection on the meaning of these events almost as they were occurring.[4] On the weekend following the attack, there was expanded attendance of worshippers at all sorts of religious gatherings who mourned the suffering and loss of life. At these events religious leaders raised and responded to questions of meaning, and provided much needed spiritual reassurance for a confused nation.

Historically, most neighborhood churches, synagogues, and mosques have attempted to help people to get through hard times, especially in sudden emergencies. Faith groups churches most frequently mention community ministries that address personal crises with material support in areas of basic need. As seen in Faith Communities Today (FACT),[5] a national inter-faith study of 14,301 congregations, local faith communities see themselves as the "safety net" for neighbors in need, offering the basics: money, food, clothing, counseling and medical care.

Table 1: Community service activities in faith communities today

Five areas of most frequent response	%Yes
Cash assistance to families or individuals	88
Food pantry or soup kitchen	85
Thrift shop/clothing closet	61
Counseling or crisis "hotline"	46
Hospital or nursing home	45

Faith Communities Today (FACT) *A Report On Religion in the United States Today, 2001*

The magnitude of the September11 attacks overwhelmed the existing emergency systems, being beyond the resources of all the churches, hospitals, and state agencies combined. In the aftermath, religious bodies are most challenged to respond to the continuing impact on the psyche and soul of Americans throughout the country. More than a natural disaster (such as an earthquake or a storm), this attack destroyed the myth of American invulnerability, which has a long-term impact on confidence and security. Literally in shock, Americans struggled to absorb and cope with the new reality that the country had been successfully attacked within its borders. Like all others, the American nation is vulnerable.

The psychic and spiritual manifestation of the event was stress akin to "combat fatigue", a condition previously known only on foreign soil, now a domestic, personal experience, appearing most frequently in populations closest to the attack. Subsequently what appeared to be terrorist attacks from unknown sources have further destabilized assumptions of personal security. These threats are aimed at highly visible leaders, but postal workers and other ordinary citizens are also vulnerable. Americans show the physical, psychological, and spiritual symptoms of stress. This stress is a medical and public health issue, and the condition is a significant faith-challenge to religious leaders as well. This chronic crisis is one element that creates a new context for all social ministries.

The events of September 11 occurred when the United States was particularly vulnerable from several destabilizing forces that were already in motion and came into focus at the same time. These were not caused by the attack, but these forces significantly escalated its devastating impact, and they must be recognized in order to understand the consequences. To appreciate the nature of these threats and possible constructive alternatives for social ministries, we will briefly list some major forces of change that converged at that particular moment in history.

INCREASING NEED, DECREASING FUNDING

At the most basic level, social ministries now face an increasing need for a wide variety of community ministries, while financial resources for responding to these have diminished. Available funding has been reallocated away from local social services toward higher national priorities. Americans have been extraordinarily generous in an outpouring of financial support to agencies that are offering direct assistance to families and individuals who have suffered loss and injury. At the same time there has been a significant reduction in available funding for many other philanthropic programs.

Even before the terrorist attack there was talk of economic recession. The war against terrorism, unlike mobilization for other wars, has not produced a robust economy at home. Rather economic disorientation has increased domestic unemployment for some, and poverty for others. Although this might have been a time for congregations to expand social ministries, their traditional funding sources are suddenly, severely limited.

Caught in a trough of non-giving following the massive wave of generosity in response to September 11 attacks, local charities across the country are now suffering a stunning loss. From soup kitchens to symphonies, from AIDS programs to animal shelters, from museums to medical research, news stories from every part of the country report a decline in anticipated financial support for local programs, and a rally among a few giants to soften the blow. Carolyn Said in the *San Francisco Chronicle* captures the essence:

> The culprit for the "perfect storm" scenario of increased need and decreased donations is already well known: The existing economic down-

turn, which was accelerated in sectors such as tourism and aviation by the Sept. 11 terrorist attacks, has led to a huge spike in joblessness. At the same time, people who are feeling the pinch are donating less to charities – or contributing to relief efforts instead of giving to local groups.[6]

Some large campaigns and crisis-related organizations (such as the American Red Cross and Salvation Army) have maintained their "market share" while other less glamorous agencies have suffered. Faith-based social ministries have been asked to do more with less. To survive in these difficult conditions, all non-profit organizations including community ministries must be more aggressive in challenging volunteers and more imaginative in funding programs.[7]

Fortunately, the spirit of community volunteering has increased at the same time. In response to the September 11 attack there has been a dramatic increase in the number of people who feel moved to volunteer in community service. Thus Capital Research reports:

> Charities are reporting that volunteerism is up. Robert Goodwin, President of the Points of Light Foundation in Washington, D.C., says the organization has been flooded with calls from people looking to volunteer. The KeyCorp company reports that 10,000 of its 22,000 employees turned out for the company's volunteer day recently, up from 8,000 last year... Steve Cultertson, president of Youth Service America, is pleased with the surge in volunteerism. "That makes me optimistic that in the long term, philanthropy will flow back into the local communities."[8]

Many volunteers are looking for ways to express their concerns, act out their beliefs, and find meaning in service to, and with, others. This enacting of faith includes participation in outreach programs that cross differences in race, class, religion, language, culture, and national origin. A wide variety of faith-based programs have provided expression for this renewal of caring in communities across the country.

In short, the need has increased, the funding decreased, and the communal spirit of volunteering appears reborn.[9]

EXPANDED PLURALISM

The working definition of religious diversity in American consciousness has changed forever as a result of the events of September 11. Although the religious landscape of public awareness was once dominated by groups of Christians and Jews, the lists of casualties and places open for community worship after September 11 included Bahá'í , Buddhist, Hindu, Muslim, and Sikh, among others. Beyond the wide diversity of religious groups, American leaders, from the President to local preachers, took great pains to recognize Muslims' place in the religious landscape.[10] Muslims, although concentrated in urban areas, now rank in number of participants on a par with each of several large and established religious groups, such as Disciples of Christ, Episcopalians, Jews, Presbyterians (but fewer than Roman Catholics, Baptists, and Methodists). More than numerical growth, it has been shown that Muslims have already assumed a significant role in communities across the country.

Table 2: Community service activities in mosques throughout United States

Five areas of most frequent response	*% Yes*
Cash assistance to families or individuals	90
Marital or Family Counseling	77
Food pantry or soup kitchen	69
Prison or Jail Program	66
Thrift shop/clothing closet	64

Council on American-Islamic Relations: *A Report from the Mosque Study Project*

Although they differ in beliefs and faith-practices (such as the head covering for women), the social ministries of Muslim congregations are remarkably similar to other religious groups in the United States. According to a study by the Council on American–Islamic Relations using FACT data,[11] like other faith communities, Muslim congregations also provide a safety net of social ministries.

In the wake of September 11, in their social ministries Muslim congregations had a similar profile to neighboring churches and synagogues. By comparison with others in the FACT data we see that Muslim faith communities report a slightly higher level of involvement in all social ministries. In their five most frequent responses, the Muslim pattern differs from the total study in only one area – the Muslim emphasis on prison-related social concerns. In the FACT data, faith communities of all sorts report high levels of response to their community social concerns. It is a premium priority for all religious groups, a natural expression of our faith in action.[12]

WELFARE IN TRANSITION

Like an aerial acrobat leaping from one trapeze to the next, even before September 11, 2001, all social welfare programs in the United States were in a precarious transition. Matched only by the impact of the Great Depression, in the past few years a combination of social, religious, economic, and political forces have led to a rewriting of the rules for developing ministries in at-risk communities in America. From the oval office in the big White House in Washington D.C. to literally thousands of little white churches (and synagogues and mosques) across the country, faith-based initiatives for community ministries had become more significant, and more controversial, than in any previous generation of living memory.

Welfare was transformed by the adoption of legislation that promised to move public assistance recipients from "welfare-to-work." In 1996 a Republican Congress passed and a Democratic President signed the bill that carried the message in its title, "Personal Responsibility and Work Opportunity Reconciliation Act." This act, which President Clinton called "the end of welfare as we have known it," provided strong incentives for state agencies to encourage welfare recipients to develop economic self-sufficiency. Further, the national legislation demanded that individual states implement terminal dates and lifetime limits for most current welfare recipients.

Based on the welfare-to-work provisions, funding that had once been available through welfare departments was shifted to programs in labor and educational agencies to support employment training, and social case workers were replaced by vocational counselors. The timing of this watershed transition is significant. By September 2001, the majority of former welfare recipients had been guided and pushed into various modes of economic independence, and, although the economy was apparently thriving, these newly trained and recently employed workers remained particularly vulnerable.

In the year prior to the September 11 attacks, I had asked the leaders of faith-based ministries in Hartford to assess the transitional situation. In general, they reported that we were in the midst of a major transition. In the process, they noted that many welfare recipients were struggling. These are typical responses: [13]

Director, soup kitchen and job training program:

> A very small percentage are doing much better; they are working and they have an improved sense of their self-esteem and are doing well; but there is a bigger percentage of people who are having a worse time than they ever had.

Executive, housing program:

> I think the theory that the state can save money by cutting welfare is true. But what is not taken into account is the measurement of the impact especially on children. You have more and more families doubling up; what is a three-bedroom unit becomes a three-family unit. A two-family house becomes a five-family house.

Manager, temporary family shelter:

> We are having more and more parents who are homeless who are coming to the shelter than we have had in the past ... People are poorer, poorer than they were before and they have less money. And then with that money that you have, you have to go to work and then you have to pay for day care and transportation costs. So your expenses have gone up and your income has gone down.

In this new configuration of social welfare, the social ministries of faith communities were among the first to feel the impact of change as they offered care and support to those caught in the transition. Political forces, seeing the church caught in the middle, made a second major change in the social services landscape.

PROMOTING FAITH-BASED MINISTRIES[14]

Into this national climate entered George W. Bush with a strong commitment to encourage faith-based ministries to take a larger share of responsibility for encouraging and, it was hoped, transforming the lives of welfare recipients. With congregations showing such a high level of involvement, especially in crises ministries, there was little wonder that the new President might be interested in sharing the load. The administration was particularly impressed by the location of congregations in areas of significant need, and the residence of members living in these neighborhoods. The presence of ministries in these neighborhoods provided a unique possibility to expand their work (such as soup kitchens and clothing pantries) to larger and long-term programs from day care and tutoring to drug abuse and job training.

For many years in cities throughout the country, local schools, police, and welfare departments have worked in and through particular congregations to offer social ministries in the community. In addition, nationally recognized religious agencies like the Salvation Army, Catholic Charities, Lutheran Family Services, and the Jewish Federation developed an enviable track record of contract-for-services to families and individuals in need. For a generation government agencies have provided oversight and assistance to faith-based educational and health programs in every kind of community, especially in the pressured areas of city centers. Legally these programs that worked with "tax dollars" were prohibited from exposing clients to sectarian religious symbols, literature or activity. They provided "services," as suggested by this ministry leader:

Congregation supporting drug rehab. program:

> Interfacing with the state sometimes you are dealing with agencies that might not feel comfortable with the spiritual component. But they don't have a problem because the roof is provided, the shelter, all the support services, heat in the winter, hot water, three meals a day for all the residents, transportation to and from clinic appointments.

In the context of that extended and pervasive working relationship, Federal welfare reform legislation of 1996 included the so called "Charitable Choice" provision requiring that religious organizations be permitted to receive funding on the same basis as any other non-governmental provider. Specifically the law would allow "charitable, religious or private organizations to apply for and receive competitive grants for services rendered." The new law, in effect, "baptized" existing practice, with one exception. To receive federal welfare funds, states would not require contractual religious groups to remove their art, icons, scripture or other religious symbols, and in the performance of these programs the line between secular services and religious practices became a grey area.

On January 29, 2001, within his first few days in office, Bush signed executive orders that established a White House Office of Faith-Based and Community Initiatives and supportive Centers for Faith-Based and Community Initiatives in five agencies – Justice, Housing and Urban Development (HUD), Health and Human Services (HHS), Labor, and Education. With this act he was greatly expanding the scope of previous charitable choice funding sources beyond the initial welfare, Temporary Aid to Needy Families (TANF), and related programs. Moreover he put the backing of his office and the prestige of his infant administration squarely behind this approach.[15]

In personal appeal to a national interfaith gathering of religious leaders at the time of proposing this new initiative, President Bush made his priorities clear:

> Everyone in this room knows there are still deep needs and real suffering in the shadow of America's affluence–problems like addiction, abandonment, and gang violence, domestic violence, mental illness and homelessness. We are called by conscience to respond ... It is one of the great goals of my administration to invigorate the spirit of involvement and citizenship. We will encourage faith-based and community programs without changing their mission. We will help all in their work to change hearts while keeping a commitment to pluralism ...
>
> Government will never be replaced by charities and community groups. Yet when we see social needs in America, my administration will look first to faith-based programs and community groups, which have proven their power to save and change lives ... We will make sure that help goes to large organizations and to small ones as well. We also value neighborhood healers, who have only the scars and testimony of their own experience.[16]

President Bush made charitable choice a primary initiative for his new administration, including a new office in the White House and expanded legislative support. As the terrorists attacks hit eight months later, Congress was debating new legislation to expand the use of contracts, vouchers, and other funding for "charitable, religious or private organizations" to provide services far beyond the initial allocation to Temporary Assistance for Needy Families, Medicaid, Food Stamps and similar programs. Every indication since has reaffirmed the President's commitment to expand faith-based ministries, even (or especially) in the post September 11 conditions.

VIEW FROM THE TRENCHES

As information concerning the prospect of charitable choice funding filtered through the media and layers of social service bureaucracy, the responses heard in congregations and agencies could be broadly clustered into two. The first concern was about religious groups receiving government money, and the second about the process by which those funds might be distributed.

Concerning the potential for new funding, the range of responses in Hartford congregations would seem to reflect the nation in microcosm. Some leaders are convinced that any compromise in the separation of church and state will undermine foundational beliefs.

Large Reform Synagogue:

> Jews feel very, very strongly about the separation between church and state. So we are not supporters of that notion of public funding through religious based organizations for social service, because there will always be some kind of content related to it.

Conservative-Evangelical Faith Based Ministry:

> Our Board feels so strongly that they did not want to compromise what they knew to be the "active ingredient," that is, faith.

The opposite view was expressed from faith-based programs that feel the need to expand their resources to meet pressing human needs, while believing that they were well protected against secular intrusion into their beliefs.[17]

Multicultural Inner City Parish:

> Would we try to get federal monies? I don't think we would have any scruples if we saw a need that was not being met and our parish could do that for the neighborhood. It certainly is one of our goals to be responsive to the needs of the community.

Large Regional Program for Youth:

> Would we have a problem in applying for government grants? Oh no! We would certainly do it if it looked like something that fits into our mission and was available to us. And we have had DCF funding since the second year we were around ... DCF requires that we fund a minimum of 25% of our budget, so we have to find it somewhere. If we could find it through federal funds that would be dynamite.

Rather than either/or responses, it was clear that existing social ministries were embedded in a network of private and public funding that made ministry possible. Some maintained the myth of autonomy by honestly reporting their condition, but with a catch. Thus:

Soup Kitchen/Job Training Center:

> We are completely privately funded. We do not have a cent of City, State or Federal money. Really, that is a wonderful comment on this

community. It really truly is. Our funding breaks down almost exactly one third, one third, one third. One third religious organizations (churches and synagogues), one third foundations and corporations; and one third in small gifts.

The director is accurate and honest, but, at the same time, most staff in the program were paid through a job-training program of federal funding, the food supply had federally funded subsidy, etc. No government money was received, but the feeding program could not operate without a wide variety of very appropriate but completely unrecognized government financial support.

Perhaps this next pastor captures the ambiguity that many feel about government funding being used to support faith-based community ministries: in a multi-national city parish with numerous "self-funding" programs, he says, "In our parish there is really a desire for separation of church and state. It is still very strong. But people get around it in other ways."

CHALLENGES FOR COMMUNITY MINISTRY

The national climate for faith-based social ministries radically changed as the result of national welfare legislation and a Bush administration, by a national (and worldwide) depression and the terrorist attack of September 11, 2001. The characteristics are:

- Increased social service needs for individuals and families moving from welfare to work, and others simply out of work in the depressed economy;
- Likely reduction in personal charity and corporate philanthropy in donations to most local non-profit groups, including faith-based ministries;
- Currently an increase in community spirit, and the number of volunteers willing to pitch in;
- Additional government funding is now possible through charitable choice for faith-based ministries, but government funding has been radically redirected by domestic security and war overseas;
- Continuing political and religious tensions about the appropriate expression "sectarian beliefs" in programs supported by government funding;
- Creative coalitions and partner-programs among government, education, commercial, philanthropic and religious groups.

The ability to make something positive out of these new conditions will depend on many factors far beyond the scope of this discussion. They include leadership and location, and a wise use of experience, politics, and resources – physical and spiritual. The congregations in our studies particularly stressed four inter-related dimensions that can carry faith-based ministries into the new era, namely:

1. diversified sources of income;
2. increased suspicion of government;
3. expanded coalitions that protect and strengthen ministry;
4. explicit spiritual satisfactions that sustain participation.

Diversified sources of income

Congregations in the pressure of congested urban communities are financed differently from suburban, mainline congregations. City churches, especially African-American, are confronted by human needs that far outrun their resources. Sensitive to God's call to care for the whole person, these congregations would like to do far more than their resources will sustain. A Black Church in the Methodist tradition, 500+ members, reported:

> We have a technology center for the community. We also have a project where we will take students and train them to fix cars and then they can buy them … We have identified about 58 ministries. We are partnering with the Board of Education, and we partner with the different social service areas, social service providers and with different churches … We have food banks, an after school tutoring program … [list of 50 plus programs].

These ministries cannot be sustained by bake sales and weekly donations in the offering plate, or even by the occasionally larger sums from gala fund-raising events and generous personal bequests.[18] Such support requires an aggressive fund-raising program from all and every source in sight. It is in the genius of the Black Church tradition to maintain multiple budgets based on different funding sources to sustain programs that are beyond the congregational capacity.[19] In observing their neighbors, one mainline congregation laid out their plan. From a United Methodist congregation in a culturally diverse community: "Our fund-raising program covers the following sources:

1. Contract and partnering organizations
2. Individuals and small businesses in the community

3.   A list of all corporations which have a relationship to the community
4.   Foundations that share our interest–local, regional, and national
5.   Public sector government agencies
6.   User fees based on a sliding scale."

A faith based ministry to drug addicts in the city reported their own concerns:

> The United Way has a program called Donor's choice. If you work for a company you can give to the United Way and designate your gift. Also we have access to a program through the State of Connecticut: it is a reimbursement program, for individuals who are going through a drug and alcohol program like this. They qualify, if they are indigent, for their costs for staying in a program of recovery via a state reimbursement to help them access the service. That has been a great help to us.

The prospect of charitable choice funding, especially in a post September 11 world, has stirred the imagination of many leaders of congregations and their faith-based ministries that are overwhelmed with unmet needs. The spark of possibility has made some congregations restless to do more, but not necessarily with government funding. A Housing Ministry in an African-American Community remarked: "I think we found over forty funding sources ... We applied, and just sent out a raft of proposals to foundations and corporations."

But religious integrity remains a primary issue, as the leader of this openly conservative and evangelical ministry makes clear:

> We have a wide variety of people who support us. Specific congregations. Congregational churches, Episcopal churches, Lutheran churches, Assembly of God churches ... I think that people recognize the work that is being done. [Although] to some people we are perhaps too socially minded and to other people we preach too much! There is evidence that we change lives. That is what we want. That's what we see. And I think that the people who want to be a part of that are glad to support us.

Increased suspicion of government

Even in the face of increasing support and confidence in government in general in the shadow of 9.11, leaders of faith-based ministries respond with a broad and emotional distrust of partnership with government agencies. Everyone had personal stories that ranged from frustration to betrayal. These reservations were not aimed at the motives of politicians in Washington, but reflected negative personal experiences. An African American pastor with ample experience reported:

With almost thirty years of ministry now, I confess to you that I am very cynical about the political process ...

The pastor of a wealthy suburban mainline church reflected similar sentiments:

I had the impression the welfare legislation was just to make the churches pick up the tab for things – and that's what I think it is, just rhetoric.

Some warned about "smoke and mirrors" on both sides, and worried if congregations were prepared for the problems they would inherit. The executive director of a metro-wide church council put his fears in these words:

So that the real question of charitable choice is I think – two sided: one side is a smokescreen – it pretends that there are alternatives to governments support for welfare, when there really are not; and the second is that the churches are conned into accepting responsibility so that the feds and the state can dump on the churches and say, "now it is your problem, not ours."

Virtually universal were concerns about program and fiscal management that are essential in accepting government funding. These are typical comments, in this case from a seasoned, African-American pastor of an urban Baptist Church:

The red tape – they give you something, and then they put so many restrictions on it, you can't use it ... Because you see, when the government gives you a dollar, they put a thousand restrictions on it. They give it to you to do this, but then they turn around and say you can't do it. So we need funds to do what we can do, what we have been designed to do – and that is, to get a child, bring him or her in, and begin with our program of training and discipline. Sometimes that does not meet with the government's standards ... I used to be a politician one time ... and I figured out that pastors ain't got no business being politicians.

One social worker-program developer on the staff of a large mainline congregation rather relished the challenge: "Maybe it is because I made that choice when I took the job, knowing that politics in Hartford is a combat sport."

Resistance by religious groups was not what President Bush anticipated in advocating faith-based initiatives in his first week in office.[20] Yet suspicion and even fear of government partnership seems an honest reflection based on prior experience. And such reservations would appear to be a healthy precaution against unfortunate abuse of the system. All the fears seem justified by a thoroughly documented report cited by University of North Carolina Professor Robert Wineburg. A well meaning congregation approached the welfare department with a faith-based initiative that both the church and the state agreed was greatly needed:

> The Department of Social Services put a $10,000 contract on the table for … a new faith based non-profit … I asked the director to look carefully at items A–H … the true cost [of developing the administrative infrastructure to implement the program according to state specifications] came to $75,000.[21]

Local congregations, even with the help of volunteers and a small paid staff, cannot be expected to play on such a large and undefined arena. Charitable choice funds are available because they are needed, and faith-based ministries have a history of positive service in difficult communities. Such services are even more frequently requested in the current crisis. But solo congregations are ill-advised to enter into such agreements alone. At this point congregations talked about working with others to protect their assets from being lost (or worse, falling into significant debt), even with the best intentions.

Expanded coalitions that protect and strengthen ministry

Coalitions among churches and faith-based agencies are essential both to strengthen and to protect local ministries. As centers of religious and social life, in most activities congregations tend to stand alone as self-sustaining organizations in their communities. Very few congregations are large enough to marshal sufficient physical, spiritual, and financial resources to carry the load of a social outreach ministry alone. In practice, larger churches with more resources are even more likely to work with other partners and allies in developing community ministry, while smaller congregations seem less inclined to including others in their ministries. Congregational leaders suggested four sorts of networks that could sustain their expanded ministries.

DENOMINATIONAL CONNECTIONS. The first inclination of many congregations is to find peer partners from others like themselves to share with them in ministry. Typically they turn to their denominational staff,[22] or to familiar peers who they know and trust. Even independent congregations have Sunday School organizations, theological school networks, and similar religious associations loosely related to the National Association of Evangelicals. These church organizations give identity, information, technical skill, and sometimes substantial financial support.

Thus it seemed natural for this inner city Catholic parish to use its denominational network to find its partners from among its suburban sister congregations.

> The tutoring program was started with the Community Renewal Team, and we have worked in conjunction with suburban parishes, which supply us with materials for the kids, notebooks, and nutritious snacks, that kind of thing, plus monies.

AFFINITY GROUPS. Even more than denominational organizations, congregations are more likely to reach out to their affinity network of neighborhood churches in other denominations. Congregational leaders find trust and social compatibility among these associations based on a common ground, real and spiritual, such as geography, culture, and ethnicity. These groups typically exist to provide personal networking and mutual support for pastors and their congregations by strengthening fellowship and social relations.

As ministry leaders reach out to Affinity Groups, they are looking for specialized skills to operate their ministries. Thus this report from the town of Canton, Illinois, is representative of many more structured partnerships.

> St. Mary's Catholic Church and the First Congregational UCC of Canton, IL (known hereafter as the partnering churches) have chosen to call their project Christian Service Program ... Pastors of the partnering churches, or their designated representatives, will be members of the Advisory Council. Other Advisory members ... would include persons with specialized knowledge in areas such as: legal matters, fund-raising, grant-writing, public relations, and human resources. Standing committees will be formed for Fund-Raising, Building Management, Publicity, Program Administration, Advocacy and Human Resources. Special committees will be appointed as needed ... Each member church and its congregation are expected to provide leadership, manpower, and financial support on specific needs and for annual operating expenses.

SOCIAL AGENCIES WITH PROFESSIONAL SKILLS.   At a low level of intervention and expertise, small soup kitchens, clothing closets, and tutoring programs can be run with a minimum of professional staff. As social ministries move toward continuity over time, or more intense intervention with clients, professional staff become necessary.[23] In these situations, ministry leaders shift their emphasis from ties with peers to partnerships with faith based non-profit social agencies. The church-sponsored program gains the "protection" of professional leadership for management of the program, record keeping, fiscal oversight, fund raising, etc. The faith-based program, in turn, can make use of volunteers recruited from constituent congregations. In a wide variety of organizational styles, the core agency becomes a "managing mediator." That is, it manages the program, and mediates between the church-based program and the various funding sources, including contracts with the government. The congregation can concentrate on what it does best, caring for those in need.

Black Church in an urban setting:

> Most of our partners are in the religious arena, [but] some of the secular groups that we partner with, their motivation is slightly different … With the Ministerial Alliance and the Board of Ed, we are forming some programs … We have a very powerful, a very strong partnership with the Jewish community especially Beth Israel.

Liberal Suburban Congregation restless for involvement:

> We wanted to find a big project and we started to educate ourselves and realized that we couldn't do this by ourselves. No more of this "Lady Bountiful" stuff, we needed to work in partnership with the community … The congregation about 4–5 years ago decided that they were not doing enough in Hartford and … so we interviewed 18 agencies of the city and chose one as the agency that we wanted to partner with. For our focus we really tried to focus on that agency as a way to get people working together on a common goal.

The importance of these mediating agencies cannot be overstressed. They enhance congregational abilities in many ways, such as training staff and volunteers; raising funds from government, business, and philanthropic bodies; developing board members in issues of vision, governance, and finance; addressing legal matters of incorporation, contract, copyright, and insurance; and facilitating strategic planning and program evaluation. In essence, mediators directly or by monitoring lift the burden of administration from the congregation, thus liberating faith communities to spend their energies in areas of greatest strength – ministry.

AD HOC PARTNERS – ALL OF THE ABOVE. Ad hoc groups emerge in response to community crises or recognized need. Based on their common perception of an issue, their survival depends upon the ability of their initial leadership to develop administrative infrastructure that will sustain the broad coalitional character of their composition. As indigenous, value-based institutions, congregations are essential to these ad hoc coalitions. They often include a unique mixture of business and labor, of government and private sector, of educational and philanthropic institutions – united in a common cause.[24]

In rural areas and small towns where the leaders of social, financial, political, and religious organizations are well known to each other, these ad hoc groups have been functioning for decades unnoticed. Now these multi-disciplinary patterns have been reinvented in the complexity of urban life. In following rural partnership, the number of people involved was fewer than the number of organizations listed – some individuals simply wore two hats:

> To date we have commitments for support and volunteers from the Burnettsville Town Board, Burnettsville Community Board, Washington Township Trustee, Burnettsville State Bank, Burnettsville Senior Citizens Club, and the Burnettsville Mennonite Fellowship. We expect to work closely with them in operation and fund-raising.

This kind of pragmatic "*ad hocracy*" gains momentum when it catches the spark of community concern around a particular problem or issue, receiving their initial energy boost from that crisis and the passion of local leaders. Its endurance as faith-based ministry depends heavily upon the ability of initial leadership to develop and shift the administrative work beyond pastoral leadership to a mediating organization that can implement and sustain the ministry. "Pastors alone are ill-equipped for this aspect of ministry," concluded H. Dean Trulear in his overview of faith-based ministries. In particular he cited a well known faith-based program:[25]

> The work of the Ten Point Coalitions in a variety of cities across the country exemplify such an initiative. These coalitions consist of congregations that focus specifically on juvenile violence reduction,

and reclaiming high-risk youth. Galvanized by the crisis of juvenile violence, these congregations found the need to come together and pool their resources in order to develop a seamless web of services for youth. They also realized the need for centralized staff to handle issues such as fund raising, facilitating cooperation between law enforcement, juvenile justice, community organizations and the congregations. Since they are task based, their missions are specific, they possess significant ability to be productive and efficient in the development and implementation of programs."

Many sorts of coalitions can help congregations to develop faith-based community ministries, and all are better than going it alone.

Explicit spiritual satisfactions that sustain participation

Social ministries are amazing when you count the cost! Given that outreach community ministries require such effort and constant infusion of resources and negotiation among partners with mediators, why do so many congregations keep on doing it? Because it is scriptural and it is needed. But more, they do it because touching the lives of others is spiritually satisfying in ways that are different from worship and prayer, different from fellowship and study. Social ministries carry their own uniquely transforming power to all who participate in these communities of the Spirit.[26]

As the emotional turmoil from the 9.11 emergency settles into the psyche of the nation, more people are willing to volunteer for mundane roles in caring ministries, if and when they are asked. Significant relationships occur among volunteers and other participants of community ministries. Little things do make a difference. The act of touching another person means being touched in return, and in that physical contact, participants feel spiritually nurtured.

Further, congregations are the safety net for individuals in crises, and, in many communities, they are the steeple or dome that symbolizes refuge from the worst and hope that the world can be a better place, individually and in community. That spark of hope keeps community ministries alive in difficult times, and the warmth of that hope feels real in fleeting moments of success.

Beyond their communities, congregations take an even longer view by making a difference in the next generation. A review of the kinds of ministries that congregations accept reflects their commitment to education and nurture for children, and willingness to work within prison and immigrant ministries – long term investments that can only be sustained by a vision for a better world, someday.

TRANSLATING DIVERSITY INTO ENERGY

In the ripples of September 11 and the shadow of charitable choice legislation, we live with a new climate in community ministries across the country. It is characterized by the integrity of faith and action, by the authenticity that allows participants to express openly beliefs without demanding conformity. These are comfortable expressions of spirituality that accompany many social ministries – as if the two are twin expressions of one common impulse to embrace both God and neighbor, "naturally."

All the material of this study points to a strong religious commitment to "both/and," not "either/or." We find:

- *both* particular faith expressions (Christian, Jewish, Muslim) *and* interfaith coalitions working together for common causes,
- *both* racial solidarity *and* cultural diversity (in the same ministry),
- *both* commitment to individuals (compassion) *and* intervention toward transformation (justice),
- *both* spiritual nurture *and* community ministry, *both* evangelism *and* social action,
- *both* ministries that are located in urban areas *and* cross-cultural flow of volunteers from suburban congregations,
- *both* church and state, both faith-based programs *and* government funds in common ministry.

These liaisons are not based on eliminating the differences, not just "standing in the middle of the bridge." Rather their common commitments in ministry provide a spiritual bridge that makes the connection possible. For most there is a primary emphasis on making the faith visible "in the streets."

What we have found by adopting a street is being visible in the community. People begin to look at the church in a more positive view because when you think that you are just inside and don't care about people on the outside. So in order to do that, to fight that mindset, you have to be visible. That's the object. So we try to revitalize and transform this neighborhood. That is what church is all about.

Other people report a long term commitment to be here as long as it takes, until the children of next generation come into their own:

Welfare Reform I think will probably have very little positive effect on the adults who are involved in it because most of them are going through such a difficult time ... I hope that their kids will benefit by that whole sense of going to work, a good attitude toward work – and I think *that* is where Welfare to Work is going to make a difference, and I think that is wonderful. But I think this generation is pretty much lost to a real change for the better.

Agency leaders admit significant satisfaction in seeing congregations discover the power of their own faith-in-action as they are touched in the act of touching others.

The clergy and the congregation members have often said, "This has revitalized us!" or "This has brought a new perspective to our outreach ministry." That is wonderful. That is what we intended to do. It is extremely rewarding ... a shot in the arm in connecting their faith to the purposes that they felt were very important ... The other piece is the satisfaction of gaining the entry into the congregation to help them realize that the children are suffering, and ... there are things they can do to alleviate that.

For some spiritual satisfaction rests in the re-affirmation of relationships (Divine and human), the transforming quality in divine activity, and the need for focus in our busy lives:

[Three new priorities:] One is the importance of volunteers, recognizing that their sense of relationship is critical to what we do; second, we are a faith-based organization and we want to affirm that in ways that change peoples' lives, without proselytizing; and third is we want to go deeper rather than broader.

In a surprisingly ecumenical embrace, one leader reverses the common equation of churches depending on government funding, and explains why the energy flows in the other direction, and has for a long time:

But the need is greater than our ability to meet the need. We know that we are not able to do it alone. We are not the only church in Hartford. There are many churches, thank God. Really the State is counting on the church, they might not want to acknowledge that they do. But the church has always been there. There are some regulations about receiving money, but something has happened to the people we work with. I can't just ignore that or act like it didn't happen, or act like it is attributable to something else because that would be to take away the heartbeat of the motivation.

These spiritual affirmations would seem to support the motives that initiated charitable choice for faith-based ministries. From these examples we might doubt if government funding works equally well for everyone, for "both large and small" congregations, as the President proposed. The legislation, however, pushes all congregations to ask the right questions, to reconsider their priorities, and to imagine new possibilities. Despite the complications and limitations of social ministries in conditions of this post 9.11 world, these faith-based programs would appear to be remarkably effective and spiritually satisfying for those who are moved to participate.

NOTES

1. This chapter is abridged from *Community Ministries: Proven Steps and New Challenges in Faith Based Initiatives* (Bethesda, Md.: Alban Institute, 2002), used by permission.

2. "Faith-based" community ministries designate social service or outreach programs that are supported or find their identity in a religious tradition, as distinguished from social service agencies that have secular or government support and identity. For an excellent, current examination of Faith-Based Organizations in social ministry, see Amy Sherman, *Reinvigorating Faith in Communities* (Indianapolis, IN: Hudson Institute, 2002).

3. See Miriam Therese Winter's description in "Witnessing to the Spirit: Reflections on An Emerging American Spirituality," chapter 6 in this volume.

4. For a more extended discussion of the issues raised (and neglected), see Heidi Hadsell "Internal Security and Civil Liberties: Moral Dilemmas and Debates," chap. 12 in this vol.

5. Faith Communities Today (FACT) includes 14,301 congregations from 41 denominational and faith communities, see Carl S. Dudley and David A. Roozen, eds, *Faith Communities Today (FACT) A Report On Religion in the United States Today* (Hartford CT: Hartford Institute for Religion Research, Hartford Seminary, 2001), on line www.fact.hartsem.edu/

6. Carolyn Said, "Foundations launch campaign to support safety net charities," *San Francisco Chronicle,* December 5, 2001, from web site www.sfgate.com

7. For example, "Weathering Funding Reductions," A Raffa Workshop, October 19, 2001 at www.raffa.com

8. *Philanthropy Notes,* December, 2001, Washington, D.C.: Capital Research Center, www.capitalresearch.org

9. See Nancy Ammerman's chapter (3), on recovery of latent social capital after September 11. In her emphasis on texture of congregational life, Ammerman provides significant collateral evidence on congregations as "first response" in

crisis situations, cooperation among congregations in social ministry, and expansion of inter-faith consciousness after 9.11.

10. For the need to appreciate Muslim history from its own perspective, see Ibrahim M. Abu-Rabi's chapter 2 in this volume. For the heightened tensions inherent in this expanded pluralism, see Ian Markham, chapter 10 in this volume.

11. From "The Mosque in America: A National Portrait," using data gathered in cooperation with Faith Communities Today study (above note 5), published in *A Report from the Mosque Study Project*, Washington, DC: Council on American-Islamic Relations, April, 2001. On line at www.cair-net.org

12. For an inclusive, interfaith portrait of congregations in community ministry, see Victor N. Claman and David E. Butler, *Acting On Your Faith: Congregations Making a Difference* (Boston: Insights, 1994).

13. Quotes from congregations and agencies are drawn from Carl S. Dudley, *Welfare, Faith-Based Ministries and Charitable Choice* (Hartford Institute for Religion Research, Hartford, CT, March, 2001), on line www.hirr.hartsem.edu. Also from Dudley, *Basic Steps in Community Ministries*, (Bethesda; Md: Alban Institute, 1991) and *Next Steps Toward Community Ministry* (Bethesda, Md: Alban Institute, 1996), and from Dudley, and Sally A. Johnson, *Energizing the Congregation: Images that Shape Your Church's Ministry*, (Westminster/John Knox, 1993).

14. For current advocacy materials for charitable choice and government support of faith-based ministries, see The Center for Public Justice at www.charitablechoice.html. For research papers with a more balanced view, see Nonprofit Sector Research Fund (Aspen Institute Publications), www.nonprofitresearch.org.

15. Ronald J. Sider, Philip N. Olson and Heidi Rolland Unruh, *Churches that Make a Difference: Reaching Your Community with Good News and Good Works* (Grand Rapids: Baker Books, 2001). For a less enthusiastic view, see "Congregations and Social Services: What They Do, How They Do it, and with Whom," *Nonprofit and Voluntary Sector Quarterly*, 30, December, 2001.

16. White House press release, January 29, 2001.

17. For an early and solid analysis of what constitutes a faith based ministry, see Thomas Jeavons, *When the Bottom Line is Faithfulness*, (Indiana: Indiana University Press, 1993).

18. For a discussion of these financial conditions, and some alternative approaches, see John Perkins, *Beyond Charity* (Grand Rapids: Baker, 1993); Robert Wuthnow, *Poor Richard's Principle* (Princeton: Princeton University Press, 1996); and *The Crisis in the Churches: Spiritual Malaise, Fiscal Woe* (Oxford, 1997).

19. See Ram A. Cnann and Stephanie C. Boddie, "Black Church Outreach: Comparing How Black and Other Congregations Serve Their Needy Neighbors" (University of Pennsylvania, CRRUCS Report 2001–1).

20. White House staff addressed the reluctance to participate within the first six months, see "Unlevel Playing Field: Barriers to Participation by Faith-Based and

Community Organizations in Federal Social Service Programs" (The White House, August, 2001).

21. Wineberg, Bob, "The Spirit of Charitable Choice" (Occasional Paper, Greensboro, NC: School of Social Work, University of North Carolina Greensboro, 1999).

22. For a history of denominational strategies, see Clifford J. Green. *Churches, Cities, and Human Community: Urban Ministry in the United States 1945–1985* (Grand Rapids, MN: William B. Eerdmans, 1996).

23. For an exceptionally clear and practical approach, see Bennett Harrison and Marcus Weiss, *Networking Across Boundaries: New Directions in Community Based Job Training and Economic Development* (Boston: Economic Development Assistance Consortium, 1998).

24. For a strong, focused position, see Ryan Streeter, *Transforming Charity: Toward a Results-Oriented Social Sector* (Indianapolis IN: Hudson Institute, 2001). For a richer more comprehensive view, see Mark R. Warren and Richard L. Wood, *Faith Based Community Organizing: The State of the Field* (Jericho, NY: Interfaith Funders, 2001).

25. H. Dean Trulear, "Faith-Based Institutions and High-Risk Youth" (Philadelphia: Public/Private Ventures, Field Report Series, Spring, 2000). Dean Trulear's views have strongly influenced this section.

26. Three excellent resources suggest the diversity of available material: Gary Gunderson, *Deeply Woven Roots: Improving the Quality of Life in Your Community* (Minneapolis: Fortress Press, 1997); Claudia Horwitz, *A Stone's Throw: Living the Act of Faith: Social Transformation through Faith and Spiritual Practice* (Durham, N.C.: Stone Circles, 1999); and Paul Rogat Loeb, *Soul of a Citizen: Living with Conviction in a Cynical Time* (New York: St. Martin's Griffin, 1999).

PART II

THEOLOGICAL REFLECTIONS

5

STOPPING OPPRESSION: AN ISLAMIC OBLIGATION

Ingrid Mattson

A person should help his brother, whether he is an oppressor or is being oppressed. If he is the oppressor, he should prevent him from continuing his oppression, for that is helping him. If he is being oppressed, he should be helped to stop the oppression against him.

The Prophet Muhammad[1]

The terrorist attacks of September 11 have raised important questions about the role of Muslim leaders in shaping a responsible discourse of resistance to oppression and injustice. In this chapter, I will examine some of the issues that have been raised in this regard and will consider the question, what kind of leadership do Muslims need in the face of oppression? In particular, I will consider the role of American Muslims in the context of world events following the terrorist attacks of September 11. I will acknowledge that since Muslim leadership must be responsive to events, this question cannot be answered completely in isolation of specific circumstances. The appropriate response will necessarily depend on the nature of the threat. At the same time, any truly appropriate response must be firmly rooted in faith. A faith-based response is one that recognizes the omniscience of God, and the limits of human understanding. Faith urgently demands that we recognize the omnipotence of God, and the limits of human authority. Finally, faith demands that we acknowledge the absolute accountability of each individual before God, and that communal solidarity should never impede honest self-criticism, nor should it lead to injustice against other groups.

Within hours of the September 11 attacks, Muslim leaders worldwide, including the Chief Mufti of Saudi Arabia and the leaders of all major Islamic organizations in the United States, issued strong statements denouncing the attacks as sinful and illegal. In the weeks and months following the attacks, Muslim scholars and leaders wrote articles analyzing the Islamic legal basis for classifying these acts as terrorism or brigandry. War (*jihad*) is permitted in Islamic law, they explained, but only a legitimate head of state can conduct a war. They further argued that there are strict rules in Islamic law governing the conduct of warfare; for example, civilians must not be targeted and property must not be wantonly destroyed.[2] This was an entirely appropriate and correct response.

At the same time, many Muslim leaders have not felt comfortable with the American military response to the acts of terrorism, apprehensive that it will lead to further interventions in Muslim lands that will only increase the suffering of ordinary people. In addition, Muslims perceive that Israeli aggression against Palestinians continues without American sanction; indeed, enormous financial and military support for Israel has continued. It seems that any Palestinian resistance to Israeli occupation is termed "terrorism," and is responded to with overwhelming force. The result is the Palestinians themselves are increasingly showing less restraint in the force they employ to defend their families and lands.

How should American Muslims respond to this expansion of American military force, to this increase in Israeli action, and to the further radicalization of Muslim resistance in Palestine and elsewhere? In the heightened tension that has ensued since the terrorist attacks, many have argued that it has become more important than ever for American Muslims to act as ambassadors for America to the Muslim world, and as ambassadors for Islam to the American public. This is a natural role for American Muslims, but it will have efficacy only if they are perceived as sincere advocates for, and honest critics of, each community to which they belong.

To a great extent, the terrorist attack on September 11 exacerbated a double bind American Muslims have been feeling for some time now. It has seemed, so often in the past, that we American Muslims have had to apologize for reprehensible actions committed by Muslims in the name of Islam. We would tell other Americans, "People who do these things (oppression of women, persecution of religious minorities, terrorism) have distorted the 'true' Islam." And so often we have to tell other Muslims throughout the world, that America is not as bad as it appears. We tell them, "These policies (support for oppressive governments, enforcement of sanctions against Iraq, lack of support for Palestinians) contradict the 'true' values of America." The line between apologetics and the desire to foster mutual understanding has not always been clear.

What is needed now from American Muslims, therefore, is to pay serious heed to the words of the Prophet Muhammad. If we really want to help our "brothers," not only must we support them against those who would harm them, but also we must stop them from committing oppression against others. The critical situation we find ourselves living in today is the result, to a great extent, of allowing injustice and oppression to continue unchecked. Muslims, for example, did not criticize the Taliban strongly enough for their oppression of many groups of people in Afghanistan, thinking that they should "support" the struggling rulers in a chaotic situation. The American government has not criticized sufficiently the brutality of the Israeli government, believing that it needs to be "supportive" of the Jewish state. The result is that oppression, left unchecked, can increase to immense proportions, until the oppressed are smothered with hopelessness and rage.

The first duty of Muslims in America, therefore, is to help shape American policies so that they are in harmony with the essential values of this country. In the realm of foreign policy, this "idealistic" view has been out of fashion for some time. Indeed, the American Constitution, like foundational religious texts, can be read in many different ways. The true values of America are those which we decide to embrace as our own. There is no guarantee, therefore, that Americans will rise to the challenge of defining themselves as an ethical nation; nevertheless, given the success of domestic struggles for human dignity and rights in the twentieth century, we can be hopeful.

At the same time, on the pragmatic level, there are strong arguments for the benefits of upholding international law and fostering human rights in foreign relations. As Robert Crane, President of the Washington-based Islamic Institute for Strategic Studies, has argued, it is truly in the best interest of the United States to act according to a consistent moral standard in international relations.[3] The United States has learned a hard lesson that international cooperation is essential in the fight against terrorism. Other nations will be more willing to cooperate with us on this issue if we compromise on issues important to them, even if we can achieve short-term gains pushing our own agenda. The best strategy for achieving national security needs to be reconsidered in an age of trans-national terrorism and narcotic networks, and proliferating nuclear, chemical, and biological weapons.

If Muslim Americans are to participate in such a critique of American policy, however, they will only be effective if they do it, according to the Prophet's words, in a "brotherly" fashion. This implies a high degree of loyalty and affection. This does not mean, however, that citizenship and religious community are identical commitments, nor that they demand the same kind of loyalty. People of faith have a certain kind of solidarity with others of their faith community that transcends the basic rights and duties of citizenship. But most faith groups, including Islam, obligate believers to honor their covenants and contracts, including those that entail obtaining permission to enter a country as a visitor, or by becoming a citizen. Islam further obligates the believer to provide for his neighbors and make them feel secure, without regard to their religious status or identity. The Prophet Muhammad said, "None of you believes who eats while his neighbor goes to bed hungry," and he said, "None of you believes whose neighbor does not feel secure from (your) harm." It is therefore a religious obligation for Muslims in America to promote what is in the best interest of the American people, in terms of their security and basic needs. Muslim Americans cannot be a special interest group concerned only with the rights of Muslims in America and abroad.

At the same time, Muslims in America urgently need to address injustice when it is committed in the name of Islam. The most difficult part of fulfilling this responsibility is to achieve recognition, by other Muslims, that one is speaking about Islam with some authority. After all, Islam is not self-explanatory; it is a religious tradition that needs to be interpreted and claimed. As a practicing Muslim, I believe that there is a core of fundamental beliefs and practices that distinguish authentic Islam from deviations. I also believe that apart from this essential core, the task of interpreting the application of Islamic norms to human society is an enormously complicated task, which inevitably leads to a broad range of opinion and practice. I agree with " Sunni" Muslims, the majority of the Muslim community worldwide, that after the death of the Prophet Muhammad, no one has the right to claim infallibility in the interpretation of sacred law. At the same time, this does not mean that all opinions are equal, nor that everyone has the ability to interpret law. Without the intense study of Islamic texts and traditions under qualified scholars and without the presence of a stable Muslim community through which one can witness the wisdom of the living tradition, the chances of an ordinary believer arriving at a correct judgment about most legal issues are slim. This is one of the reasons why revolutionary leaders who arise in periods of great instability often are accused of having superficial knowledge of sacred texts, and little knowledge of the actual application of law, despite being apparently sincere in their desire to relieve people of oppression.

It is also the case that it is often exceedingly difficult to sustain a self-critical attitude within revolutionary movements. When external threats are immense, dysfunction within a community is usually given little attention. This difficulty is apparent in any nation that faces a challenge to its security. Even many Americans have little patience for complaints about violations of immigrants' rights, racist profiling or transgressions of internationally recognized rights of war captives in the wake of September 11. The international Muslim community, feeling under siege for centuries since the beginning of European colonial rule, has similarly had great difficulty sustaining a self-critical attitude. Bold, charismatic revolutionary leaders have won the hearts of the people because they have given some hope for success against oppression. The inability of such leaders to address internal dysfunction has seemed less important for many people.

A number of scholars have pointed out that the revolutionary discourse of many modern Muslim leaders has most in common with the ideologies of resistance employed by Third World national liberation and self-determination movements. Khaled Abou El Fadl writes that, "modern nationalistic thought exercised a greater influence on the resistance ideologies of Muslim and Arab national liberation movements than anything in the Islamic tradition. The Islamic tradition was reconstructed to fit Third World nationalistic ideologies of anti-colonialism and anti-imperialism rather than the other way around."[4]

Before colonialism, authority was acquired by religious leaders in a much more subtle process, and religious leaders who advocated extreme hostility or aggression against the state were usually marginalized. After all, most Muslims did not want to be led into revolution, they simply wanted their lives to be better. In general, the most successful religious leaders were those who, in addition to serving the spiritual needs of the community, were able to moderate how state power was exercised over ordinary people, and in some sense, acted as intermediaries between the people and state. However, at those times when forces hostile to the practice of Islam attacked or occupied Muslim lands, for example, during the Mongol invasions, (Christian) Crusades, European colonialism, and the Soviet invasion of Afghanistan, meaningful mediation was often impossible. At such times, the people needed revolutionary leaders.

Leaders who were not able to stand against occupying forces were marginalized, and their opinions were considered lacking in authority.

Many historically Muslim lands have undergone unending turmoil since the beginning of European colonialism. Continued occupation and imperialism by foreign powers has allowed revolutionary discourse to take firm root in much of the Muslim world. Oppressive circumstances have disabled many Muslims, making them blind to the effectiveness of peaceful avenues of change, and deaf to the arguments of generations of Muslim scholars that revolt and lawlessness usually cause more harm to society even than government corruption. At the same time, when corruption is severe, when people are suffering under an oppressive government, a scholar who remains silent will lose all authority with the majority of people.

This is the reason why it is so difficult to find authentic, authoritative Muslim voices advocating peaceful resistance to oppression. Religious leaders who speak out in a peaceful way against injustice will remain marginalized if their speech has no effect. The majority of Muslims simply will not recognize such people as religious leaders. At the same time, in many parts of the world, even those who speak out against corruption in a peaceful manner are jailed, tortured, and killed. Anwar Ibrahim, former Minister of Finance of Malaysia, for example, is widely believed to have been the victim of a state conspiracy in 1998 to prevent him from publicizing proof of widespread government corruption linked to the President of Malaysia.[5] After the September 11 attacks, he published an article, in which he linked the growth of extremism to such repression by the state, saying:

> Bin Laden and his protégés are the children of desperation; they come from countries where political struggle through peaceful means is futile. In many Muslim countries, political dissent is simply illegal. Yet, year-by-year, the size of the educated class and the number of young professionals continue to increase. These people need space to express their political and social concerns. But state control is total, leaving no room for civil society to grow.[6]

In such circumstances, very few people – only those who are willing to risk losing everything: their property, their families, their security and their lives – will continue to speak out. Such individuals rarely limit their attempts to change state behavior through speech, because they have seen it to be ineffective. Indeed, in such circumstances, "extremism" might seem to be the only rational choice, because extreme actions are the only actions that seem to have an effect.

In this context, Muslim Americans need to deeply consider what kind of leadership they can and should exercise in the Muslim world. First of all, it is clear that we need to be lovingly self-critical of our own flaws, and of the errors committed by fellow Muslims, even those in difficult circumstances. We cannot allow unsubstantiated suspicions, vague accusations of conspiracies, and exaggerated protests of attempts to ensure security to be used as excuses for violating the rights of women, non-Muslims, and others. According to the words of the Prophet Muhammad, we are truly helping our fellow Muslims when we insist that they cease their injustice and oppression of others. During the Prophet's own life, despite persistent external attacks on the Muslim community, the Prophet did not shy from addressing injustice committed by individual Muslims. Indeed, by helping his companions leave their old culturally acquired practices of brutality, he helped them develop a communal solidarity that was the key to the security of the state.

At the same time, by focusing on the absolute primacy of an individual's relationship with God, the Prophet gave the early Muslims a measure of success that was not dependent on political achievement. Soumayya, the first martyr in Islam, a slave-woman who was killed by her polytheist owner, was "successful" because she recognized only God as her true master. The Prophet Muhammad was unable to stop Soumayya from being oppressed and killed, because he had not yet been successful in establishing a state ruled by law; indeed, his own security was tenuous. All he could say to Soumayya and her husband Yassir as they were being killed was, "Patience family of Yassir, for verily Paradise is yours."

Certainly Muslim Americans must, in the first place, pray for their oppressed brothers and sisters, and assure them that God will reward them if they suffer innocently. But what if such people react to their oppression with a brutality of their own? We need to examine the argument that oppressed people must use only non-violent means of resistance, or confine military action to what is permitted by the law of war, even when such limited methods appear to be totally ineffective in stopping oppression. Is it possible that usual standards of morality in warfare and conflict must be ignored when it appears that great suffering cannot be stopped if resistance and retaliation is limited by these norms? This argument has been made many times in periods of crisis, leading the United States, for example, to drop atomic bombs on Japan, knowingly killing thousands of innocent civilians in the most horrible fashion.

Some Muslim leaders, using the same logic, have argued that standard Islamic limits on the means employed in warfare must be set aside if the brutal oppression of ordinary Muslims is to be stopped. They argue that in the Palestinian case, for example, peaceful means have not led to a lessening of Israeli oppression. During fifty years of diplomacy at the United Nations numerous resolutions have been passed in support of Palestinian statehood and in condemnation of Israeli oppression, which the UN has been unable, or unwilling, to enforce. Millions of Palestinians continue to live in squalid refugee camps, and in daily humiliation and insecurity under Israeli rule. Faced with this reality, they suggest that Palestinians have no choice but to use any means to destabilize Israeli society, to force the Israelis to back off out of a desire to protect their own interests and to provide true security for their citizens.

I believe this argument is flawed because it confuses the need to under-stand what might compel a desperate person to commit indiscriminate acts of violence, and the need to provide strategies, which can be justified by faith, that might relieve such a person from suffering. Before we consider such strategies, however, we must seriously consider the deep suffering experienced by those who suffer persistent abuse and humiliation. We should not be surprised that extremely oppressive circumstances might lead an individual to disregard any moral code. To illustrate this point, we might want to consider this statement, made by a man who fled from American slavery to safety in Canada in the early nineteenth century:

> The abuse a man receives at the South is enough to drive every thing good from the mind. I sometimes felt such a spirit of vengeance, that I seriously meditated setting the house on fire at night, and killing all as they came out. I overcame the evil, and never got at it – but a little more punishment would have done it. I had been so bruised and wounded and beset, that I was out of patience. I had been separated from all my relatives, from every friend I had in the world, whipped and ironed till I was tired of it. On that night when I was threatened with the paddle again, I was fully determined to kill, even if I were to be hanged and, if it pleased God, sent to hell: I could bear no more.[7]

Reading such a statement from an Islamic perspective, it occurs to me that certainly one could say that such an act of violence, and other acts of terror-ism, might lead a person to hell. It is also possible that God will forgive even such grave sins. But what if another individual, appalled, for example, at the treatment of this slave, unable to compel the abusive master to free him, encouraged him to commit this act of violence? What would be the weight of sin on such a person? At the same time, would it not be wrong for such a person to simply condemn as a grave sinner the desperate slave who has lashed out not only at his oppressor, but has inflicted violence on all those around his oppressor?

If we return once more to the example of the Prophet Muhammad for guidance, we see that he used a variety of techniques to relieve the suffering of the unjustly oppressed, depending on his ability to help them. For the early martyrs, all he could do was pray for them and reassure them. Once he was recognized as a prophet by the people of Medina, he was able to do much more. Still, it has been argued convincingly by a number of scholars that political power was relatively decentralized during the time of the Prophet, and he often could use only moral persuasion and shaming to stop certain individuals from acts of oppression.[8] Thus, Abu Masud al-Ansari, one of the early Muslims from Medina related:

> I used to beat a young slave of mine until once I heard a voice behind me saying, "Know Abu Masud that God is more powerful over you than you are over him." I turned and lo and behold it was the Messenger of God. So I said, "He is free, Messenger of God, for the face of God." The Prophet said to me, "If you had not done so, hell-fire would have covered you."[9]

In other reports about the Prophet, we see him directly ordering a person to free a slave he has struck in anger.[10] In these cases, perhaps, the Prophet had the *political* authority to enforce such an order.

What we learn from the Prophet's example is that Muslims are required to help the oppressed within the limits of authority they possess. Thus, Muslims in America must demonstrate their empathy with their oppressed brethren through prayer and encouragement. They must use their legal rights to free speech to publicize the oppressors and shame them. They must work for a just political order, and in particular, encourage their government to make universal human rights a priority in foreign policy.

Americans, Muslims and non-Muslims, are not neutral outsiders to the conflicts in Muslim lands that have come to threaten our security. The United States government has a long history of negative interventions in the Middle East. Muslim Americans, too, have supported resistance movements with words and, in some cases, with money. What is of primary importance is that we ensure that our "help" does not in fact increase oppression and injustice.

During the Soviet occupation of Afghanistan, the United States gave support to a resistance movement that desperately needed to succeed.

Nevertheless, enough care was not paid to the way this support could increase internal oppression among the Afghan people. In my own small way, I learned this lesson too. In 1988, I was working in an Afghan refugee camp in northern Pakistan. Part of my job was to register women for monthly widow's benefits. One day, a woman who had received her payment the day before walked into our office with a black eye. She told us that her brother-in-law had tried to take her money, and when she refused, he beat her up. When we investigated further, we discovered that in some areas, corrupt tribal leaders were seizing all the widows' benefits and using the money to increase their power to oppress others. What this taught me is that one can do a little good to relieve the suffering of others, or one can do a great deal of harm.

We pray that Americans, Muslims and non-Muslims, will have the wisdom to know what is good, and the courage to stand up to oppression, whatever form it takes.

NOTES

1. *Sahih Muslim: being traditions of the sayings and doings of the Prophet Muhammad as narrated by his companions and compiled under the title* al-Jami'-us-Sahih, trans. and edited by 'Abdul Hamid Siddiqi, 4 vols. (Beirut: Dar al-Arabia, n.d.), 4, 1367.
2. The articles, op-eds, press releases, and statements are so numerous that the best way to access them is through links collected on the "Muslims Against Terrorism" web-site: www.matusa.org. A brief overview of the statements made by major Muslim leaders was published in a full-page ad in the *New York Times* and other major American newspapers on October 17, 2001.
3. Robert Crane, "A Wake-up call for America and Muslims World-Wide," in September 2001 issue of *Islam21* on-line magazine, http: //www.islam21.net/pages/keyissues/key7–2.htm.
4. Khaled Abou El Fadl, "Islam and the Theology of Power," *Middle East Report*, 221, Winter 2001.
5. His story is told in *Renaissance Man: Dato Seri Anwar Ibrahim, Former Deputy Prime-Minister of Malaysia*, UASR Regional Report Series, 3 (Springfield, VA: UASR Publishing Group Inc., 2001).
6. *Time* (Asian edition), October 15, 2001, 158, no. 15.
7. Benjamin Drew, *The Refugee* or *the Narratives of Fugitive Slaves in Canada related by Themselves with An Account of the History and Condition of the Colored Population of Upper Canada* (Toronto: Prospero, 2000), 220.
8. W. Montgomery Watt, *Muhammad at Medina* (Oxford: Oxford University Press, 1956), 228–38.
9. Muslim, v. 3, 883–84.
10. Muslim, v. 3, 883.

6

WITNESSING TO THE SPIRIT: REFLECTIONS ON AN EMERGING AMERICAN SPIRITUALITY[1]

Miriam Therese Winter

September 11, 2001. It began like any other day as the sun moved resolutely westward across the American landscape, but it was in reality a day without precedent in the history of the United States. Well before midmorning, thousands of lives were suddenly hurled from here into eternity. Our flesh and blood, our unfulfilled hopes, our best laid plans went up in smoke as towering infernos and flaming fields turned vital shards of the American dream into dust and ashes. It was a harrowing moment, a moment of mourning, of terror and tears, of sorrow and anger and disbelief. At the same time it was a turning point in the heart of a pioneering people. Despite theological ambiguities concerning God and good and evil unleashed in the conflagration, many of us knew instinctively that we who had come this far by faith[2] would somehow muddle through it; that God, in Whom we trust, in Whom we live and move and have our being, did not bring us this far just to leave us. This defining moment for people of faith saw the spirit of America rise up like a phoenix from the ashes, cohesive and compassionate and determined to begin again.

What follows is a focused reflection on the implications of this catastrophe while the wound is still wide open. From the perspective of spirit and spirituality, an attempt will be made to uncover what might serve as a light to our path as we move forward into the future. To do this it will be necessary to situate September 11 within a much wider context, seeing it momentarily not only at the epicenter of American concern, but as part of a global reality that exists within an expanding universe that has a lengthy relationship with galaxies beyond our own. A brief consideration of the value and the limits of organized religion in a time of national crisis will prepare the way for positing the importance of a distinctively American spirituality. Further analysis will show that such a spirituality is emerging and that this rudimentary phenomenon, which manifested itself prior to the events of September 11, has come of age within them.

Two primary convictions underlie these reflections on an emerging American spirituality, namely, that such a channeling of the American spirit in ways that unify is a legitimate and inclusive means of filling the current void caused by legislative curtailment of the sacred within our public sphere; and that a nation founded on principles that honor diversity and plurality can find within its rich and multifaceted collective consciousness appropriate elements for a meaningful response to events of significance.

THE WORLD OF THE TWENTY-FIRST CENTURY

When the first astronauts soared into space and orbited our planet, they saw with their own eyes what mystics have intuited and scientists are discovering, that in essence there are no boundaries. Earth from a distance gives no indication of geographical borders, no lines of demarcation that apportion and divide. The stunning blue orb adrift in space that so transfixed the explorers continues to symbolize the impossible dream of one unsegregated world.

That image is a visual reminder of a time long before recorded time when the continents of Earth were joined together and its waters intermingled, a period billions of years before the evolution of the human species and the advent of civilizations with all of their complexity and differentiation.[3] Humanity's expansion from tribe to village to urban setting to urban metropolis and into the modern era's global societies gives our twenty-first century world historically unique characteristics. Now nations are at once connected to and yet disconnected from one another, largely by means of socio-political/economic realities and the technological omnipresence of the internet's worldwide web. Conflicting currents of globalization increasingly traverse our planet, promoting a future that is said to be beneficial to all. Such claims carry within them the confluence of an overwhelming number of diverse experiences and unrealized expectations, raising hopes that almost always crumble of their own accord. Within this vortex the violent events of September 11 took sinister shape and spewed forth with venomous fury. From the same wellspring, however, also poured forth an avalanche of life-giving response. Our twenty-first century world is one in which good and evil, life and death, those that have enough and more than enough and those that are deprived live in close proximity, no matter how far apart. An axiom of our present era can surely be stated this way: how we live as individuals, what we do as a society, is bound to affect us all.[4]

This snapshot of the world today is not the total picture. If all we knew of our world were limited to what we could see from where we stand with feet firmly planted, we would know little of who we are and are capable of becoming. There is so much more to reality than what is visible to the eye. Beyond the horizons, beneath the surface, within the core of all that exists are unseen forces shaping our world in ways that challenge our assumptions and our priorities, inviting us to reconsider our physical world from the inside out. It may sound as though this reflection has slid into the realm of spirituality, but for the moment, it has not. What follows is strictly scientific.

Science has made a significant contribution to our knowledge of the origins of life, the nature of the universe and its unfolding story, and the inner reality and interrelationship of all life forms on our planet. The following aspects of quantum theory, rooted in quantum physics, have particular relevance here.

On the quantum or subatomic level at the core of all that is, where the fundamental elements of life remain invisible to the naked eye, nothing is fixed or static. All is in flux. Anything is possible. There is unlimited potential to change. Particles of energy constantly move in and out of relationship, manifesting potential as this or that and carrying within them the memory of what was made manifest. Waves of energy, packets of potential, comprise a variety of energy fields that fill the space within us and beyond us and throughout what was once thought to be the cosmic void, forming an invisible web of interconnectedness. Chaos, not control, is a basic principle, for what unfolds is unpredictable, yet chaos does not mean out of control, for that which exists contains within itself the ability to order and renew itself and to achieve a transformation. The most minute disturbance can trigger a systemic response that may prove to be beneficial. A local change can influence the whole and have impact at a distance because of a fundamental interrelationship and interconnectedness.[5]

The scientific perspective of the inner workings of ourselves and the world around us suggests some vital linkages to the conversation at hand. It may require a quantum leap for some to perceive the connections between scientific theory and an emerging American spirituality, but the relationship is crystal clear. Conversations on the relevance of the new science to spirituality and attempts to articulate a quantum theology are already well underway.[6] It is here that spirit and spirituality experience an energizing transformation with the potential to radiate out and into the hearts of the American people, a point that will be developed more fully later on.

Individual and systemic behaviors and beliefs are integrally related to how we view and understand our world. We have seen how the world around us has changed and is continually changing. Before proceeding to the specifics of an American spirituality, it is necessary to reflect briefly on religion, and more directly, religion in America, which is such a significant presence in so many of our lives.

RELIGION AND SOCIETIES

From the dawn of civilization, individuals have responded collectively to manifestations of the sacred in a manner that bound them together and set them apart as a group. In diverse ways and in various settings, experience and interpretations of experience were codified over time in rites and creeds and canons. Lives were ordered according to precepts supporting mythological expectations, and shared convictions were periodically expressed in symbolic and ritual forms.[7]

Religion has played a central role in the evolution of civilizations, the shaping of societies, and the transmission of cultural values. It has been morally and ethically central to the way humans have behaved. From generation to generation, religion has brought out the best in us, at times evoking, at other times mandating concern for one another through specified services to those who are in need. However, at the same time, it has also given rise to the worst in us, spawning all manner of confrontation and less than civil behavior. Religious wars have been among the bloodiest and most brutal in human history. Countless lives have been sacrificed on the altars of religion while invoking one of the many names humanity has for God. Nevertheless, it would be hard to conceive of society without religion, for its capacity to contribute to the good of the whole ordinarily outweighs other factors.

It is perhaps more accurate to speak of "religions" rather than "religion," for there is much that distinguishes one religion from another in theology and in praxis, a point we need to keep in mind as ecumenical and interfaith efforts explore common ground. There were those in archaic societies before recorded history who celebrated the myth of eternal return around an *axis mundi*, and there was the cultic worship of the goddess in numerous places throughout all those centuries when God was depicted as a woman, as indicated by artifacts and figurines from archaeological finds.[8] Today there are countless traditional religions among the world's indigenous peoples that are distinct from one another and that differ dramatically from the religious traditions represented by churches, basilicas, stupas, temples, synagogues, and mosques. The locus of the sacred, ways of knowing and naming God, rites and rituals and symbols and songs from time immemorial have yielded a multitude of perspectives that shape reality. More often than not a particular approach is considered to be the right way, even the one and only way, if not for everyone, then surely for those who are said to belong. To complicate things even further, there are a growing number of syncretistic expressions where elements of more than one tradition have been blended to create hybrid forms that adherents find meaningful for the moment. There are also multiple ways of being a practicing Christian – of being a Catholic or a Protestant or an Orthodox Christian – and more than one authentic way to be a Muslim or a Jew. Of particular importance are the experiences and perspectives that gender, race, culture, and ethnicity bring to traditional understandings, initiating processes of ethical, theological, and ritual change. No wonder it is so difficult for us to enter into genuine dialogue or to unite in support of a cause.

Nevertheless, on September 11 and during the weeks that followed, individuals and communities of faith from a broad spectrum of religious traditions, without hesitation and with no strings attached, gave of themselves and their resources tirelessly and generously, bringing a dimension of hope to quell the temptation to despair. It was America at its finest as citizens from various faith perspectives came together as one.

It has not been an easy journey for religion in America. The Pilgrims who arrived in 1620 to begin a new life in a new world came seeking freedom to practice their religion and found it, for themselves, but only for a time. The fierce repression of indigenous peoples who had practiced their religions freely for centuries before the settlers arrived; the witch hunts throughout the colonies that led to the trials, torture, and execution of women for speaking up and acting out of their own religious convictions; and the despicable treatment of African slaves that deprived them of physical, social, psychological, and religious freedoms indicate that historically, in America, religious freedom has been a whole lot freer for those within the dominant religion than for those who are outside.

Freedom of religion in America is a constitutional guarantee embodied in the First Amendment, which reads: "Congress shall make no law respecting an establishment of religion [Establishment Clause] or prohibiting the free exercise thereof." [Free Exercise Clause] To ensure this freedom the courts enforce a separation of church and state. But as Stephen Carter points out in *The Culture of Disbelief*, what that actually means in practice is often quite complex. "The metaphorical separation of church and state originated in an effort to protect religion from the state, not the state from religion."[9] An unfortunate consequence of this basic liberty often has been freedom *from* religion and its expression in the public domain rather than freedom *for* it. Although not the intended outcome, one can argue it is nonetheless inevitable as long as religion in America retains its historically Christian bias. The current push by the Christian religious right to have the Ten Commandments posted in schools, courtrooms, and other public places as a sign of our nation's allegiance to God and to basic Christian values illustrates how difficult it is to be religiously inclusive in a religiously pluriform nation. American civil religion is indicative of how we as a people have often dealt with this.

The term "civil religion," which first appeared in J. J. Rousseau's *The Social Contract* in 1762, refers to "the beliefs, symbols, rituals and institutions which legitimate the social system, create social solidarity and mobilize a community to achieve common political objectives."[10] The signs, symbols, and rituals of an American civil religion are present all around us. The phrase "In God we trust" is stamped on all our currency. The nation observes Thanksgiving Day as a time to gather and give thanks for all our many blessings. We recognize our union "under God" every time we pledge allegiance to our flag and to the United States of America. In the aftermath of September 11, flags appeared everywhere in unprecedented numbers together with the phrase, "God bless America," which was and is ubiquitous. The flag, a national and political symbol, is also considered sacred. Many of the symbols and rituals of American civil religion are unabashedly patriotic and often political. In many instances it is difficult to separate patriotic from religious, and we may not always want to. The recent outpouring of patriotic fervor has been a cathartic response to the evil perpetrated on America. It helped affirm our solidarity as a people and our allegiance to our nation, an important step in the healing process and in our commitment to carry on.

WITNESSING TO THE SPIRIT

The ash had not yet settled on Ground Zero and its surroundings when the site was awash with the signs and symbols of an invincible American spirit, as young and old, rich and poor, blue collar worker and CEO, those at a distance and those nearby rose up *en masse* to help repair the hole in the nation's heart. At the Pentagon, in a Pennsylvania meadow, and up and down the sidewalks of New York, courage, a rugged determination, a sudden surge of neighborliness, and an incalculable generosity kept alive what might have died along with those who were lost. Much has already been written, powerfully and poignantly, about what has transpired since that devastating day, so there is no necessity for simply a descriptive reiteration here. What I will offer is a perspective on this witness to the spirit – individual spirit, the American spirit, the spirit of God or Holy Spirit – knowing it will be one among many, because in the realm of spirit and spirituality, personal perspectives abound.

The response to September 11 will be reviewed through the interpretive lens of the Spirit, so that sacred and sacramental realities in the midst of secular settings might be identified. This may help us to see more clearly the transforming impact of what transpired, so we might trust that the Spirit will be with us should it ever happen again. Sacred here is understood to mean in and of the Spirit. The use of the word sacramental suggests a glimpse into another and unfamiliar level of reality, whereby something in our physical world bridges the expanse between seen and unseen in ways that evoke new meaning, enriching the here and now. The sacred was made manifest in many ways and in many places September 11, 2001 and during the weeks that followed. Through symbol and symbolic action, which at the time seemed to be simply the necessity of the moment, America was able to express its grief and to do what needed doing. Here are some of the means whereby the human spirit and the divine spirit converged to strengthen and inspire.

Sacred space

Too often in attempting to discern the sacred we tend to ignore the ordinary. More often than not we think the sacred is anywhere else but here. The last place we would look for God is in the wreckage of Ground Zero, and that's where we were wrong. God was right in the midst of things, neither willing nor preventing, but as Being at the core of those precious beings who, unexpectedly and irrevocably, ceased to be as they had been and came to be as they are. In the cries of terror, in the tears of regret, in the words spoken silently or aloud to loved ones left behind, God wailed, wept, whispered to them, then welcomed them home beyond the veil where now, no longer wounded but whole, they are in a place of peace. And God was there in the heroic efforts to salvage life from the rubble, in the outpouring of compassion, in the agony of loss. God was, is, and always will be at the heart of life as we know it, no matter how it unfolds, because God is life generating life, pulling from the debris we leave behind infinite possibilities to begin again anew.[11] We will remember these sites as sacred spaces, if only for a time: the void where once twin towers stood, the gaping wound of the Pentagon, a field of fallen heroes. If ever a place was holy ground it is there in the belly of Manhattan. In this hallowed place blood, sweat, tears intermingle, and deep within its aching womb, love lies interred.

Story

The story of life – our story, God's story – is a sacred story, although we seldom speak about this with the life-stories we have known. It is time to change that now. Life-stories are potentially life-changing for others, for stories are ways in which the Spirit transmits wisdom and meaning, which is why scriptural stories have such a capacity to empower. Every life lost that fateful day, every life that lost a loved one that day, every life that reached out to another that day and in the days that followed is part of a larger story that has become a primary source of inspiration for us all. So many of the narrative accounts in the news, in the eulogies, in shared memories were just like those heard in former times about the lives of saints and martyrs, who once were one of us. We must never stop telling these stories, for telling the story of those who are gone keeps their memory alive and their spirit here among us.

Candles

There is something primal about fire, something mysterious about the flame's ability to ignite a spark within us and to link us to worlds beyond ourselves. There is something about a candle. A microcosm of cosmic light. Our kinship with a distant star. Prelude to the rising sun when the wavering voice within us says there will be no morning after. Promise to oneself at night not to be afraid of the dark. Bolt of light in a violent storm. Vigil lamp in memory of a loved one not returning. Radiant witness to life beyond life. Beacon illuminating our way. Glimmer of hope. Ray of relief. A burning passion to never give up but to live life regardless. Everywhere and anywhere, people came together. They came carrying candles. Flickering light. Rippling light. Rivers of light. Holy light. Sometimes the only comfort we know is a candle in the wind.

Shrines

There is a lengthy, unbroken tradition going all the way back to ancient times behind the practice of memorializing an experience with a shrine. In the biblical era and long before, stones would often mark the place where someone had encountered the sacred or had wrestled with the divine. Throughout history and around the world shrines have taken many shapes and forms, from wooden markers and wayside altars to chapels and basilicas, sacred icons, the Taj Mahal, a black granite wall with the names of those who died in the Vietnam war, a tombstone or a mausoleum, a room, a plaque, a flowering tree. Some shrines were meant for the moment and have since passed into history. Others like the Oklahoma memorial were erected to live on. Memorials are sacred places that put the living in touch with that which only the heart can see. They capture a timeless moment in time, invite us to return and remember, are visible witness to the passerby to stop and pay attention, for once upon a time something of utmost importance happened here. The shrines that sprang up spontaneously in response to the experience of September 11 are living memorials of lives lost and of spirit living on. The photos, flowers, and artifacts, the relics of those remembered, help integrate the before and after, providing an opportunity for holding close, letting go, moving on.

Sound

The sound of steel smashing into steel, of fuselage exploding on impact, of towers crumbling, sirens wailing, people screaming, children crying, whether or not we heard it, no matter how far away we were, reverberates within us, for the violent wounding of America is personal pain to all. Those who were in the midst of it have unique issues to deal with. For the rest of us, the media made it feel like we were there. The sound of human voices. Healing sounds, encouraging sounds. Conversations. Consoling words. A word of thanks. A whispered prayer. Sounds of recovery helped us move to another phase with familiar sounds, yet one sound in particular will remain long after the rest fade away – the tolling of the bells. The sound of a bell includes within it the full range of harmonic overtones, unlike musical instruments, all of which resonate with a partial overtone series. The bell towers of New York rang in harmony with the tolling of the bell to herald a new beginning. The haunting, penetrating sound at and around the site of Ground Zero symbolized the inclusion of all Americans who cherish liberty. Steeple bells. The Liberty Bell.[12] Ring the bells to honor our dead. Ring the bells to proclaim our freedom. Ring the bells to celebrate solidarity in the midst of our differences. Far and near, glad tidings tell. For this, the tolling of the bell.

Silence

There is no more riveting sound than the hollow sound of silence. Within silence we are able to hear the sounds of generations before – their songs, their celebrations – and we open ourselves to the song of the universe and the silence of the spheres. Be still and know that I am God, the psalmist prayed before us.[13] Be still and receive insight from God – a flash of intuition, heightened imagination – for wisdom waits in silence for an occasion to be heard. We bring to the surface discarded dreams when we listen for signs of their stirring. We find a way where there is no way of getting up and moving forward. We still the urge to take revenge, to retaliate, to get even. When we take time to be silent, we hear one another into hope, for silence is the only way for another to be heard. Silent vigils. Silent witness. Those rituals of silence in past months that marked our solidarity in spirit and brought us to this moment revealed to us that in the silence we sensed something new about ourselves and learned to live with it.

Service

From September through December, the dominant image of American response was that of selfless service. The numbers of those responding to the clarion call to action are already legendary – more than anticipated, more than was needed, far more than could be utilized – yet still they continued to come. There were those engaged in public service who went the extra mile and then kept on going. From the swamps of the deep south, they came; from the wilderness out west, they came; from the coastal regions and from the plains and all across the middle, they came; from the north and throughout the northeast, they rolled up their sleeves and got to work, expecting nothing, giving their all, stooping to pick up the pieces, helping to put those broken in spirit back together again. Emergency service. Military service. The many facets of public service. Liturgical and worship service. Funeral services, *ad infinitum*. Countless acts of kindness. Performing *mitzvot*. Giving alms. Whenever we begin to get down on ourselves for all the things we are lacking, there is an image that can move us to tears or to lift up our hearts in thanksgiving. There was a call to action, and everybody came. Even those who had nothing to give, nothing to do, nowhere to go, made their contribution by being there in spirit. All over America, spirit called out to spirit and everybody came. It was this power of presence, this witness to the spirit, that turned our nation around. It was and is a tribute to that which is the best in us, that which had been there all along. How good it was to see it.

Ashes

One stark and penetrating symbol emerging from September 11 is the thick covering of ash all around Ground Zero. Reflecting on this phenomenon, we are forever reminded that we are dust and ashes, that this is the matrix from which we come and to which we will return. What we don't often talk about is the fact that we here on earth are intrinsically related to the stars, for the dust of earth is stardust, gift from some far galaxy in some primordial time. We come from light and return to light, radiant with love. The ash that blocked the New York sun and settled everywhere is visual reminder that those who are gone are still right here among us and will be absorbed into whatever it is that we in the future become. We breathe in the remains of their vibrancy, breathe in their valiant spirits, breathe in the ways they influence and inspire in the tragic wake of their passing. Their spirits merge with our spirits, transcending the limitations and separations of finitude, and we continue on together, one with the spirit of God.

Such is the way of Spirit, who infuses elements of our everyday world with sacramental potential to energize and inspire. The sacred symbols and rituals of service emanating from this decisive event have the power to evoke within us a wealth of associations that give meaning to our lives. What we do during these days is not just for now but forever. The passing of time will embellish the myth and reinterpret the symbols, so that those we have known appear larger than life to succeeding generations. But that is exactly what happens when transforming events occur. We can only hope that one day we can all look back on the recent devastation as a time of saving grace.

AN EMERGING AMERICAN SPIRITUALITY

Spirituality means different things to a lot of different people. The tendency today is to distinguish between spirituality and religion. Spirituality is spontaneous, dynamic, and always open to change, with freedom to follow the Spirit, often discerned intuitively and now and then through signs. Religion is formal, fairly set in its ways, and follows established traditions. The two are not mutually exclusive. In fact, they are often compatible, for many who practice spirituality within the framework of their religion find that both approaches meet their needs. The terms are often used interchangeably in print and in conversation, contributing to the confusion about precisely what spirituality is and what the word really means.

There are those who would dismiss spirituality as frivolous and ephemeral, saying it is too subjective, that its emphasis on finding one's personal path is isolating and narcissistic, that it ignores critical issues and the needs of the wider world. Feminist women in particular counteract this critique by insisting that "the personal is political,"[14] that spirituality provides a forum, freedom, and opportunities to address those very things. A study of American women who participate in feminist spirituality groups documents a strong correlation between spirituality and social justice, noting a high level of engagement in actions oriented toward systemic change.[15] The proliferation of spirituality groups indicates that these are or can be alternatives to isolation, offering those who feel alone a secure setting in which to safely engage with other people. In fact, a strong sense of community is a hallmark of women's spirituality and of small faith communities seeking to live authentically.

There are multiple paths and myriad ways to approach spirituality according to the present generation of seekers.[16] Most profess a concern for this world, a desire for peace and justice and a sensitivity to environmental issues, often seeking to live by faith in a manner that integrates body, mind, and spirit. In the present context it would not be unusual for a distinctively American spirituality to emerge as a way of meeting our need as a people to come together in public places and acknowledge that we are "one nation," that we are "one nation *under God*," that we are "one nation under God, *indivisible* ..." There are signs of such a spirituality in our national response to September 11. Its expression is shaped by and takes place within the raw realities of the moment and reflects the following characteristics: spontaneity, generosity, hospitality, compassion, courage, sense of community, adaptability, and patriotism. These eight gifts of the American spirit, bedrock virtues and values, have the potential to unite us in spirit under the guidance of God's spirit in ways that further the welfare and well-being of our nation.

Spontaneity

This is something that Americans are known for all over the world. It reflects a willingness to take a chance, to risk pioneering ventures. It got us to the moon and back and into other situations where no one has gone before. The downside is our propensity for instant gratification. We want things fast – fast food, fast forward, extremely fast computers and cars – and are quick to tire of our latest successes. Ours is a culture of impermanence. Just look at our fashions and fads. Yet there are many positive aspects to our spontaneity. It is why we are quick to jump in or reach out or to act instinctively. We respond to emergencies, we volunteer, we gamely roll with the punches, and when things don't go according to plan, well, we improvise. On September 11 our spontaneity was a paramount virtue. Spontaneous prayer. Spontaneous rituals. Spontaneity is a welcome trait in spirituality.

Generosity

Whatever else we might say about America, we have to admit we are generous. Philanthropy, foreign aid, tithing, almsgiving, organ giving, the giving of blood, our daily sharing of our goods and of ourselves are acts that flow from a quality that is core to our understanding of who we are as a people. This is not always apparent. Our basic inclination to accumulate and to horde and our fear that enough will never be enough mask our innate altruism, particularly in the global arena, where we often give aid with one hand and collect interest with the other, thereby driving those already destitute more deeply into debt with our consumer-driven economy, or gobble up most of the world's resources to support our national interests to the detriment of our planet. That said, there are many throughout our nation who advocate forgiving the debt of the world's poorest nations, who insist we act more responsibly in relationship to the environment, and who promote a more just and equitable distribution of our resources, both at home and abroad. We need to be reminded, we who are so accustomed to the practice of reciprocal giving, which means, if I give something to you, well then, you had better give something to me … we need to be reminded that in gift-giving societies, the one who receives a gift is expected to give a gift of equal or higher value in return, but not to the original donor. It is given to someone else, perhaps even a stranger, perhaps anonymously, so that the giving goes on. A gift in gift-giving societies is to be given away again, freely given away with no expectation of return. America was originally a gift-giving society. The early settlers discovered this among the indigenous people and it took them a while to adjust.[17] Some of that gift-giving spirit remains embedded in our psyche. It shapes our Thanksgiving Day observances. It surfaced again full force last fall. We who have been given so much are compelled to give in return. A generous spirit – a giving spirit – is a vital and valued characteristic of spirituality.

Hospitality

In essence hospitality means our door is always open, the kettle is hot, the welcome is warm, there is always room at the table. Genuine hospitality would add that the heart is always open. The bruised and broken spirit knows it can find sanctuary there. American hospitality placed an ad on a billboard on a statue in the New York harbor that reads:

> Give me your tired, your poor,
> Your huddled masses yearning to breathe free,
> The wretched refuse of your teeming shore,
> Send these, the homeless, tempest-tossed to me,
> I lift my lamp beside the golden door![18]

We need to remind ourselves that there was a time in our country when it was safe to talk to strangers, when we invited them in, welcomed them home, and made them part of us. We need to recreate a climate where strangers again feel safe among us, where those who are different in any way feel acceptance and respect. When we stared death in the face last fall and searched frantically for the missing, we wept and prayed for everyone, accepted help from anyone, were hospitable to all. Hospitality does not victimize our innocent brothers and sisters because of ignorance and fear, but says to prejudice and xenophobia, "You are not welcome here." Without genuine hospitality, spirituality is only a six-syllable word.

Compassion

The word means to feel sympathy, to have sorrow for the sufferings of others. It also means to suffer together and is accompanied by an urge to help.[19] We can safely say we have been there. We have had compassion, individually and collectively, so many times in so many ways for so many different reasons and for so very many people right here in America and all around the world. Compassion for women and children who are victims of violence and desperately poor ignites anew our desire to help and to make a difference. Compassion is more than just doing good. It seeks to have an impact, to affect systemic change. Compassion knit us together as one in our response to September 11. Our compassion for families in their tragic loss and also for one another softened our rough edges. We need to do more of that. We need to push ourselves to a more sympathetic response to the wounds of the world and to a more empathetic concern for those disadvantaged here at home. If we say we are a compassionate people, then let us take an inventory of when and where and how. Whose suffering have we felt? Whose suffering are we feeling? Who needs our sympathy now? A spirituality of compassion could turn the world around.

Courage

You can feel it. You can taste it. You know it when it's there. It is at the heart of all we have been able to do and be as a nation. With courage we overcame our fears when we had to cross the great divide and embark upon the wilderness: over sea and land and then out into space, moving through uncharted waters to create a national entity that would encompass all manner of diversity with freedom and justice for all. Courage gives us the right stuff to do what it takes to save lives, expand our horizons, ensure liberty. The courageous were where they needed to be on September 11. The courage of those living and dead gives us the courage to continue on. The courage to act. The courage to accept. The courage to live life justly. The courage to forgive one another when we fall short of our goal. Commitment to a transforming spirituality is also a call to courage.

Sense of Community

When something of significance is on the line, we hunker down together, garner strength from community, and work to get things done. Shoulder to shoulder, hand over hand, bucket by bucket, the heartbreaking task of digging friends out of the rubble could be done because of community. Anything is possible when ordinary people are committed to work as a team. We discover that the gift each person brings is precisely what we needed. Warm socks. A hot meal. A massage for weary shoulders. Someone who will sit and hear us out, or whisper a prayer, or hold our hand. These symbols of solidarity are characteristic of community and they are surfacing everywhere. I have never seen anyone bowling alone, but I do see people in many places finding ways to be together. We seem to be cultivating a whole new set of habits of the heart.

Adaptability

Versatile. Changeable. Handy. We have learned to live with that. There are times when it does come in handy, our ability to adapt, our capacity to change, our versatility. How often have we found ourselves cut off or up against a wall and managed to find a way out? Survivors craft alternatives. Those who have hope savor the opportunity for a second chance, for they know the future belongs to the ones who can facilitate and adapt to change. We did not antici- pate the carnage that interrupted and brutally rearranged our lives, but we managed to make the adjustment. That kind of versatility requires imagina- tion and a willingness to give it a try. A spirituality that is dynamic and contin- ually evolving is congruent with who we are.

Patriotism

Many would agree that patriotism is one of our more dynamic traits, but can it really be considered a characteristic of our spirituality? After careful consider- ation, I would have to say, why not? Consider our patriotic fervor. It's every- where. We're good at it. It is one thing at which we excel. Put aside for the moment the critical issue of who feels comfortable within the metaphor and who has opted out and why. What we have at the heart of American society is a mechanism for making things happen. While patriotism means different things to different people and functions in a variety of ways, not all of them gratifying, it does have unifying strength and unlimited potential to evoke and engage the spirit. For many of us we mean it to mean we're proud to be an American, and that can be a virtue if we choose to make it so. The more we take time to think about it, the more it makes sense to say that an American spirituality, to be viable and valid, would have to reflect a deep integration of patriotic values and a faith-based response. This presumes a patriotism free of political manipulation, a stream within the mainstream that is capable of expressing patriotic dissent to ensure that principles of justice will not be compromised. Such a commitment would prepare the way for embracing what Michael Lerner calls "the politics of meaning." One of the goals of the nation-wide movement based on his initiative is "to create the social, spiritual, and psychological conditions that will encourage us to recognize the unique- ness, sanctity, and infinite preciousness of every human being, and to treat them with caring, gentleness, and compassion."[20] Such an outcome is the intended effect of our emerging spirituality.

    Imagine what it would be like if we took certain symbols seriously, ones we don't really see any more, even though they are all around us, symbols that could add depth and new meaning to our patriotic bent. What if we were to reenergize the symbols that have become peripheral so they effect what they signify? For example, look closely at the coins in your pocket and the dollar bills in your wallet, in fact all the bills that are in your purse. On every single one appears the phrase, "In God we trust." We could not ask for a better prayer in times such as these. Why not use our money to trigger an awareness of God, and instead of choosing between God and money, invoke God when using money. We might think twice about how we spend it, might remember to share more liberally with those who are in need. The street word for money would give our financial transactions a whole new meaning. "Give us this day our daily bread."[21] Give us enough to pay the rent, put food on the table, make ends meet. Suddenly that which is engraved with symbols becomes in itself a symbol, acquiring new associations that can change the way we relate to money and the role it plays in our lives. Symbols integral to daily life are potentially sacramental. They have the capacity to open us to one another and to God.

There are other ways of integrating the secular and the sacred and of blurring the lines between patriotism and spirituality. For example, our Pledge of Allegiance in which we the people publicly affirm that our nation is "under God." And "God bless America." These words we so easily say or sing have become habitual and are appropriate anywhere, even in the classroom. God in these contexts seems to have been liberated from the conundrum of theology in a way that allows the reality to function unencumbered. It is possible for all who participate to embrace this God as their own, if they choose to do so. There is freedom to mentally embellish the word with an image or a name, or simply to feel a connection to the Sacred through the word. In some strange way the patriotic here is functioning as spirituality would, transcending the inherent divisiveness of theological interpretations to facilitate an interconnectedness among us and between us and God. What is needed now is to prevent the words "God bless America" from becoming a cliché or simply another slogan or something one says without thinking. We need to pay attention, to invoke God's name with awareness as in a mantra or in prayer, thereby giving moments such as these some sacramental substance. These are precious opportunities either to pray or to center ourselves, if only for an instant. Such moments in time are potentially occasions of divine blessing, when words are no longer simply words but vehicles of grace. There is a poignant irony in this paradoxical juxtaposition of patriotism and spirituality, with each contributing to the other's growth in authenticity.

Symbols achieve their purpose through the integrity of their application and with consistent practice. They shape a spirituality by continuity and habituation. Through elements such as prayer and song and rites and rituals, an underlying spirit is embodied and made visible through core characteristics such as those previously described. These enact and reiterate the values, ideals, and assumptions of an underlying myth.

The power of myth is legendary. It is a fundamental perspective at the core of a culture, a religion, or a nation and is very slow to change. There are many underlying myths that shape our image of America and our understanding of ourselves. For example, the myth of American supremacy. It is expressed in the manifold ways we as individuals and as a nation strive to be number one, an image that disrupts dialogue and mocks equality. Or the myth that implies that there really is equitable liberty and justice for all. Tell that to the descendants of slaves, to indigenous tribal nations, to lesbians and gays, and to those who are devastatingly poor or in other ways disadvantaged. For reasons both historical and personal, there are those who reject patriotic trappings because they feel that much of what these represent does not apply to them. It is necessary for such myths to change before their metaphors and symbols can release their power to transform us. Sometimes the problem is not the myth but its interpretation and distorted applications. The myth of liberty and justice, to be valid in principle and not simply an ideal, must be applicable to all.

It is important to point out that this reflection on patriotism and its implications for an emerging spirituality that is distinctively American is simply the opening word in a much lengthier conversation, one that must move immediately toward locating our nation more realistically within the context of the rest of the world. Step one is to access and release spirit on personal and national levels. Step two is to harness that energy to bring about good in the world. This brings us back to the question of myth. Joseph Campbell, an authority on mythology, writes: "The only myth that is going to be worth thinking about in the immediate future is one that is talking about the planet, not the city, not these people, but the planet, and everybody on it."[22]

That is indeed our agenda. We can begin by ensuring that our enthusiasm for our nation is not isolationist or disproportionate. When we say "God bless America," why not extend the blessing to "God bless America, and God bless everyone," or something along those lines. Add a global perspective to prayer, choose planetary symbols. Sing songs about the world and our responsibility to it.

> O for a world where everyone respects each other's ways,
> where love is lived and all is done with justice and with praise.
>
> O for a world where goods are shared and misery relieved,
> where truth is spoken, children spared, equality achieved.
>
> We welcome one world family and struggle with each choice
> that opens us to unity and gives our vision voice.

The poor are rich, the weak are strong, the foolish ones are wise.
Tell all who mourn: outcasts belong, who perishes will rise.

O for a world preparing for God's glorious reign of peace,
where time and tears will be no more and all but love will cease.[23]

A FINAL WORD

Quantum theory may be relatively recent, but its roots extend all the way back
to the first cosmic whimper. An intuitive understanding of the innerconnect-
edness of all life forms is the birthright of life itself and a source of hope within
us. Wise women and men through time perceived what the eye failed to see
and the mind dared not imagine. Scientists identified energy as primary
source, as wellspring of life. Mystics experienced the mystery and knew that it
was God.

I am that supreme and fiery force
that sends forth all the sparks of life ...
I shine in the water,
I burn in the sun and the moon and the stars.
Mine is the mysterious force of the invisible wind.
I sustain the breath of all living.[24]

It is remarkable that in an age of skepticism the pragmatic mind of the scientist, the philosophical soul of the theologian, and the passionate faith of the
mystic overlap in conversations about the reality of God.[25]

When one considers the universe,
can anyone be so simple-minded as not to believe
that the Divine is present in everything,
pervading, embracing and penetrating it?[26]

At the heart of authentic spirituality is the desire to be one with God. It is the
impetus for ordering our lives according to what we believe God's expectations to be. There is an integral relationship between our understanding of the
Divine and how we view the world around us. The converse is also true, for we
necessarily image God in ways congruent with our worldview. For the greater
part of Christian history, the spiritual focus within institutional religion was
on other-worldly matters. To be spiritual, the goal of spirituality meant feeling
disdain for the things of this world and living for the hereafter. My understanding of spirituality springs from the root words "spirit" and "ritual." An

applied spirituality in the midst of this world, one that is committed to transforming the world, is open to God's spirit and to spirit everywhere. What
follows from that is life in the Spirit energized through life-giving rituals of
spirit in which God's spirit, one's own spirit, and the inner spirit of all that
lives overlap and intertwine. It is through this ongoing celebration of the
liturgy of life with its cosmic implications and global applications that
mystery is made manifest. Within this primal connection to and through the
Divine Spirit, we are one in spirit with all that lives and with all who have gone
before us. It is here that the events of recent months are invested with deeper
meaning. It is here that our experiences of the sacred, in and through things
we may not understand, receive power to transcend the limitations of our
theologies and become graced theophanies. It is here we are energized to
answer God's call to be agents of wholeness and healing in a war-weary, war-
worried world.

It may be easier to embrace spirituality than it is to understand it. Defining
it is like trying to catch a butterfly with your hand. Rabbi Lawrence Kushner
writes: "Spirituality is where you and God meet – and what you do about it."[27]
This is exactly what happened in the fall of 2001. Without warning we were
confronted by the incomprehensible ways of God, and we did something
about it. Millions of Americans went to work rebuilding a slice of our nation,
while giving an earful to God. People from a multitude of religious traditions,
people with no formal religious affiliation, people on diverse spiritual paths
worked together and wept together in solidarity as a nation. They were visible
witnesses to the spirit of God in the spirit of God's people. Characteristic of an
authentic spirituality is its capacity to invite into community people from all
walks of life who arrive by different paths. It rejoices in diversity, which it sees,
not as divisive, but as manifestation of the divine. Perhaps one day we will
look back to September 11 and recognize it as foundational for a new way of
being in relationship with the sacred, with one another, and with the world.
We may also perceive the beginnings of a distinctively American spirituality,
and we will be amazed at how reluctant we were to even suggest such a thing at
the time.

To be changed as a people, transformed as a nation, it is wise to use those
vehicles that already have power to persuade us. It makes the process more
integrated and the effects more enduring. When we channel energy to bring to
birth a more just and compassionate world, suddenly an impossible dream
awakens to a new day dawning. We are able to see that a spirit of liberty, a spirit
of love, a wholesome and holy spirit of life are already here among us. God

bless America. God has blessed America. May God continue to bless us with generosity and compassion and give us the grace to be less self-centered and more responsive to others. May blessings extend through our concerted efforts to heal the brokenhearted and transform a divided world into an oasis of peace. God bless our world and all that lives with bountiful, beneficial blessings. God bless us all, healing us all at the level of our deepest need, making us living witnesses to the spirit of Shalom.

NOTES

1. This article © the Medical Mission Sisters.
2. Adaptation of the opening line of a song text by Albert A. Goodson (© Manna Music Inc. 1965).
3. See James Lovelock, *The Ages of Gaia: A Biography of Our Living Earth* (New York: Bantam, 1988); Brian Swimme, *The Hidden Heart of the Cosmos: Humanity and the New Story* (Maryknoll, NY: Orbis, 1996); Brian Swimme and Thomas Berry, *The Universe Story: From the Primordial Flaring Earth to the Ecozoic Era: A Celebration of the Unfolding of the Cosmos* (SanFrancisco: Harper and Row, 1992).
4. For further reflection, see: Anne Lonergan and Caroline Richards, eds, *Thomas Berry and the New Cosmology: In Dialogue with Gregory Baum, James Farris, Stephen Dunn, Margaret Brennan, Caroline Richards, Donald Senior, and Brian Swimme,* (Mystic, CT: Twenty-Third Publications, 1987); Thomas Berry, *The Great Work: Our Way into the Future* (New York: Bell Tower, 1999); David Toolan, *At Home in the Cosmos* (Maryknoll, NY: Orbis, 2001).
5. For an introduction to quantum theory, see: David Bohm, *Quantum Theory* (London: Constable, 1951); Paul Davies, ed., *The New Physics* (Cambridge: Cambridge University Press, 1989); Nick Herbert, *Quantum Reality* (London: Rider & Co., 1985); Tony Hey and Patrick Walters, *The Quantum Universe* (Cambridge: Cambridge University Press, 1998); J. P. McEvoy and Oscar Zarate, *Introducing Quantum Theory* (Totem Books USA, 1996). For some applications of quantum theory, read: Margaret J. Wheatley, *Leadership and the New Science: Learning About Organization from an Orderly Universe* (San Francisco: Berrett-Koehler, 1992); Danah Zohar, *The Quantum Self: Human Nature and Consciousness Defined by the New Physics* (New York: Quill/William Morrow, 1990); Danah Zohar and Ian Marshall, *The Quantum Society: Mind, Physics, and a New Social Vision* (New York: Quill/William Morrow, 1994).
6. John David Ebert, *Twilight of the Clockwork God: Conversations on Science and Spirituality at the End of an Age* (Tulsa, OK: Council Oak Books, 1999); David Lorimer, ed., *The Spirit of Science: From Experiment to Experience* (New York: Continuum, 1999); Andrew Newberg, M.D., Eugene D'Aquili, M.D., and Vince Rause, *Why God Won't Go Away: Brain Science and the Biology of Belief* (New York:

Ballantine Books, 2001); Diarmuid O'Murchu, *Quantum Theology: Spiritual Implications of the New Physics* (New York: Crossroad, 1997).

7. Joseph Campbell, *The Masks of God: Creative Mythology* (New York: Viking Press, 1968); Mircea Eliade, *Myth and Reality* (New York: Harper and Row, 1963).

8. Riane Eisler, *The Chalice and the Blade: Our History, Our Future* (New York: Harper and Row, 1987); Mircea Eliade, *The Myth of the Eternal Return: Or, Cosmos and History* (Princeton: Princeton University Press, 1954); Mircea Eliade, *The Sacred and the Profane: The Nature of Religion* (New York: Harcourt, Brace & World, 1959); Marija Gimbutas, *The Language of the Goddess* (San Francisco: Harper and Row, 1989); Merlin Stone, *When God Was a Woman* (New York: Harcourt, Brace, Jovanovich, 1976).

9. Stephen L. Carter, *The Culture of Disbelief: How American Law and Politics Trivialize Religious Devotion* (BasicBooks/HarperCollins: 1993), 105.

10. Refer, the web's reference engine (www.xrefer.com/entry/104898).

11. Most of this paragraph and part of the subsequent section on ashes first appeared in my column entitled "Another Perspective" in *American Catholic* (published in Connecticut: October 2001).

12. Commissioned by the Pennsylvania Assembly in 1751 to commemorate the 50-year anniversary of William Penn's 1701 Charter of Privileges, which speaks of the freedoms valued by people all over the world, the Liberty Bell sounded from the tower of Independence Hall in Philadelphia on July 9, 1776 to summon citizens to hear the first public reading of the Declaration of Independence. Engraved on the bell are these words from Leviticus 25: 10: "Proclaim Liberty throughout all the Land unto all the Inhabitants thereof." Information courtesy of www.ushistory.org

13. Psalm 46: 10.

14. Sheila D. Collins, "The Personal is Political". In Charlene Spretnak, ed., *The Politics of Women's Spirituality: Essays on the Rise of Spiritual Power within the Feminist Movement,"* (New York: Doubleday: Anchor Books, 1982), 362–367.

15. Miriam Therese Winter, Adair Lummis, Allison Stokes, *Defecting in Place: Women Claiming Responsibility for Their Own Spiritual Lives* (New York: Crossroad, 1994).

16. For example: Maria Pilar Aquino and Elisabeth Schussler Fiorenza, eds., *In the Power of Wisdom: Feminist Spiritualities of Struggle* (London: SCM, 2000); Joan Borysenko, *A Woman's Book of Life: The Biology, Psychology, and Spirituality of the Feminine Life Cycle* (New York: Riverhead Books, 1996); Stephen C. Barton, *The Spirituality of the Gospels* (Peabody, Massachusetts: Hendrickson, 1992); Joseph Epes Brown, *The Spiritual Legacy of the American Indian* (New York: Crossroad, 1991); Robert McAfee Brown, *Spirituality and Liberation: Overcoming the Great Fallacy* (Louisville: Westminster, 1988); Barry L. Callen, *Authentic Spirituality: Moving Beyond Mere Religion* (Grand Rapids: Baker Academic, 2001); Joan Chittester, *Heart of Flesh: A Feminist Spirituality for Women and Men* (Grand

Rapids: Eerdmans, 1998); Kenneth J. Collins, ed., *Exploring Spirituality: An Ecumenical Reader* (Grand Rapids: Baker, 2000); Elizabeth Conde-Frazier, *Crossing the Wilderness and Desert Toward Community: The Spirituality of Research and Scholarship* (Princeton: Princeton University Press, 2000); James Conlon, *The Sacred Impulse: A Planetary Spirituality of Heart and Fire* (New York: Crossroad, 2000); Joann Wolski Conn, ed., *Women's Spirituality: Resources for Christian Development, second edition* (New York: Paulist, 1996); Lawrence S. Cunningham and Keith J. Egan, *Christian Spirituality: Themes from the Tradition* (New York: Paulist, 1996); Robert S. Ellwood, ed., *Eastern Spirituality in America: Selected Writings* (New York: Paulist, 1987); Michael Thomas Ford, *Paths of Faith: Conversations About Religion and Spirituality* (New York: Simon and Schuster, 2000); Matthew Fox, *Creation Spirituality: Liberating Gifts for the Peoples of the Earth* (San Francisco: Harper and Row, 1991); Urban T. Holmes, *Spirituality for Ministry* (San Francisco: Harper and Row, 1982); Cheslyn Jones, Geoffrey Wainwright, Edward Yarnold, eds., *The Study of Spirituality* (New York: Oxford, Oxford University Press, 1986); Rabbi Lawrence Kushner, *Jewish Spirituality: A Brief introduction for Christians* (Woodstock, Vermont: Jewish Lights Publishing, 2001); Steven J. Land, *Pentecostal Spirituality: A Passion for the Kingdom* (Sheffield, England: Sheffield Academic Press, 1993); Ian Markham, "Spirituality and the World Faiths." In Mark Cobb and Vanessa Robshaw, eds, *The Spiritual Challenge of Health Care* (Edinburgh: Churchill Livingstone, 1998); Francis X. Meehan, *A Contemporary Social Spirituality* (Maryknoll, New York: Orbis, 1982); Diarmuid O'Murchu, *Reclaiming Spirituality: A New Spiritual Framework for Today's World* (New York: Crossroad, 1998); Virginia Ramey Mollenkott, *Sensuous Spirituality: Out From Fundamentalism* (New York: Crossroad, 1993); Seyyid Hossein Nasr, ed., *Islamic Spirituality, Volume I: Foundations* (New York: Crossroad, 1987); Seyyid Hossein Nasr, ed., *Islamic Spirituality, Volume II: Manifestations* (New York: Crossroad, 1991); Parker J. Palmer, *The Active Life: A Spirituality of Work, Creativity, and Caring* (San Francisco: Harper & Row, 1990); Peter J. Paris, *The Spirituality of African Peoples: The Search for a Common Moral Discourse* (Minneapolis: Fortress Press, 1995); Joan Puls, *Spirituality of Compassion* (Mystic, Connecticut: Twenty-Third Publications, 1988); Ronald Rolheiser, *The Holy Longing: The Search for a Christian Spirituality* (New York: Doubleday, 1999); Ronald Rolheiser, *Spirituality for a Restless Culture* (Mystic, Connecticut: Twenty-Third Publications, 1991); Wade Clark Roof, *A Generation of Seekers: The Spiritual Journeys of the Baby Boom Generation* (San Francisco: Harper and Row, 1993); Mary Hembrow Snyder, ed., *Spiritual Questions for the Twenty-First Century: Essays in Honor of Joan Chittester* (Maryknoll, New York: Orbis, 2001); Carlyle Fielding Stewart, III, *Soul Survivors: An African American Spirituality* (Louisville: Westminster, 1997); Wayne Teasdale, *The Mystic Heart: Discovering a Universal Spirituality in the World's Religions* (Novato, California: New World Library,

1999); Phyllis A. Tickle, *Re-Discovering the Sacred: Spirituality in America* (New York: Crossroad, 1995); John R. Tyson, *Invitation to Christian Spirituality: An Ecumenical Anthology* (New York: Oxford University Press, 1999); Nicki Verploegen Vandergrift, *Organic Spirituality: A Sixfold Path for Contemplative Living* (Maryknoll, New York: Orbis, 2000); John Welwood, ed., *Ordinary Magic: Everyday Life as Spiritual Path* (Boston: Shambhala, 1992); Winter, Lummis, and Stokes, *Defecting in Place*; Miriam Therese Winter, *The Singer and the Song: An Autobiography of the Spirit* (New York: Crossroad, 1999); Robert Wuthnow, *After Heaven: Spirituality in America Since the 1950s* (Berkeley: University of California Press, 1998); Takeuchi Yoshinori, ed., *Buddhist Spirituality: Indian, Southeast Asian, Tibetan, and Early Chinese* (New York: Crossroad, 1993).

17. Lewis Hyde, *The Gift: Imagination and the Erotic Life of Property* (New York: Vintage Books, 1979), 3–5.

18. These last five lines of the sonnet entitled, "The New Colossus," by Emma Lazarus, who emigrated to the United States, are engraved on the Statue of Liberty. *The Story of America* (Pleasantville, New York: The Reader's Digest Association, 1975), 329.

19. Webster's New World Dictionary, 1974.

20. Michael Lerner, *The Politics of Meaning: Restoring Hope and Possibility in an Age of Cynicism* (Reading, MA: Addison-Wesley, 1996), 56–57.

21. A phrase from "The Lord's Prayer," also known as the "Our Father" in the Christian tradition.

22. Joseph Campbell, *The Power of Myth* (New York: Doubleday, 1988), 32.

23. "O for a World," hymn text by Miriam Therese Winter, set to the hymn tune AZMON, in *Songlines: Hymns, Songs, Rounds and Refrains for Prayer and Praise* (New York: Crossroad, 1996); recorded on *Hymns Re-Imagined* (www.medicalmissionsisters.org or http: //mtwinter.hartsem.edu), © Medical Mission Sisters 1990. Also available in these collections (see below) is Miriam Therese Winter's adaptation of the text to "America the Beautiful" by Katherine Lee Bates. "How Beautiful" © Medical Mission Sisters 1993.

> How beautiful, our spacious skies, our amber waves of grain;
> our purple mountains as they rise above the fruitful plain.
> America! America! God's gracious gifts abound,
> and more and more we're grateful for life's bounty all around.
>
> Indigenous and immigrant, our daughters and our sons:
> O may we never rest content till all are truly one.
> America! America! God grant that we may be
> a sisterhood and brotherhood from sea to shining sea.
>
> How beautiful, sincere lament, the wisdom born of tears,
> the courage called for to repent the bloodshed through the years.

America! America! God grant that we may be
a nation blessed with none oppressed, true land of liberty.

How beautiful, two continents, and islands in the sea
that dream of peace, non-violence, all people living free.
Americas! Americas! God grant that we may be
a hemisphere where people here all live in harmony.

24. Hildegard of Bingen (1098–1179), *Liber divinorum operum*: Patrologia Latina, volume 197.

25. For some recent conversations, see: Marcus Borg and Ross MacKenzie, eds., *God at 2000* (Harrison, Pennsylvania: Morehouse, 2000); Marcus Borg, *The God We Never Knew: Beyond Dogmatic Religion to a More Authentic Contemporary Faith* (San Francisco: Harper and Row, 1997); Donald Dorr, *Divine Energy: God Beyond Us, Within Us, Among Us* (Liguori, Missouri: Triumph Books, 1996); Patrick Glynn, *God: The Evidence: The Reconciliation of Faith and Reason in a Postsecular World* (Rocklin, California: Prima, 1997); Elizabeth A. Johnson, *She Who Is: The Mystery of God in Feminist Discourse* (New York: Crossroad, 1992); Sally McFague, *The Body of God: An Ecological Theology* (Minneapolis: Fortress, 1993); Sallie McFague, *Models of God: Theology for an Ecological, Nuclear Age* (Philadelphia: Fortress, 1987); Henry Margenau and Roy Abraham Varghese, eds., *Cosmos, Bios, Theos: Scientists Reflect on Science, God, and the Origins of the Universe, Life, and Homo sapiens* (Chicago: Open Court, 1992).

26. Gregory of Nyssa (c. 330–395), *The Great Catechesis of Gregory of Nyssa*, chap. 25.

27. Rabbi Lawrence Kushner, *Jewish Spirituality: A Brief Introduction for Christians* (Woodstock, Vermont: Jewish Lights Publishing, 2001), 9.

7

VIOLENT FAITH

Kelton Cobb

I must begin with a confession. I am a Christian. I believe in a loving and just God who created all things, cares for all things, and is the destiny of all things. I also believe that religions are good for us. They teach us how to live, how to recognize the humanity in each other, how to respect properly all of creation, how to cope with the passing of all that we love, and ultimately with our own deaths. I am partial to monotheistic religions, and for that reason consider myself a descendant of Abraham – along with Jews and Muslims. These three faiths share the conviction that the God who reached out to Abraham, Sarah, and Hagar is the origin and destiny of all reality, and is to be trusted.

It is important for me to state these convictions up front because everything that follows will sound, and is, critical of religion but I am trying to understand some things.

The argument in this chapter is that religion lends itself to violence. Before I lift the curtain on such an unpleasant piece of news, it is important for me to say that religion also inspires peace and goodwill. In fact, the record of religions for instructing human beings in the personal, social, and global conditions that are necessary for peace, and for infusing us with the goodwill to pursue peace, dwarfs the record of religions for inspiring violence. And, to come at it another way, the record of conscientiously *non*-religious leaders and movements for attaining the peaceable kingdom is not encouraging. Adolph Hitler, Joseph Stalin, Mao Tse-tung, and Pol Pot are responsible for 100 million deaths in the last century. Standing at the beginning of the twenty-first century we have the benefit of hindsight with these several large scale non-religious social experiments – each driven by a vision of justice for society – that have now run their miserable courses to sober us up regarding how wonderful life might be if we could rid our social orders of religious principles, prohibitions, and hopes.

In the aftermath of the September 11 attacks, there has been much good coverage in the news stressing the fact that the vast majority of Muslims are as horrified by the actions of the terrorists as everyone else. Their moral outrage and bewilderment is genuine, and arises not only from whatever innate moral sense that human beings have been given, but beyond that, and intensifying their horror, by the ethical universe in which they live as the result of having been shaped by all the values, writings, prophets, and prayers of Islam. It is as incomprehensible to Muslims as it is to Christians and Jews that a good God would not release his hand to divert these hijacked jets, or to soften the hearts of the hijackers.

Many times in the last months, I have heard the Qur'an quoted to the effect of saying that the murder of one innocent person is equivalent to the destruction of all humanity, and that this terrorist attack has nothing to do with true Islam. This distancing of violence from the heart of Islam is an essential point to emphasize at this moment, given that many Americans equate Islam with the taking of hostages and terrorist bombings, with no remainder.

I have to admit that my own response to this is yes, and no. If Islam does not condone such violent acts, why do they occur? How are we to account for the assassination of Anwar Sadat, the student-held hostages in Iran and Lebanon, the *fatwa* against Salmon Rushdie, the 1993 World Trade Center truck bomb, the 1997 ambush of tourists in Egypt, the amputations of limbs, destruction of ancient Buddhist statues, and persecution of women under the Taliban regime, and now the body count from the attacks of September 11? If Islam does not lend support to such actions, on what grounds do members of al-Qaeda, Hamas, Hezbollah, and al-Jihad identify themselves as dedicated Muslims who follow in the footsteps of Muhammad and his Companions?[1] Without a doubt the formation of these organizations was precipitated by oppressive political situations. Nevertheless, the perpetrators of these crimes certainly believe about themselves that they are devout Muslims carrying out the will of God in designing and executing these acts of terror, that their actions are sanctioned by Islamic law.[2] They are readers of the Qur'an and followers of recognized mullahs, scholars, and jurists, some with credentials from the most respected institutions in the Muslim world.[3] We can presume they observe the five pillars of Islam – bearing witness to God and Muhammad as God's prophet, daily prayers, almsgiving, fasting, and pilgrimage. Communities out of which suicide bombers have come regard them as martyrs who have now found their place in paradise. To be sure, these clerics, communities, and ways of reading the Qur'an occupy a place on the edges of Islam. But are these edges so remote that we are justified in viewing them as having nothing to do with true Islam, that they are as remote from Islam as is *feng-shui* or the art of the samurai?

The letter that was discovered in Muhammad Atta's car found parked at Logan Airport, which contained final instructions for how the hijackers should conduct themselves immediately before and during the operation, was a document on spiritual direction. The hijackers were instructed to read and meditate on *surahs* eight and nine of the Qur'an, the traditional war chapters that excoriate unbelievers and command the followers of the Prophet to "strike terror into the enemy of God and your enemy," to "arrest them, besiege them, and lie in ambush everywhere for them," and to trust that those who fight for God's cause have been promised "gardens of eternal bliss where they shall dwell forever." The letter coaches them to pray through the night, purify their souls, read Qur'anic verses into their hands and then rub their hands on their clothes, knives, and passports to bless them, to shout "*Allahu Akbar!*" (God is greater) when the hijacking begins "because this strikes fear into the hearts of the non-believers," and to end their own lives by praying in the "seconds before the target ... 'There is no God but God, and Muhammad is His messenger.'" In short, they are admonished to get spiritually prepared to fight this battle for the sake of God. No other motives are named.[4]

Clearly, those involved presumed they were being good Muslims – in fact, that they were being the best of Muslims, the most devoted to the teachings of their faith. That does not mean they were right. In fact, I believe they were wrong, both in their overall understanding of Islam, and in their high esteem for themselves. But that is not to say that they are not real Muslims. Certainly they do not represent the golden mean of historical Islam, nevertheless this particular letter, and an abundance of lengthier and more substantial writings that lie behind it and argue for *jihad* against the West to protect the lives and honor of Muslims, and seek to return Islam to world supremacy through whatever means necessary, falls within the boundaries of Islam.[5] In the months following the attacks there have been worldwide Muslim demonstrations in support of Osama bin Laden and al-Qaeda, and websites that advocate *jihad* are flourishing on the Internet. It must be faced that there is a movement among a significant minority of Muslims defending the extremist groups. On what basis can it be said that they are not true Muslims and that their Islam is not true Islam? What is true Islam? For that matter, what is true Christianity? Or true Judaism? We are all divided up within our traditions into factions, and issuing bulls of excommunication to each other has seldom clarified the "true" center of any faith. More often it engenders bitterness and clarifies nothing.

Every religion has its heresies, and heresies must be marked and remembered as out of bounds. Heresies are always children of the religion from whence they come – rogue children, but genetic heirs nonetheless. Heresies are usually borrowed elements of their parent religions, but elements that are broken off and isolated from counter elements that moderated them. Better than charging these radical Islamists[6] with not being true Muslims would be to ask questions like: What components of this faith lend themselves to these distortions? What counter elements that might keep them in check are being neglected? What dangerous traps lie hidden in its scriptures? What responsibility do the bearers of a religious tradition have for the distortions in its transmission?

The Islam of these terrorists does not do justice to the magnificent, civilized, and peace-loving past of Islam, but it has to be recognized as a "real strand" of Islam. Every religion is like a rope, woven from many strands. Christianity is a weave of the teachings of Jesus, the theology of Paul, the neo-platonism of Augustine, Constantine's conversion, the *Little Flowers* of St. Francis, the icononography of the Copts, the Crusades, the Inquisition, the piety of the Puritans, the Ku Klux Klan, the Civil Rights movement, Jerry Falwell, and Archbishop Romero. I don't like several of these strands, but when I study them I discover that they contain fibers I recognize in my own faith. Inside the racism of the Ku Klux Klan one can find firm beliefs surrounding Elijah's contest with the prophets of Baal, divine election, God's sovereignty over all reality, hatred for the devil, absolute faith in the resurrection of Christ, the importance of purity and righteousness, and the lordship of Jesus Christ. The Klan did not come out of thin air; it is a development within Christianity which I abhor, but in calling myself a Christian I am complicit and have to answer for it.

This chapter examines the bloodier strands of two of the religions that have been inspired by Abraham: Judaism and Islam. I will approach them in two ways: *first*, I will consider the role that a selective use of founding stories plays in the interpretation of present conflicts; *second*, I will examine the mechanism of sacrifice that is at work in religion.

With equal vigor and justification a parallel case could be made with respect to any of several violent strands within Christianity, such as the anti-semitism which it sustains like an obstinate weed. Christianity has always had its violent activists who have persecuted Jews, attacked Muslims, and declared holy war against all manner of offenders. During the Crusades, Christian warriors descended on the Holy Land to claim it for the Church and to empty it of all infidels, i.e., all Muslims and Jews. In the words of Pope Urban II, who issued the first call for a military expedition to Jerusalem in 1095: "Enter upon the road to the Holy Sepulchre, wrest that land from the wicked race, and subject it to yourselves. The land which, as the Scripture says, 'flows with milk and honey,' was given by God into the possession of the Children of Israel." Christians, of course, were the rightful "Children of Israel." As the waves of Crusades progressed, the idea arose that killing any Jew was a merit-worthy act, and pogroms began occurring in Europe. While the Church hierarchy disapproved of these attacks on Jews, it was not hard for rank and file Christians to find sufficient justification for these massacres in the Gospels and the writings of Paul. The Jews are clearly depicted in the New Testament as having rejected Jesus as their messiah and conspiring to put him to death. This amounted to deicide – they had rejected and killed God – a crime of unimaginable monstrousness and ingratitude. Their culpability in this murder was reinforced everytime the Mass was performed. For this they have been cursed until the end of time, and deserve to be dispersed, oppressed, humiliated, and treated as outcasts. After the Crusades, pogroms periodically erupted in response to various calamaties that swept through Europe, for example the plague, tax riots in Paris, schisms in the Church, wars, and economic depressions. This crested, of course, in the twentieth century with the Holocaust. It could be argued that among the Abrahamic faiths, Christianity has generated the greatest amount of suffering through its violent strands – if only because it has wielded more power than Islam and Judaism for the last three hundred years.[7]

THE ROLE OF FOUNDING MYTHS

Our scriptures are full of wars, great bloody conflicts between those whom God has elected and those whom God has rejected. In their details, these chronicles of holy war present a variety of precipitating causes, motivations, surrounding circumstances, and strategies. These records of conflicts provide every subsequent generation of the faithful with a repertoire of war scripts, such as the crossing of the Red Sea, the battle of Jericho, David and Goliath, the Babylonian invasion, the Battle of the Trench, Armageddon. There are huge defeats and glorious victories, there are battles that achieve peace and battles that breed other battles, and there is every mixture of human heroism and divine intervention to explain the outcomes. To this day, Jews, Christians, and Muslims, in both our personal lives and our geopolitical lives, have the scripts of these archetypal conflicts playing and guiding our discernment whenever we meet a threatening situation. Much rests on the battle we select as most analogous to our present crisis. In summoning it up, we settle into a pattern of strategies and expectations that will determine the history to follow.

I am not suggesting that in the war rooms of the great powers of today our leaders are openly discussing or even conscious of these scriptural contests. But I am suggesting that these archetypal hostilities are engrained in our cultures, and at the deepest level influence the sense we make of unfolding crises.

For the moment, however, I'll make the more obvious case that with respect to Zionism and radical Islamism, isolated founding stories have been used to justify the worst aspects of our present conflicts.

Zionism

SECULAR ZIONISM. In 1896, Theodor Herzl, a journalist writing from Paris for a Viennese newspaper, wrote a pamphlet he called, "The Jewish State," in which he laid out a plan for the return of Jews dispersed around the world to Palestine to create a Jewish nation-state of Israel. The return, he proposed, should be gradual, stretched over several decades. "The poorest will go first and cultivate the soil. They will construct roads, bridges, railways, and telegraph installations, regulate rivers, and provide themselves with homesteads, all according to predetermined plans. Their labor will create trade, trade will create markets, and markets will attract new settlers – for every man will go voluntarily, at his own expense and his own risk. The labor invested in the soil will enhance its value ... the emigrants standing the lowest in the economic scale will be gradually followed by those of the next grade. Those now in desperate straights will go first."[8] There were at that time movements of Jews colonizing land in both Argentina and Palestine, fleeing the latest wave of pogroms in Europe and Russia. But Herzl recognized that for the mass migration he envisioned, of such numbers that the creation of a sovereign state would be viable – a state in which Jews might "live at last as free men on our own soil, and in our own homes peacefully die"[9] – required the ancestral pull of the "Promised Land." Therefore he favored Palestine. He was aware that this would necessitate some displacement of the "native populace." But he was confident that once a Jewish majority was in place, and the wealth and expertise of the Jewish professional classes began developing the land and its resources, this local resistance would happily acquiesce. "We could offer the present authorities enormous advantages," he wrote, "assume part of the public debt, build new thoroughfares, which we ourselves would also require, and do many other things. The very creation of the Jewish State would be beneficial to neighboring lands, since the cultivation of a strip of land increases the value of its surrounding districts."[10]

Indeed, the early Zionists believed their cause overlapped with the interests of the local Arabs. Arab lives could only be improved by having brothers-in-arms against the corrupt Ottomans, and later the imperialist British, as well as the brains and capital of the Jews to develop the land. The Arab reception of the growing influx of Jews was, however, that of resistance, and eventually armed resistance. This gradually wore many Zionists down until they could conceive of their goal only in opposition to Arabs. This was clarified further in the 1930s when, as their ideals for a pluralist society were fading, they began to feel pressure from another front, from Jews fleeing the Holocaust. This intensified the basic Zionist conviction that Jews needed a Jewish state if they were to survive as a people: a conviction with ample supporting evidence from history. Mass immigration and colonization of Arab lands in Palestine, in violation of quotas on Jewish immigrants established by the British Mandate, became the strategy of the Zionist organizations. Vladimir Jabotinsky, a leader of various Zionist parties and organizations, was adamant about this, and in 1937 testified openly about it in London before the Peel Commission, the body whose charge it was to find a way beyond the impasse that had been reached between Arabs and Jews. He pushed the idea of a population transfer, relocating Palestinian Arabs to existing Arab nations in order to open land to Jewish settlers. "I fully understand that any minority would prefer to be a majority," he testified,

> it is quite understandable that the Arabs of Palestine would also prefer Palestine to be the Arab State No. 4, No. 5, or No. 6 – that I quite understand; but when the Arab claim is confronted with our Jewish demand to be saved, it is like the claims of appetite versus the claims of starvation. No tribunal has ever had the luck of trying a case where all the justice was on the side of one party and the other party had no case whatsoever.[11]

In answer to a question from the Chairman of the Commission suggesting that these recommendations would drag Britain into armed conflict with "world Islam," Jabotinsky denied that this would necessarily follow. He proposed this "compromise":

> Tell the Arabs the truth, and then you will see the Arab is reasonable, the Arab is clever, the Arab is just; the Arab *can* realize that since there are three or four or five wholly Arab States, then it is a thing of justice which Great Britain is doing if Palestine is transformed into a Jewish State. Then there will be a change of mind among the Arabs, then there will be room for compromise, and there will be peace.[12]

David Ben-Gurion, the first Prime Minister of Israel, carried this concept forward after the establishment of the state of Israel in 1948. Transferring the Arab population was imperative, given their refusal to assimilate to the new Jewish state. The colonization of Jews alongside Arabs was a temporary measure. Taking a long view, the Arabs had to go. "It is clear," he wrote in 1954, "that England belongs to the English, Egypt to the Egyptians and Judea to the Jews. In our country there is room only for Jews. We will say to the Arabs: 'Move over'; if they are not in agreement, if they resist, we will push them by force."[13]

Had the State of Israel not been born in circumstances where all of its neighbors wanted to destroy it, a *full-bodied* pluralist state may have stood a better chance. But it did not have this good fortune. Nevertheless, Israel was a nation that needed to be born, given the number of perennially displaced Jews who needed a safe place to live, and the particular gravity of the moment due to the Holocaust. It deserves to be recognized, furthermore, that there is historical legitimacy in their claim to Palestine – it is their ancestral home, the site of their most sacred symbols and history, and home to a continuous community of Jews. And, theologically, given the constant theme in scripture of God blessing Israel with the land of their ancestor Abraham, it is not out of the question to suggest that the return to *this* land was an act of divine providence.

RELIGIOUS ZIONISM.   For the first fifty years of the Zionist movement, its champions were defiantly secular; more sympathetic with Marx than Moses. In fact, most religious Jews felt great reluctance toward the state-creating ambitions of the Zionists. The Orthodox viewed Zionism as a heresy. For centuries they had internalized the prophetic admonishment that their exile was a sentence for their sins, for the fact that their ancestors had abandoned the covenant, as Moses had predicted they would, and turned to worship other gods. But they also believed the promise which followed: If they returned to God and obeyed God with all their hearts and souls, then:

the Lord your God will restore your fortunes and have compassion on you, gathering you again from all the peoples among whom the Lord your God has scattered you. Even if you are exiled to the ends of the world, from there the Lord your God will gather you, and from there he will bring you back. The Lord your God will bring you into the land that your ancestors possessed, and you will possess it; he will make you more prosperous and numerous than your ancestors (Deut.30: 1–5).

This promise was reiterated by the prophets, and remained the hope of all praying Jews. But for the Orthodox, the understanding was that this gathering in and return to Zion would come about by means of an obvious act of divine intervention, through the coming of the messiah. Certainly the political maneuverings of the secular Zionists did not qualify as the stirrings of the messiah whose appearance would usher in a new age for all creation. It was not until after the establishment of the state of Israel in 1948 that religious Jews began to reconsider their resistance to Zionism. With the creation of a sovereign homeland, they began to see the hand of God, and the formation of the State of Israel as a penultimate move in the direction of the divine promise.[14]

In short, the early Zionists were political pragmatists. They recognized their precariousness in the diaspora, and like many others at the turn of the century, desired to attempt a new social experiment, one that would include the Arabs and, they imagined, elevate the conditions of their lives as well. The deep historical pull toward Palestine was strong, but more out of momentum from past generations with their attachment to the region than out of piety. Religiously devoted Jews were suspicious of the movement. It took several decades for the social experiment to fuse with the religious mythos that God was the force behind this return to the Promised Land, and give rise to messianic Zionism.

Messianic Zionism really came into its own following the Six Day War in 1967. In the swiftness with which the "biblical territories" were "reconquered," many saw the hand of God and an approaching messianic redemption. In the 1970s and 1980s a solid bloc of Zionists on the religious right emerged with Meir Kahane and the Kach party, and the Gush Emunim ("the bloc of the faithful"), a movement of aggressive and messianic Zionists that formed in 1974. While Zionism had from the beginning embraced the ideal of a pluralist state (albeit with a few notable exceptions), the new religious right pursued a policy of cleansing the Promised Land of all Arabs and non-Jews as a biblical imperative. Kahane promoted the deportation of all Palestinians. "God wants us to live in a country of our own," he claimed, "isolated, so that we live separately and have the least possible contact with what is foreign, and so that we create as far as possible a pure Jewish culture based on the Torah."[15]

The Gush Emunim view it as imperative that the biblically defined land mass of Israel, and particularly the West Bank (which they refer to by its biblical names "Judea and Samaria") come fully under Jewish control. Their primary strategies are staging demonstrations, illegally squatting on Palestinian properties, and recruiting Jews in the diaspora to immigrate and join them – actions that frequently descend into violence and require intervention by the Israeli military. There is also an underground unit of the Gush Emunim that has conducted terrorist actions, including car bombings of Arab mayors and a foiled attempt to blow up the Dome of the Rock. The Intifada is the Arab response to their activities. Joshua, the successor of Moses and military commander who engineered Israel's conquest of Canaan, is a pivotal figure for the Gush. Journalist Ellen Cantarow sheds light on this biblical patron of the settlers, observing that Joshua "is the prototype of the powerful Jew bringing redemption with the sword, taking back what is rightfully his, consigning forever to the past the *shtetl* Jew cowering in his *stibl* while peasants and soldiers come to make pogroms."[16] Given their conviction that God has given this land to the Jews, the Gush are unapologetic about their aim to empty Israel of Arabs. One Gush activist in Kiryat Arba explained to Cantarow:

> There were Arabs living here. By what right did we throw them out? And we *did* throw them out. We threw them out of Jaffa. We threw them out of Haifa. Of course there were excuses. We threw them out because there was a war. Or we threw them out because we bought land. It's a very nasty story, isn't it, from the moral point of view? All the stuff about socialism, about national redemption may be true, but that's only one part. The fact is, we returned here because the Eternal gave us the land. It's ridiculous, stupid, simplistic, but that's what it is. All the rest is superficial. We came back here because we belong.[17]

Mark Juergensmeyer describes a visit he made in 1995 to Baruch Goldstein's grave in Kiryat Arba. Goldstein had gunned down thirty Muslim worshippers at the Tomb of the Patriarchs in Hebron in 1994. Paying his respects at the grave was one of the settlers, Yochay Ron. Juergensmeyer initiated a conversation with Ron and pressed him on his attachment to the land

and the violent measures that he obviously endorsed to wrest it from the Arabs. Ron explained that the land must be liberated in order for there to be a spiritual liberation – a standard messianic reply. Then he continued, "the biblical lands – specifically the ancient towns and sites on the West Bank – are sacred, and .,. Jews are under God's requirement to occupy them."[18] For Ron and other Zionists on the religious right, Juergensmeyer explains, the war with the Arabs "goes back 'in biblical times'... indicating that the present-day Arabs are simply the modern descendents of the enemies of Israel described in the Bible for whom God has unleashed wars of revenge."[19]

CORROBORATIVE SACRED NARRATIVES. It is in these developments that it becomes clear the extent to which the biblical report of ancient Israel's conquering of Canaan is providing a script for the present. After the exodus from Egypt the tribes of Israel wandered through the wilderness for forty years. Their wanderings brought them to the plains of Moab, on the east bank of the Jordan River. It was here that Moses summoned Joshua and charged him to "go with this people into the land that the Lord has sworn to their ancestors to give them" and to take possession of it. Then Moses addressed the Israelites and said to them, as God had instructed him:

> When you cross over the Jordan into the land of Canaan, you shall drive out all the inhabitants of the land from before you, destroy all their figured stones, destroy all their cast images, and demolish all their high places. You shall take possession of the land and settle in it, for I have given you the land to possess ... But if you do not drive out the inhabitants of the land from before you, then those whom you let remain shall be as barbs in your eyes and thorns in your sides; they shall trouble you in the land where you are settling (Numbers 33: 51–55).

Shortly after this, Moses died and Joshua led Israel across the Jordan to the city of Jericho. Following God's instructions, they marched around the city for seven days, at the end of which the priests blew trumpets, the people shouted, and the walls of Jericho fell. Then Joshua's army set upon all inhabitants of the city, men, women, young and old, oxen, sheep, and donkeys, and killed them. This was in accord with the instructions that had been given to Moses regarding how the military campaign in Canaan was to be pursued: "you must not let anything that breathes remain alive. You shall annihilate them just as the Lord your God has commanded, so that they may not teach you to do all the abhorrent things that they do for their gods, and you thus sin against the Lord your

God" (Deut. 20: 16–18). Thus began the campaign to take possession of Canaan. Next on their route, moving up the Jordan Valley, was the city of Ai. Here Joshua divided his army into two units, and with one lured the inhabitants of Ai out of the city to do battle, while the other entered the city and set it on fire. As with Jericho, all the citizens of Ai were slaughtered and their king was hanged, but the livestock were taken as booty.

City by city, the Israelites moved through Canaan defeating its inhabitants and dividing up the land into territories for each of its tribes. Subsequent assaults were not always as thorough as Jericho and Ai, as the Canaanites organized themselves against the invading armies of Israel and put up a better fight. Moreover, Israel entered alliances with some of the towns, and learned to live with them as neighbors, trading partners, and as a peasant class.[20] Many years later, when the vigorous period of the conquest was over and Joshua was an old man, he summoned the elders of the tribes to meet with him to remind them what God had done for them. "Thus says the Lord, the God of Israel," he told them:

> I brought your ancestors out of Egypt ... you lived in the wilderness for a long time. Then I brought you to the land of the Amorites, who lived on the other side of the Jordan; they fought with you, and I handed them over to you, and you took possession of their land, and I destroyed them before you ... I gave you a land on which you had not labored, and towns that you had not built, and you live in them; you eat the fruit of vineyards and oliveyards that you did not plant. Now therefore revere the Lord (Joshua 24: 7–8, 13–14).

With this recitation of God's activity on their behalf, the elders of Israel renewed their covenant, and Joshua then sent them away "to their inheritances."

In short, the land God had promised to Abraham and his descendants was not a pristine, unpopulated place that was ready for these immigrants to simply show up and inhabit. It never was, not when Abraham first settled there, nor when the exiles from Egypt arrived, nor, later, when the Jews returning from the Babylonian exile found their way back. Each time the land had to be reconquered and recolonized, and this required all manner of intrigue, espionage, diplomacy, divine intervention, military cunning, violence, and faith.

Each phase of return and settlement in biblical Israel provides archetypes for how Zionists might attempt to understand their present situation. A multitude of approaches to this can be found in the biblical accounts, ranging from absolute holy war, taking no prisoners, to gradual absorption and assimilation. The Zionism of groups such as the Kach Party and the Gush Emunim have taken Joshua's campaign as their plotline for how to conquer and settle "Judea and Samaria." They are bound by God to occupy this sacred land and to "create as far as possible a pure Jewish culture based on the Torah." Certain civilizational restraints prevent them from a full application of God's command to "not let anything that breathes remain alive," but they are nevertheless pursuing a strategy of purification based on religious identity.

All nations and civilizations have bloody histories. They come into existence by way of migrations, invasions, and armed struggle. Indigenous populations are either decimated, expelled, or absorbed. This is the way of the world; this is the history of the United States, a history which has borne me into existence, and which I seldom second-guess. It is also a way of behaving that is contrary to the sense of egalitarian justice that, ironically, has entered human consciousness through the Jewish scriptures. As the covenant is clarified in the Torah and the writings of the prophets, Israel is commanded to set the oppressed free, to shelter the homeless and share bread with the hungry, to never shed innocent blood, and, always reminded of their own experience as exiles in a strange land, to act justly and show mercy toward strangers. Nevertheless, there is this deep and not unimportant "archaeological" layer of stories in the Bible which stands in tension with the Bible itself. Both of the injunctions – cleanse the land of its native inhabitants and act with justice toward resident aliens – are found unambiguously in scripture as divine commands. Moral discernment which holds itself answerable to the Bible requires finding a point of balance between these two. Most Jews, even most Zionists, have sought a position of compromise between these poles.

Islamism

GRIEVANCES.   Among the grievances against the United States that have been identified as motivating the recent actions of radical Islamists are the way it meddles in the governments of the Islamic world against the will of the people and on the side of tyrants.[21] There is a perception that our foreign policy, corporations, and culture industries are the apotheosis of arrogant power, the belief that we are indifferent to the suffering of Muslims. The effects of U.S.-led globalization, which inspires social mobility and cosmopolitan loyalties, are viewed as destabilizing traditional societies. Osama bin Laden, in a 1998 interview that appeared on PBS's *Frontline*, made the following charges:

They rip us of our wealth and of our resources and of our oil. Our religion is under attack. They kill and murder our brothers. They compromise our honor and our dignity and dare we utter a single word of protest against the injustices, we are called terrorists ... The leaders in America and in other countries as well have fallen victim to Jewish Zionist blackmail. They have mobilized their people against Islam and against Muslims ...We are a nation whose sacred symbols have been looted and whose wealth and resources have been plundered. It is normal for us to react against the forces that invade our land and occupy it.[22]

The U.S., then, has plundered the wealth, denied the political self-determination, and defiled the sacred symbols and dignity of Muslim peoples, all the result of Jewish influence.

THE TREACHEROUS JEW.   Developing his incriminations against the Jews, bin Laden continues:

We believe that this [Clinton] administration represents Israel inside America. Take the sensitive ministries such as the Ministry of Exterior [*sic*] and the Ministry of Defense and the CIA, you will find that the Jews have the upper hand in them. They make use of America to further their plans for the world, especially the Islamic world. American presence in the Gulf provides support to the Jews and protects their rear. And while millions of Americans are homeless and destitute and live in abject poverty, their government is busy occupying our land and building new settlements and helping Israel build new settlements in the point of departure for our Prophet's midnight journey to the seven heavens. America throws her own sons in the land of the two Holy Mosques for the sake of protecting Jewish interests.[23]

And what are these Jewish interests, what is it that the Jews want? According to bin Laden, it is to reconquer the entire Arabian Peninsula in an "expansion of what is called the Great Israel":

We know at least one reason behind the symbolic participation of the Western forces and that is to support the Jewish and Zionist plans for expansion of what is called the Great Israel. Surely, their presence is not out of concern over their interests in the region ... Their presence has no meaning save one and that is to offer support to the Jews in Palestine who are in need of their Christian brothers to achieve full control over the Arab Peninsula which they intend to make an important part of the so called Greater Israel.[24]

Perhaps more striking than the grievances listed against the U.S. in many of the radical Islamist proclamations is this persistent accusation that Israel and the Jews are working behind the scenes for a full-fledged war against Islam. For bin Laden, Jews use the U.S. government as an instrument to achieve control of the Arabian Peninsula. In Pakistan, in the weeks following the September 11 attacks, word spread through the madrassas that it was, in fact, Jews who piloted the planes. According to one journalist, who was in Pakistan at that time, the head of one madrassa in Peshawar, Al-Sheikh Rahat, assured him of this. "'The Jews have done this,' he said, calling the attacks a plot by Israel to draw the world into war. It is repeated madrassa by madrassa, the company line of the militants and the poorer classes from which they come, spreading out from the student body to the shops and foot traffic." Some of the teachers explained that "even though the Jews flew the planes into the towers, it was Allah's will. Allah, the teachers said, put the idea in the minds of the Jews. Allah, in his wisdom, knew that the Muslims would perhaps be briefly discredited, the students said, but that when the truth comes out, it would ultimately destroy the Jews."[25]

While astonishing in the credulity this displays for conspiracy theories, it is a view not limited to isolated madrassas in South Asia. The Egyptian Sheikh Muhammad Al-Gamei'a, who served until November as the representative of Al-Azhar University to the U.S. and as the Imam of the Islamic Cultural Center of New York City, was interviewed three weeks after September 11 for an unofficial University website. In the interview he reports back to his Egyptian audience that most Americans know or suspect that "the Jews were behind these ugly acts," but they won't admit to it in public because "the Zionists control everything – political decision making, the big media organizations, and the financial and economic institutions." The American public lacks the courage to speak out against this array of power. With Jews occupying all the key positions of power in the U.S., he claims, this attack was not so difficult to stage. In a like manner, he goes on, the Jews have always ridden on the back of the world powers. "These people always seek out the superpower of the generation and develop coexistence with it. Before this, they rode on the back of England and on the back of the French empire." Moreover, he goes on, it is the Jews who are everywhere "disseminating corruption, heresy, homosexuality, alcoholism, and drugs. Because of them there are strip clubs, homosexuals, and lesbians everywhere. They do this to impose their hegemony and colonialism on the world." And he claims to have heard that some Jewish doctors are known to have poisoned sick Muslim children.[26]

While the hatred for the U.S. is formidable in radical Islamist circles, the hatred for Jews is monumental. When Muslim explanations are offered for it, they harp backward to the Jewish tribes in the Arabian Peninsula during the life of Muhammad. Typical of this is an editorial that appeared in an Iranian newspaper associated with Seyed Ali Khamenei and the Council of Guardians of the Islamic Revolution, saying, "The history of the beginnings of Islam is full of Jewish plots against the Prophet Muhammad and of murderous attacks by the Jews ... unequivocal verses in the Qur'an speak of the hatred and hostility of the Jewish people agains the Muslims."[27]

In one of the most influential tracts of the radical Islamist movement, *The Neglected Duty*, the Egyptian writer Abd al-Salam Faraj argues for a literal view of jihad (the power of the sword) as what was intended in the Qur'an and Hadith. Faraj draws on both of these ancient sources, as well as on important medieval jurists, to make his case for the religious duty of overthrowing corrupt regimes which fail to govern according to *Shari'a*. The actions of Muhammad and the first generation of his followers are treated as archetypes for how to respond and interpret present political realities. In three sections, Faraj refers to Muhammad's dealings with the Jews. Twice he recounts how the Qurayzah (a Jewish tribe in Medina) had incited unbelievers against the Prophet and cooperated with an assault on Medina. The assault ultimately failed due to the cunning of the Muslim command. The Qurayzah were seditious but cowardly and not very smart. The third reference is to the Nadir, another tribe of Jews in Medina, whom Muhammad suspected were plotting to kill him and whom he promptly banished from the oasis. They resisted, withdrew into their fortress, and only complied after Muhammad began burning down their date trees, their source of wealth. Again, the Jews were treacherous, but no match for Muhammad.[28]

Another significant ideologue for the radical Islamists, Sayyid Qutb, after claiming that the Western imperialist states have been fighting against Islam for centuries, also ultimately points his finger at the Jews of Medina:

> And let us not forget the role of worldwide Zionism in the plot against Islam and in uniting the forces against it both in the Crusaderist imperialist world and in the materialist communist world. It is the continuing role that the Jews have always played since the Hijrah of the Apostle to Medina and the founding of the Islamic state.[29]

Similarly, bin Laden, in his 1996 *Declaration of War*, recalls yet a third tribe of Jews in Medina, the Qainuqa, who had humiliated a Muslim woman. In response Muhammad broke his treaty with the tribe, and banished them also from the city. Bin Laden cites this story as the grounds for viewing any treaty as dissolvable given sufficient reason. In his 1998 interview, he remarked: "The enmity between us and the Jews goes far back in time and is deep rooted. There is no question that war between the two of us is inevitable." He assured his listeners that Islam will prevail over the Jews, "as the Messenger of Allah has promised us in an authentic prophetic tradition when He said the Hour of Resurrection shall not come before Muslims fight Jews and before Jews hide behind trees and behind rocks."[30]

CORROBORATIVE SACRED NARRATIVES.   As with the Zionist settlers and the script they have found in the story of ancient Israel's conquest of Canaan, it appears the radical Islamists have found a script in the Qur'an and Hadith for their present hostility toward Jews. What is this story?[31]

After emigrating from Mecca in 622 to Medina during the *hijra*, Muhammad and his Companions entered into treaties with the inhabitants of the oasis of Medina, promising them freedom in faith and property in exchange for a military pact. Medina was the home of Arabs and Jews, and the Jews were organized into three large tribes, the Qaynuqa, Nadir, and Qurayzah, who resided in separate quarters of the oasis. At first the Jews adopted a tolerant, if not entirely friendly, attitude toward the new arrivals. Muhammad hoped that they would accept him as a prophet within their own tradition of monotheism, he even pointedly warned them to do so, but they refused and made it known that the age of the prophets was over, and that Muhammad's appropriation of their history and forebears was illegitimate. The Jews, like some other inhabitants of Medina, were also threatened by the diminution of their political position in the oasis with the arrival of the charismatic Muhammad and his Companions.

The first incident between Muhammad and the Jews occurred two years after the *hijra* in the bazaar of the Qaynuqa quarter, when a Jewish goldsmith furtively pinned the skirt of a squatting Muslim customer to her upper garment so that when she stood she was exposed. A fight broke out and both a Jew and a Muslim were killed. Muhammad arrived to arbitrate the dispute, but the Jews refused, withdrew behind the walls of their sector, and attempted to conspire with their Arab allies to join them in a rebellion against Muhammad. Their allies refused, and they found themselves alone and besieged by the forces of Muhammad. After two weeks they surrendered. Muhammad banished them from the oasis, and they migrated north and settled with other Jews in the Syrian border area.[32]

The second incident happened two years later and involved the Nadir tribe.[33] Muhammad had been warned by God that the Jews of Nadir intended to kill him by dropping a rock on his head from a rooftop as he rested against the wall of one of their houses. He arose from this spot, returned home, and sent an emissary to the Nadir notifying them that because of their planned treachery, his treaty with them was over, and they must leave the oasis. While the Nadir contemplated their response, one of Muhammad's Arab enemies in Medina met with them and offered his military support. The Nadir then refused Muhammad's ultimatum and hunkered down in their stronghold to await their allies. The allies failed to materialize and after two weeks of the siege, Muhammad ordered his men to cut down and burn the Nadir's date trees. With this they surrendered, and Muhammad banished them from Medina. They loaded their camels and migrated north to the existing Jewish settlement of Khaybar. Some travelled further to Syria.

The third incident involved the Qurayzah tribe five years after the *hijra*. The Meccans and their allies were marching to Medina with the intention of dealing the Muslims a decisive blow. Muhammad caught wind of it, and realizing his forces were outnumbered he instructed the *umma* to dig a long and deep trench on the northern edge of the oasis. This trench gave Medina an advantage because it inhibited a charge of the enemy's cavalry. The Meccans settled for a siege of the city, which they attempted to intensify by persuading the Qurayzah, who occupied the southern flank of the city, to conspire with them and invade Medina from within. Following some very clever espionage, Muhammad undermined this pact, and with a change in the weather, the Meccan confederacy went home. It was then clear to all that the Qurayzah had betrayed the *umma* and now had no allies to come to their rescue. Muhammad ordered a siege, the Qurayzah were surrounded, and after a month they opened negotiations with the Muslims, sending word that they were willing to leave Medina and never return (just as had been the arrangement with the Qaynuqa and Nadir tribes) and then they surrendered. The Muslim forces entered the fortress, handcuffed all the men, and isolated the women and children. Allies of the Muslims, the al-Aws, who had formerly been allied with the Qurayzah, pleaded with Muhammad for leniency. Muhammad agreed to let one of the al-Aws pass judgment on the Qurayzah, and they sent for one of their elders who had recently been wounded at the

Battle of the Trench. When he arrived he announced, "The men should be killed, the property divided among the Muslim warriors, and the women and children taken as captives." Muhammad pronounced that he had judged rightly, ordered that trenches be dug in the main bazaar of Medina, had the men brought out in batches, beheaded them, and buried them in the trenches.[34] Between six and seven hundred Qurayzah men were killed, and, in the words of Muhammad's biographer, Saifur Rahman al-Mubarakpuri, the "hotbeds of intrigue and treachery were thus exterminated once and for all." Medina was rid of the last of its three powerful Jewish tribes, although smaller groups of Jews did remain and lived there in peace.

A final incident occurred the following year. About seventy miles north of Medina was the oasis of Khaybar, with rich soil, flourishing date groves, fruit orchards, and seven fortresses. Khaybar was predominantly Jewish, and many of the Qaynuqa and Nadir who fled Medina had settled there. It was, according to Mubarakpuri, "a hotbed of intrigue and conspiracy" against the *umma*; in fact, in his estimation, "the continual afflictions that the Muslims had sustained were primarily attributable to the Jews" in Khaybar. Following the Hudaybiyah Peace Treaty, which had dispirited many Muslims because it prohibited them from entering Mecca that year, Muhammad decided it was time to take an army of six hundred men up to Khaybar and settle his affairs with the Jews there, with the intent of eliminating the Jewish influence in the Arabian Peninsula once and for all. When Muhammad arrived, the Jews withdrew to their fortresses, "too cowardly to meet the Muslims in open fight," according to Mubarakpuri, "but rather hurled a shower of arrows and stones on the attackers." The Muslims finally gained entry to the first fortress through the use of battering rams, whereupon "the Jews were put to rout and fled in all directions leaving behind their women and children." The siege of Khaybar lasted one month, the forts falling one by one. Many of the Jewish men were killed when the forts were breached, and the women were captured and divided up among the Muslim warriors, who were prohibited by Muhammad from having intercourse with those who were pregnant. During the latter stages of the siege, when it was clear they could not win, the remaining Jews surrendered and asked Muhammad if they might be allowed to stay and continue farming the land on the condition that half of their date crop be given to the Muslims. Muhammad agreed to these terms. He took possession of the oasis of Khaybar, allowed the Jews to remain as sharecroppers, and left them with the provision that "if we wish to expel you we will expel you."

This was an important turning point for the *umma*. The spoils taken at Khaybar and the sharecropping arrangement resulted in a new and ongoing affluence for the Muslims.[35] It also marked the end of any political threat that the Jews of Arabia had posed. Within a few years, the Jews who were left in Khaybar emigrated from the Peninsula; however, small communities of Jews remained in Arabia, on relatively friendly terms with the Muslim majority. They stopped conspiring and Muhammad and his Companions stopped besieging them.

Contemporary Islamists like bin Laden, Faraj, and Qutb draw many lessons from these ancient stories. Taken together, they portray Jews as condescending, wealthy, quarrelsome, breachers of treaties, treacherous conspirers, inept and cowardly warriors, and corrupters of divine revelation. In the sequence of incidents narrated above, Muhammad is seen to adopt different methods of dealing with the politically powerful Jews: lay siege to them; destroy their means of production; force them into exile, massacre them; or dispossess and turn them into sharecroppers. Those who convert can be assimilated. Those who refuse to convert but agree to relinquish any ambition to political power can be tolerated and allowed to practice their faith, on payment of an additional tax.

Bernard Lewis has observed that historically, by and large, Jews have received better treatment in Muslim lands than in Christian lands. He argues that this has much to do with the fact that Muslims know that their founder won his battle against the Jews and humiliated them. In the Qur'an and Hadith there are an abundance of passages describing the Jews as hostile and malevolent. Their hostility, however, was ineffective and they were put in their place. Consequently, until relatively recently, the prevailing opinion of Muslims towards Jews had to do with their unimportance in the great scheme of things – they were "weak and ineffectual – an object of ridicule, not fear."[36]

The establishment of a Jewish state on land that had been in the hands of Muslims since the seventh century (except for the ninety years when it was controlled by the Crusaders and thirty years controlled by the British) forced a reassessment of this long-held belief in the political impotence of the Jews. Coming to terms with this has brought these otherwise submerged stories of Muhammad's dealings with the Jews of Medina and Khaybar bobbing back up to the surface as crucial acts of statecraft by the founder. Whereas for centuries these stories served as reminders that Jews were no longer a force to be reckoned with, they have now resurfaced as stories about the threat that Jews eternally pose to the *umma*. And they are now functioning as archetypes for the radical Islamists as they seek to know their enemy and how this enemy is to be vanquished.

SACRIFICE

In his book, *Terror in the Mind of God*, Mark Juergensmeyer argues that the causal relationship between religion and violence can move in either direction. Religion can give rise to violence; violence can revive interest in religion.[37] In the two accounts offered above, it is my sense that it is violence that has reached out to religion for support. In both cases, founding myths were identified which have served to justify and intensify the resolve of those committing the violence, and to recruit others for the cause. The messianic Zionists discovered in their scriptures a justification for their claim on a Promised Land cleansed of all non-Jewish elements, and a spectrum of militant means to accomplish this. The radical Islamists discovered in their scriptures a justification for their suspicion that the Jews are behind the failure of their aspirations to build a *Shari'a*-governed state, and a spectrum of militant means to overcome this. Those same founding myths have been available to Jews and Muslims for centuries. They are very violent narratives, sanctioning deportations and genocide, but have not, until now, found an audience prepared to use them as weapons. It is not fair to say religion is the driving force behind the violence of these particular movements, but it is fair to say that genuine, and quite dangerous, elements of Judaism and Islam have been appropriated to justify the wars these groups are waging, and quite effectively.

Juergensmeyer also suggests that when individuals feel threatened or belittled at the deepest core of their identity, they are tempted to turn to religion to explain how this has come to pass. Religion provides a cosmology, history, and eschatology to explain their suffering. If they can then sacralize the struggle and come to understand it as reflecting a more encompassing cosmic struggle between forces of good and evil, or between forces of the elect and forces of the scorned, it becomes easier to legitimize violence, even terrorism.[38]

It is not so much that religion is violent; it is that *we* are violent. Human beings are violent. Our religions take account of this and, for the most part, moderate the violence of which we are capable. They channel it into actions that are less destructive, by placing it within a universe of symbols that are, upon inspection, designed to restrain violence. The literary theorist René Girard has written incisively about this. Human beings are creatures who covet. We desire what our neighbor has. This leads to a rivalry for the object we desire because our neighbor intends to keep it for herself, and "will not let someone snatch it away without combat." Consequently, our desire will be thwarted, but in place of accepting this and moving on to another object, "nine times out of ten" our desire will simply become more intent upon acquiring *this* object. Our neighbor, noting our desire, and thus the desirability of what she has, becomes even more determined to keep it. This results in a spiralling of desire and ultimately in violence. Magnified onto society this becomes what Thomas Hobbes described as the war of all against all.[39] But before we all kill each other and the community to which we belong is ripped apart by our aggression, the idea arises to redirect all of our hostility away from each other and onto a third party, a surrogate victim who cannot reciprocate our aggression – a scapegoat. This is the origin of all rituals of sacrifice, according to Girard, and is the unique contribution of religion. It is, in fact, the birth of religion. At an early stage in virtually all religions can be found traces of human sacrifice that served the purpose of transferring onto a single unlucky victim all of "the internal tensions, feuds, and rivalries pent up within the community."[40] Over time religions managed to propose substitutes for human victims, replacing them with animal sacrifices, and, at an even later stage of development, with abstract symbols of sacrifice. The great achievement in this was that instead of neighbor murdering neighbor and the endless feuding that would follow, a regulated system of substitutionary sacrifice was developed.

Evidence that Girard cites for this is the pervasiveness of symbols of violence in the central rituals of virtually every religious tradition. Consider the Abrahamic faiths: Jewish Passover recalls the sacrifice of both lambs and Egyptian firstborn on the eve of the Israelites' departure from Egypt; Christian Easter has at its core a crucified, bleeding God, whose body believers consume in every Eucharist; the Ramadan fast of Muslims was instituted to commemorate the battle of Badr, Muhammad's first military victory. The violent sacrifice of life which solidified each community of faith is the subtext of all three. As Girard expresses it, "The purpose of the sacrifice is to restore harmony to the community, to reinforce the social fabric."[41] Moreover, by ritualizing these original sacrifices, the cohesiveness that sacrifice produces does not require an actual ongoing spilling of blood. This is the manner in which religions moderate the violence toward which we humans are inclined.

Nevertheless, this primitive impulse to find surrogate victims onto whom we might transfer our hostilities remains a temptation. When calamity strikes, when social tensions are high, or when one's cultural identity has been insulted, scapegoating is an impulsive response. It was in the attempt to ameliorate tensions between eastern and western Christianity that the idea of launching a Crusade against the Muslims was conceived. During the Crusades, when Christians and Muslims were at war with each other, both sides made it a regular practice to massacre entire villages of Jews. Under the vindictive terms of the armistice following the First World War, Germany sought to alleviate its social turmoil through the genocide of its Jewish population. It was in the weeks following frustrating treaty negotiations with his opponents in Mecca that Muhammad conceived the campaign agains the Jews in Khaybar. In the U.S. every successive wave of immigrants has served as a scapegoat for whatever social crisis was occurring at the time.

In the case of Zionism it is worth contemplating whether longstanding tensions between Christians and Jews in Europe and Russia ultimately resulted in the scapegoating of the Arabs in Palestine. The Christians in Europe and Russia were too formidable an opponent to be taken on directly by the Jews. As Girard explains the scapegoating mechanism: "The real source of victim substitution is the appetite for violence that awakens in people when anger seizes them and when the true object of their anger is untouchable."[42] Similarly, the vilification of the Jews that can be seen in Islamist writings may be a scapegoating response arising from the real center of the conflict, which is between a fragmented Islam and Western powers. It is worth making note of the fact that the last day of the Ottoman siege of Vienna was September 11, 1683. On the following day, the Catholic King of Poland, John Sobieski, routed the Turks and permanently reversed the encroachment of Islam into Europe. Many historians mark this as a tidal shift of world dominance between Islamic and Western civilizations. The symbolism of this anniversary is probably significant in our efforts to understand the grievances of the September 11 terrorists.[43]

CONCLUSION

The attacks of September 11 are horrific instances of terrorism in the name of religion. Following the twisted logic of the hijackers' minds it is conceivable that, in the minutes before they reached their targets, they were praying in the cockpits that the sacrifice they were about to make of thousands of innocent lives would open a door in the firmament through which God would step into the world and restore justice. This is the logic of sacrifice: the shedding of innocent blood pleases the gods and restores order and peace to the community. Islam is not alone in this. There is a violent recessive gene in every religious tradition. Each religion has its militants and its own theological justifications for the use of violence. Each religion preserves a canon of warrior narratives to draw upon when it feels itself cornered or the victim of injustice. To take a sober view, there are times when it is appropriate to rehearse these narratives. An honest look at history cannot escape the fact that the best, most extensively humane periods of social order and civilization have required some passage either through war or the threat of war. But it is dangerous to rehearse these warrior narratives, and to make use of them as archetypes for our own behavior, in isolation from conflicting narratives of divine mercy and common grace. It must be remembered that with each cycle of violence a new cohort of victims is created. While we cannot close our eyes to the multiple accounts in both the Bible and the Qur'an that the God of Abraham reportedly authorized the slaughter and humiliation of whole cities of both Canaanites and Jews, this same God took an intense and abiding interest in the innocent victims of history and in teaching us the conditions that allow for peace to flourish and "justice to roll down like the waters" on behalf of all victims. We must pick our way through these incongruous scripts and injunctions, and rely on our faith that God is, indeed, good, just, and trustworthy.

NOTES

1. It is worth pointing out that while Hamas (the "Islamic Resistance Movement") was founded by Muslims, it is now composed of both Muslims and Christians who share the goal of securing rights for Palestinians. Thanks to my colleague Professor Jane Smith for drawing this to my attention.

2. In the words of Osama bin Laden, from a 1998 interview: "Our call is the call of Islam that was revealed to Muhammad. It is a call to all mankind. We have been entrusted with good cause to follow in the footsteps of the Messenger and to communicate his message to all nations ... Allah created us to worship Him and to follow in his footsteps and to be guided by His Book. I am one of the servants of Allah and I obey his orders. Among those is the order to fight for the word of Allah and to fight until the Americans are driven out of all the Islamic countries ... It is also our duty to send a call to all the people of the world to enjoy this great light and to embrace Islam and experience the happiness in Islam. Our primary mission is nothing but the furthering of this religion." See "Interview Osama bin Laden," May 1998 >http: //www.pbs.org/wgbh/pages/frontline/shows/binladen/ who/interview.html> (cited 2 January 2002).

3. E.g., Sheikh Abdullah Azzam, who is described as Osama bin Laden's "spiritual mentor." He was born in the West Bank in 1941, received a Ph.D. in Principles of Islamic Jurisprudence from Al-Azhar University in Cairo, taught in the 1970s at

King Abdul-Aziz University in Jeddah, Saudi Arabia, and subsequently moved to Pakistan to further the cause of the jihad movement in Afghanistan. He is the author of *Join the Caravan* (1987), a book that inspired Muslims from around the world to fight on behalf of Afghanistan. Other clerics of the movement include Sheikh 'Abd al-Rahman, the mufti of the Egypt-based Tanzim al-Jihad; the Egyptian Sheikh Ahmad Isma'il; Sheikh Sayyid Muhammad Husayn Fadlallah, associated with Hezbollah in Lebanon; and Sheikh Ahmad Yasin, the founder of Hamas. See R. Scott Appleby, ed., *Spokesmen for the Despised: Fundamentalist Leaders of the Middle East* (Chicago: University of Chicago Press, 1997).

4. "Full Text of Notes Found After Hijackings," *New York Times*, September 29, 2001 [http://www.nytimes.com/2001/ 09/29/national/29SFULL-TEXT.html> (cited 20 December 2001).

5. I have in mind here various treatises and pamphlets written by Rashid Rida, Maulana Maudoodi, Sayyid Qutb, Abd al-Salam Faraj, and Abdullah Azzam.

6. Throughout this chapter the term "radical Islamist" will be used to refer to radical political Islamism, of the sort observed by the various more violent movements within the Muslim world who pursue a mixture of political and religious aims. These movements identify themselves as Islamic and have a common ideology, i.e., to recast the social order along the lines of the Islamic *Shari'a*, bringing all areas of life under its rule, to overthrow regimes in Muslim countries that do not do so, to return to a purity of faith and practice that reflects the period of Muhammad and his Companions, and to resist Western influence and particularly its political, economic, and moral ideals and practices. It is important to note that not all Islamist movements have turned to violence as a means to achieve their ends. In the broadest sense, Islamism refers to a variety of revivalist movements in the modern Muslim world (beginning in the eighteenth century with the Wahabi movement). Most of Islamism in the eighteenth and nineteenth centuries was an internal critique that called for the purification of Islamic doctrine and practice – only a minority called for the establishment of an Islamic political system. This political edge of the revival, calling for an Islamic state or states governed by the *Shari'a*, has really gained its voice in the twentieth century, in response to both colonial and post-colonial pressures in Muslim lands. But there are still many Islamist movements that are not interested in establishing an Islamic state, and concentrate instead on a reinvigoration of Islamic doctrine, science and piety. My thanks to the co-editor of this volume, Ibrahim Abu-Rabi', for clarifying this.

7. See Karen Armstrong, *Holy War: The Crusades and Their Impact on Today's World* (New York: Anchor Doubleday Books, 1991); Bernard Lewis, *Semites and Anti-Semites: An Inquiry into Conflict and Prejudice* (New York: W.W. Norton, 1999); and Rodney Stark, *One True God: Historical Consequences of Monotheism* (Princeton: Princeton University Press, 2001).

8. Theodor Herzl, "The Jewish State." In Arthur Hertzberg, ed., *The Zionist Idea*, (New York: Atheneum, 1959), 221.

9. Ibid., 225.

10. Ibid., 222.

11. Vladimir Jabotinsky, "Evidence Submitted to the Palestinian Royal Commission," in Hertzberg, ed. *Zionist Idea*, 562.

12. Ibid., 569.

13. Quoted from Ben-Gurion's *The History of the Haganah*. In Colin Chapman, *Whose Promised Land?* (Oxford: Lion Publishing, 1989), 49.

14. This interpretation of the provisional role of the state of Israel in the divine scheme of redemption is generally attributed to Rabbi Abraham Isaac Kook (1865–1935).

15. Meir Kahane, quoted in Armstrong, *Holy War*, 306.

16. Ellen Cantarow, "Gush Emunim: The Twilight of Zionism?" *Media Monitors Network*, February 27, 2001 >http: //www.mediamonitors.net/cantarow1.html> (cited 18 December 2001).

17. Ibid.

18. Mark Juergensmeyer, *Terror in the Mind of God: The Global Rise of Religious Violence* (Berkeley: University of California Press, 2000), 52.

19. Ibid., 153.

20. Whether the indigenous people of Canaan were defeated or revolutionized into an egalitarian society by the appearance of Israel is debated by biblical historians and archaeologists. See Norman K. Gottwald, *The Tribes of Yahweh: A Sociology of the Religion of Liberated Israel, 1250–1050 B.C.E.* (Maryknoll, N.Y.: Orbis Books, 1979). But on the face of it, the Bible records it as a clear defeat of the idolatrous peoples of Canaan. It is this mythological portrayal of what occurred, more than any historical reconstructions, that is relevant to my argument here.

21. E.g., the 1953 overthrow of the democratically elected Mossadeh government in Iran; support of Israel in 1967 war; opposition during the Cold War to Islamic nationalism; support of repressive regimes such as Saudi Arabia and Egypt; and sanctions on Iraq following Gulf War.

22. Interview Osama bin Laden, *Frontline*.

23. Ibid.

24. Ibid.

25. Rick Bragg, "Shaping Young Islamic Hearts and Hatreds," *New York Times*, 14 October, 2001, sec. A, p. 1.

26. Interview dated October 4, 2001, translated from Arabic by the IMRA (Independent Media Review Analysis) http: //www.imra.org.il/story.php3 (cited 15 December, 2001). According to Bernard Lewis, the word on the street is even more colorful and disturbing. Stories circulate through the Muslim world of Israelis deliberately infecting girls with AIDS and syphilis and packing them off to Egypt to spread the diseases. "They are also accused of supplying Egyptian women

with hyper-aphrodisiac chewing gum which drives them into a frenzy of sexual desire, while at the same time selling hormonally altered fruit that kills male sperm." They are likewise charged with exporting carcinogenic shampoos and cucumbers. A French convert to Islam, Roger Garaudy, in his book, *The Founding Myths of Israeli Politics*, offers a debunking of the founding myths that prop up Israel in the eyes of the West: the myth of Chosen People and Promised Land; the myth of Holocaust; and the myth of the modern Israeli miracle. He has been fêted by governments and literary circles in Lebanon, Syria, Jordan, Iran, and Egypt, including receiving the Egyptian Writers Award. See Lewis, *Semites and Anti-Semites: An Inquiry into Conflict and Prejudice*. (New York: W. W. Norton, 1999), 265–68.

27. *Jumhuri-I Islami* (8 January, 1998), quoted in Lewis, 265.

28. Abd al-Salam Faraj, *The Neglected Duty*, §108, 116, 117, 126. Translated by Johannes J. G. Jansen, in *The Neglected Duty: The Creed of Sadat's Assassins and the Islamic Resurgence in the Middle East* (New York: MacMillan, 1986).

29. Sayyid Qutb, *Social Justice in Islam*, §8.74. Translated by William E. Shepard, in *Sayyid Qutb and Islamic Activism: A Translation and Critical Analysis of Social Justice in Islam* (Leiden: E. J. Brill, 1996), 288.

30. Osama bin Laden, "Declaration of War Against the Americans Occupying the Land of the Two Holy Places," August 1996 < http: //www.azzam.com/html/articlesdeclaration.htm> (cited 12 December 2001).

31. Narration of the following events is a compilation of materials drawn from A. Guillaume's *The Life of Muhammad: A Translation of Ishaq's Sirat Rasul Allah* (London: Oxford University Press, 1955); Karen Armstrong's *Muhammad: A Biography of the Prophet* (San Francisco: Harper Collins Publishers, 1992); Muhammad Husayn Haykal, *The Life of Muhammad*, translated by Isma'il Razi A. al-Faruqi [http: //www.witness-pioneer.org/vil/books/MH[rule]LM> (cited 3 January, 2002); and Saifur Rahman al-Mubarakpuri, *The Sealed Nectar: Memoirs of the Noble Prophet*, translated by Issam Diab [http: //www.witness-pioneer.org/vil/Books/SM[rule]tsn> (cited 3 January, 2002).

32. *Surah* 5 was revealed during the period of the Qaynuqa uprising, and much of this surah serves as an interpretation of the Jews refusal to recognize Muhammad as an apostle of God, just as their predecessors had failed to grasp the prophethood of Moses, and had subsequently confounded the teachings he had given them. Moreover, the Jews, according to this surah, had refused to believe and had put to death many of God's messengers before Muhammad. In the depiction of Jews here the emphasis is on their stubbornness and treachery, and their habit of making "a jest and a pastime" of true religion.

33. *Surah* 59 was written in reference to this episode.

34. *Surah* 33 contains the revelations to Muhammad that pertain to this event. "He brought down from among their strongholds those who had supported them from

among the People of the Book and cast terror into their hearts, so that some you slew and others you took captive. He made you masters of their land, their houses, and their goods, and of yet another land on which you had never set foot before" (33: 26–27).

35. *Surah* 48 contains references to the Khaybar campaign, such as "God has promised you rich booty, and has given you this with all promptness. He has stayed your enemies' hands, so that He may make your victory a sign to true believers" (48: 20).

36. Lewis, *Semites and Anti-Semites*, 129.

37. Juergensmeyer, *Terror in the Mind of God*, 161.

38. Ibid., 162f.

39. René Girard, *I See Satan Fall Like Lightning*, translated by James G. Williams (Maryknoll, N.Y.: Orbis Books, 2001), 8.

40. René Girard, *Violence and the Sacred*, translated by Patrick Gregory (Baltimore: Johns Hopkins University Press, 1977), 7.

41. Ibid., 8.

42. Girard, *Satan*, 156.

43. Juergensmeyer suggests that there is this dramatic aspect to terrorism – anniversaries are crucial to understanding the message of the action: "To capture the public's attention through an act of performance violence on a date deemed important to the group perpetrating the act, therefore, is to force the group's sense of what is temporally important on everyone else." See Juergensmeyer, *Terror in the Mind of God*, 133.

8

RELIGIOUS LEADERSHIP IN THE AFTERMATH OF SEPTEMBER 11: SOME LESSONS FROM JESUS AND PAUL

Efrain Agosto

INTRODUCTION

In the aftermath of the tragedies in New York, Washington, and Pennsylvania on September 11, 2001, major historical, political, and religious questions emerged. "How could this happen to us?" "What is it in the history of our relations with Islamic nations and radical forces within those nations that could engender such horrific plans?" "Why would anybody hate us so?" Theologically, people of faith, and even those without, asked, "How could God permit such a thing?" "If God is real, how could such a thing happen to so many innocent people in such a horrible way?"

No easy answers emerged for such questions. Almost immediately, scholars and practitioners of Islam across the country tried to explain the tenets of their faith and disassociate it and themselves from the perpetrators of the terrorist attacks. In the climate of renewed patriotism overwhelming the grieving nation, some of the braver souls among the Islamic apologists dared to remind us, against the choruses of protest, of years of what they perceived as benign neglect over justice issues in the Middle East, for example, with regard to the Palestinian question. The "why do they hate us" question required such stark reminders, as much as the nation would not hear it.

With regard to the equally difficult questions of theodicy, "Why did God allow this?", various responses included the harsh tones of Christian conservatives like Jerry Falwell and Pat Robertson, "it is the judgment of God for our nation's sins." Of course, the "sins" decried by the likes of Falwell and Robertson included abortion, homosexuality and secularism in general. At the other end of the theological spectrum, the sermons of more mainline religious leaders called for peace, understanding, and patience with each other, consoled the grieving, and reminded us that while God may not intervene with the exercise of human free will, God was present with those dying and is present with those grieving in the aftermath.

And, of course, we heard the voices of our political leaders, especially the U.S. president, George W. Bush, who consoled the grieving, but also galvanized and prepared the nation for an all-out "war on terrorism" as a response to the September 11 attacks. Mayor Rudolph Giuliani, on his way out as mayor of New York City due to term limits, received so many accolades for the way he handled the crisis that he almost pursued a waiver of the term limits so he could stay on as mayor.

Whatever the questions, whatever the responses, it seemed like this was and continues to be a time for leaders of all types, religious, political, military, to step forward, climb up on a lectern (as well as climb down into the pits to help recovery workers) and confront the demons surrounding our tortured souls. What's a leader, especially a religious leader, to do? What do we say?

While books of sermons and speeches from the days and weeks following the tragedies are hastily being put together, this discussion seeks to take a step backward and reflect on the biblical, specifically New Testament, Christian sources for understanding the role of religious leadership in times of crisis. In particular, it will outline and discuss the leadership attributes and affirmations of Jesus, the founder of the religious renewal movement that became Christianity, and the Apostle Paul, one the movement's earliest and most successful missionaries, authors, and theologians. Questions I will ask of these seminal Christian figures and the written sources by or about them include: What does it take to be a leader in a crisis? What are some of the *sine qua non* of religious leadership in particular? Perhaps such reflection, from a Christian perspective, can help guide us to exercise appropriate religious leadership in the months and years ahead as we continue to respond in the aftermath of September 11, 2001.

JESUS — LEADERSHIP IN RESPONSE TO IMPERIAL DOMINATION

Recent studies on the historical Jesus have reminded us that he emerged in the midst of the domination system that was the Roman Empire.[1] Rome exercised imperial domination by extreme oppression of the poorest of the poor, including heavy tax burdens on the peasant population of Palestine, in collusion with Israel's elite leadership – both political and religious. As a result, various grassroots resistance and reform movements emerged throughout the period of the early empire in and around first-century C.E. Palestine. The leaders of such movements included "bandits," "prophets," and "messiahs" such as Hezekiah, Judas, his son, Galilean Cave Brigands, Eleazar ben Dinai, "the Samaritan," and John the Baptist.[2] All of these, in one form or other, tried to respond to the imperial oppression in the Palestinian countryside by resisting Roman domination either through social banditry (as in the legend of Robin Hood in a later time and place) or religious renewal movements, such as those calling for a restoration of Israel's long-gone glory days of King David. An example of the latter is those communities represented by the Dead Sea Scrolls with their messianic expectations. Lastly there was the option of outright revolt. The latter, prefigured by such groups as the Sicarii with their assassination tactics in the fifties C.E., and other such temporary violent forays, developed into full-fledged war in the late sixties, culminating in the horrific sack and destruction of Jerusalem by Titus's Roman forces in 70 C.E.

How did the leadership of John the Baptist and later, one of his followers, Jesus of Nazareth figure into all of this? The Jewish historian, Josephus, an apologist for the Roman presence in Palestine, described John the Baptist as "a good man, who demanded that the Jews be intent on virtue, conduct themselves with justice toward one another and piety towards God ... But when others rallied behind him – for they were greatly stirred by his speeches – Herod [one of the Jewish Roman puppet kings in Judea and Galilee] feared that such convincing eloquence among the people might lead to some sort of uprising, for they seemed to heed his every word" (*Antiquities* 18.116–9).

Indeed the gospel stories about John the Baptist corroborate this tendency in John to challenge the powers of his day because of their oppression of the masses in Palestine. Matthew reports these challenging words of John to local, elite, religious leaders:

> But when he saw many Pharisees and Sadducees coming for baptism, he said to them, "You brood of vipers! Who warned you to flee from the wrath to come? Bear fruit worthy of repentance. Do not presume to say to yourselves, 'We have Abraham as our ancestor'; for I tell you, God is able from these stones to raise up children to Abraham. Even now the ax is lying at the root of the trees; every tree therefore that does not bear good fruit is cut down and thrown into the fire (Mt 3: 7–10).

Luke adds an ethical edge to John's challenge to the leadership of his day:

> And the crowds asked him, "What then should we do?" In reply he said to them, "Whoever has two coats must share with anyone who has none; and whoever has food must do likewise." Even tax collectors came to be baptized, and they asked him, "Teacher, what should we do?" He said to them, "Collect no more than the amount for you." Soldiers also asked him, "And we, what should we do?" He said to them, "Do not extort money from anyone by threats or false accusation, and be satisfied with your wages" (Lk. 3: 10–14).

Whether religious, financial or military leaders, John the Baptist pronounced a word of judgment and justice. In particular, the word of justice entailed attention to those with less by those with more. Indeed, such a cry for justice by the "voice in the wilderness" eventually led to his death at the hands of those political leaders whom he denounced (Mt. 14:3–12; Mk. 6: 17–29). This attention to the poor and oppressed was a fundamental criterion of leadership proclaimed by not only John, but also Jesus, his follower and successor in the reform movement John founded and Jesus enhanced. Like John, Jesus was executed for proclaiming this message of justice.

When the time came for Jesus to take over the leadership mantle from John, John tested Jesus' commitment to this cause with a series of questions, to which Jesus replied by recounting his acts of compassion for the poor and oppressed:

> When the men had come to him, they said, "John the Baptist has sent us to you to ask, 'Are you the one who is to come, or are we to wait for another?'" Jesus had just then cured many people of diseases, plagues, and evil spirits, and had given sight to many who were blind. And he answered them, "Go and tell John what you have seen and heard: the blind receive their sight, the lame walk, the lepers are cleansed, the deaf hear, the dead are raised, the poor have good news brought to them. And blessed is anyone who takes no offense at me" (Lk. 7: 20–23).

Thus, in many ways, but especially in this concern for those to whom nobody else paid attention ("the poor"), in Roman-controlled and dominated Israel, Jesus followed in the footsteps of John.

GATHERING A TEAM

However, Jesus did not carry out his mission alone. He soon gathered around him a group of followers that the gospels refer to as disciples, because they not only did what Jesus did, but listened to what he said. Theirs was a teacher–student relationship.

One of the fascinating aspects of the stories about Jesus and his disciples is who constituted this band of followers. They were not the "cream of the crop" from among Israel's constituencies. They included fishermen, the hated tax collectors, and women disciples. The established leaders of the community questioned the quality of such supporters:

> When the scribes of the Pharisees saw that he was eating with sinners and tax collectors, they said to his disciples, "Why does he eat with tax collectors and sinners?" When Jesus heard this, he said to them, "Those who are well have no need of a physician, but those who are sick; I have come to call not the righteous but sinners" (Mk. 2: 16–17).

The disciples, then, the future leaders of the movement, actually came from among the target audience for Jesus' ministry, such as the peasants of the countryside and the overtaxed working class of the local fishing and building trades. (Jesus himself was a carpenter.) John Dominic Crossan has called the Jesus movement, including his disciples, "a kingdom of nobodies."[3] In fact, much of the gospel record depicts these disciples as failures in understanding Jesus and his ultimate mission. When Jesus speaks in parables to outsiders to see if they really understand the heart of his message, he has to interpret not only for them, but also for his disciples! "Do you not understand this parable? Then how will you understand all the parables?" (Mk. 4: 13) Later, when Jesus calms a storm in their presence, the disciples stand amazed asking, "Who then is this, that even the wind and the sea obey him?" (Mk. 4: 41) Jesus wonders about them too, however, "Why are you afraid? Have you still no faith?" (Mk. 4: 40) Repeatedly in Mark, as well as in the other Synoptic Gospels, although less so, the disciples lack the vision and faith to rightly perceive the true nature of the mission of Jesus.

All three gospels attest that the disciples even failed to see the heart of Jesus' message, which was directed precisely at their own people! When Jesus rebuked a "rich young ruler" who wanted to become a disciple, but on his own terms, the disciples could not understand how Jesus could reject him:

> Jesus, looking at him, loved him and said, "You lack one thing; go, sell what you own, and give the money to the poor, and you will have treasure in heaven; then come, follow me." When he heard this, he was shocked and went away grieving, for he had many possessions. Then

Jesus looked around and said to his disciples, "How hard it will be for those who have wealth to enter the kingdom of God!" And the disciples were perplexed at these words. But Jesus said to them again, "Children, how hard it is to enter the kingdom of God! It is easier for a camel to go through the eye of a needle than for someone who is rich to enter the kingdom of God." They were greatly astounded and said to one another, "Then who can be saved?" Jesus looked at them and said, "For mortals it is impossible, but not for God; for God all things are possible." (Mk.10: 21–27; cf Mt. 19: 21–26; Lk. 18: 22–27).

Although they may not always have understood, Peter, in this context, recognized that at least Jesus' disciples had taken the step of faith and sacrifice, and followed Jesus: "Look, we have left everything and followed you" (Mk. 10: 28). Jesus acknowledged Peter's commitment and added, "But many who are first will be last, and the last will be first" (Mk. 10: 31). Thus the point of the pericope is clear: all-out commitment is needed for leadership in this movement, even if it comes from those at the bottom of the social rung. The rich young ruler lacked that commitment, exemplified by his unwillingness to give of himself and his possessions to the poor and oppressed in Palestine. Thus, Jesus must rely on the poor themselves, even if they more often than not failed to understand. But, at least, they had the commitment. Peter himself, the seemingly most committed of all, failed to understand that Jesus must face the ultimate sacrifice for the cause, and Jesus must rebuke him too ("Get behind me Satan," Mk. 8: 33; Mt. 16: 23). Nonetheless, Peter's consistent failures did not preclude him from ultimately being a major movement leader in the aftermath of Jesus' departure from the scene.

ASSIGNING A MISSION

Not only did Jesus surround himself with a band of future leaders; he gave them a clear mission to carry out, and that mission was intimately tied up with Jesus' concern for the poor and oppressed of Palestine. First of all, after gathering the disciples, he commissioned them:

> He called the twelve and began to send them out two by two, and gave them authority over the unclean spirits. He ordered them to take nothing for their journey except a staff; no bread, no bag, no money in their belts; but to wear sandals and not to put on two tunics. He said to them, "Wherever you enter a house, stay there until you leave the place. If any place will not welcome you and they refuse to hear you, as you

leave, shake off the dust that is on your feet as a testimony against them." So they went out and proclaimed that all should repent. They cast out many demons, and anointed with oil many who were sick and cured them (Mk. 6: 7–13).

By living the life of itinerant preachers ("wandering charismatics"[4]), who worried not about possessions and depended on their constituencies for physical needs, the disciples could best identify with the target audience of their, and Jesus', ministry – the poor, peasant population among Palestine's people. By healing physical maladies and exorcising evil spirits, they symbolically challenged the powerful human forces that controlled and oppressed the lives of the masses.[5]

Given the radical nature of this mission, however, the disciples could not expect a grand and glorious reception, but rather, in fact, ignominy:

James and John, the sons of Zebedee, came forward to him and said to him, "Teacher, we want you to do for us whatever we ask of you." And he said to them, "What is it you want me to do for you?" And they said to him, "Grant us to sit, one at your right hand and one at your left, in your glory" (Mk. 10: 35–37).

This was their expectation for all their trouble on behalf of the messianic mission that Jesus had presented to them – glory and power – however, this contradicted the very nature of their mission – a challenge to the hegemony and power of their oppressors. So Jesus had to set them straight:

But Jesus said to them, "You do not know what you are asking. Are you able to drink the cup that I drink, or be baptized with the baptism that I am baptized with?" They replied, "We are able." Then Jesus said to them, "The cup that I drink you will drink; and with the baptism with which I am baptized, you will be baptized; but to sit at my right hand or at my left is not mine to grant, but it is for those for whom it has been prepared" (Mk. 10: 38–40).

For all their bravado about accepting the challenge without much glory ("We are able"), Jesus had to elaborate on the nature of their mission as one of sacrifice:

Jesus called them and said to them, "You know that among the Gentiles those whom they recognize as their rulers lord it over them, and their great ones are tyrants over them. But it is not so among you; but whoever wishes to become great among you must be your servant, and whoever wishes to be first among you must be slave of all. For the Son of Man came not to be served but to serve, and to give his life a ransom for many" (Mk. 10: 42–45).

In many ways, this is the key text for an understanding of leadership in Jesus and the gospels. The disciples had to understand that the nature of their leadership would run counter to "business as usual" in the Roman Empire, or else they would risk repeating the same mistakes of their oppressors and become oppressors themselves. "Lording over" their charges was not the way of the gospel, but rather servanthood. To be first, to be a leader, entails the sacrifice of service on behalf of those most in need.

THE ULTIMATE ACT OF LEADERSHIP

Ultimately, this is what Jesus himself had to do. After gathering and commissioning a team of future leaders around him, he set about their training through modeling for them a ministry of service and sacrifice for the "least of these" among their peers in Palestine. Indeed, Jesus taught his disciples that their ultimate victory depended upon their treatment of those whom nobody else in the empire was paying attention to:

> Then the king will say to those at his right hand, "Come, you that are blessed by my Father, inherit the kingdom prepared for you from the foundation of the world; for I was hungry and you gave me food, I was thirsty and you gave me something to drink, I was a stranger and you welcomed me, I was naked and you gave me clothing, I was sick and you took care of me, I was in prison and you visited me." Then the righteous will answer him, "Lord, when was it that we saw you hungry and gave you food, or thirsty and gave you something to drink? And when was it that we saw you a stranger and welcomed you, or naked and gave you clothing? And when was it that we saw you sick or in prison and visited you?" And the king will answer them, "Truly I tell you, just as you did it to one of the least of these who are members of my family, you did it to me" (Mt. 25: 34–40).

Jesus showed the way toward this vision, not only by healing and preaching to the neglected masses, but by challenging their oppressors right in their own seat of power. When Jesus entered Jerusalem for the last time, to the cheering throngs of his many followers and supporters during the Passover feasts, the eyes and ears of the Roman and Jerusalem elite perked up with concern. But, then, when he entered the temple in Jerusalem and turned over the tables of the money-changers, merchants, and tax-collectors, Jesus challenged the imperial financial, religious, and political power over his people. He drew the wrath of those in power, and their plot to kill him intensified. Both the Roman forces, represented by the proconsul Pontius Pilate, and the Jewish hierarchy of the city, those whose seat of power was the temple, colluded in the arrest, trial and execution of Jesus.[6]

Despite the horrific death of Jesus at the hands of the Roman military forces and those who colluded with them from among the temple elite, his followers picked up where he left off after his death. They believed in his ultimate vindication by means of resurrection and return, even though most had initially fled the scene of his crucifixion (all except the women disciples, the gospel accounts agree). Nonetheless, despite this initial fear, the disciples do come forward to carry on the traditions that Jesus left for them, that of preaching, teaching, and caring for the "least of these" within the world of the Roman hegemony in Palestine. They too faced sacrifice and persecution, but they remembered the words of Jesus with regard to the nature of gospel leadership: "For the Son of Man came not to be served but to serve, and to give his life a ransom for many" (Mt. 10: 45).

LESSONS FROM JESUS

The key to the leadership of Jesus was that he carried out his mission in direct contrast to the established leadership of his day. He followed John the Baptist, chose his own disciples, and trained and commissioned them with the express purpose of providing relief to those who were suffering as the result of failed religious and political leadership.

Therefore, anytime we ask ourselves what kind of religious leadership we want, especially in times of crisis, like those we face now in the aftermath of September 11, among Christians, a christological question needs to be asked. Who is attending to the poor and oppressed? What in our actions and policies is creating more or less justice, or injustice? Can we, dare we, rise to the occasion, even ride against the tide, and ultimately call for, attention to those whom nobody else considers in our society, in our world? Can we demand that this be the clarion call of gospel leadership, whether or not it be politically or religiously acceptable in mainstream circles? To invoke the name of God and not call for justice for the neglected masses is to shortchange a christological definition of leadership.

Thus, it may be that the U.S. response to the September 11 attacks with a "war on terrorism" is justifiable on some political level or maybe even moral level in the eyes of some, but *not* without a consistent, accompanying question. What is demanded from us on behalf on those who suffer ongoing persecution, poverty, rejection, and turmoil? Without such a question, our leadership, religious, but also political, is not complete.

Now, it may seem to some that the actions of Jesus, as described here, are comparable to those of the September 11 terrorists, especially the main suspect, Osama bin Laden. After all, like the Jesus described above, did not bin Laden pursue justice on behalf of a people ultimately oppressed by an imperial, hegemonic body, the United States of America specifically, and the West in general? In general terms, this may be true, Jesus and bin Laden exercise leadership on behalf of an oppressed and neglected people. However, Jesus never sought to use violent action against innocent people. In fact he defended the innocent, not killed them. For Jesus, the ends never justified the means. He never joined groups advocating violent action against the Romans. Indeed, that may have motivated one of his disciples to betray him (Judas Iscariot). Like bin Laden and the September 11 terrorist cause, violent action may have done more harm to the cause of the poor in Palestine in the long term than good. The utter destruction of Jerusalem four decades after Jesus by descendants of his violent compatriots in the twenties and thirties proves the point. No, leadership for Jesus entailed a very different route from that of bin Laden.

How did the Jesus movement, then, beyond its initial stages, continue to carry out his clarion call for justice for the poor and oppressed of his society? There was a variety of emerging Christian communities that had various answers to this question. Perhaps the best documented in the New Testament are those who followed the Apostle Paul. We turn to his writings for a brief review of leadership in the Pauline communities to continue our quest for some answers with regard to the religious and political leadership needed in the aftermath of September 11.

LEADERSHIP IN PAUL

Some preliminary considerations

Although Paul's ministry took place in the same climate of Roman imperial hegemony in which Jesus carried out his ministry, there were some distinctions. Paul took the Jesus movement (albeit he was not the only one, but certainly the best attested one) beyond the immediate beginnings in Palestine into large areas of the Empire. In particular, Paul devised a strategy in which he would preach and establish Christian communities in the major cities of the empire, including Thessalonica, Philippi, Corinth, Ephesus, and Colossae. He also expected to visit, after completing his ministry in the eastern Mediterranean, the capital of the Empire, the city of Rome, in order for the churches there to finance his mission trip west to Spain (cf. Romans 15: 23–24). Thus, Paul cleverly utilized all the benefits of the Roman imperial hegemony – good roads with military security, prosperous cities, individuals with financial means – to support and enhance his Christian gospel mission.

Secondly, like Jesus, Paul did not go about his mission alone. He too surrounded himself with a group of associates, whom he regularly called "co-workers" (cf. Rom. 16: 3, 9, 21; 2 Cor. 8: 23, Phil. 2: 25, 4: 3; 1 Thess. 3: 2; Phlm. 1, 24), and upon whom he depended in order to nurture and instruct the congregations he founded. The qualities Paul expected of these leaders shows that he did not rely on typical Greco–Roman expectations of class and status in order to select his associates or endorse their leadership to his churches. Rather, like Jesus, Paul selected and endorsed leaders from among those whom he served. He expected them, as he did of himself, to disinterestedly serve the Pauline congregations, even to the point of sacrifice and risk.

In what follows, I will briefly explore what Paul expected of himself with regard to his own leadership qualities and then what he expected of his associates and co-workers. I will also discuss the ultimate goals of Paul, his leadership and that of his associates, before outlining some implications for leadership in times of crisis today.

Paul's statements about his own leadership

Paul alludes to the nature of his leadership in a variety of places in his letters. First of all, early in his ministry he found himself defending the nature of the Pauline mission, including himself and his associates. He writes to the Thessalonians:

> You yourselves know, brothers and sisters, that our coming to you was not in vain, but though we had already suffered and been shamefully mistreated at Philippi, as you know, we had courage in our God to declare to you the gospel of God in spite of great opposition For our appeal does not spring from deceit or impure motives or trickery, but just as we have been approved by God to be entrusted with the message of the gospel, even so we speak, not to please mortals, but to please God

who tests our hearts. As you know and as God is our witness, we never came with words of flattery or with a pretext for greed; nor did we seek praise from mortals, whether from you or from others, though we might have made demands as apostles of Christ. But we were gentle among you, like a nurse tenderly caring for her own children. So deeply do we care for you that we are determined to share with you not only the gospel of God but also our own selves, because you have become very dear to us. You remember our labor and toil, brothers and sisters; we worked night and day, so that we might not burden any of you while we proclaimed to you the gospel of God (1 Thess. 2: 1–9).

Several factors stand out in this passage. First, Paul and his missionary associates were willing to suffer on behalf of the gospel mission. As we shall see, Paul also expected his leaders to confront similar mistreatment on behalf of the gospel with courage and integrity. Integrity represents the second emphasis in this passage. Neither "deceit," "impure motives," or "trickery" motivates the missionary enterprise, but rather the desire to serve God's people which is in fact God's desire and God's calling. Ultimately, God motivates the Pauline missionary enterprise, not personal gain or greed.

Finally, the passage refers several times to the missionary love for their constituents. Their love and concern, "like a wet nurse caring for her own children" (1 Thess. 2: 7, my translation) for the Thessalonians and their spiritual well-being lies behind Pauline missionary activity, so much so that they did manual labor to support the ministry and not be a financial burden to the Thessalonians (2: 9).

Early in Paul's ministry, then, the issues of suffering, integrity, and finances confronted his missionary efforts, and therefore demanded a defense, which he makes here in 1 Thessalonians (most likely his first extant letter). He affirmed honest efforts in doing God's will through his preaching ministry, genuine love for his converts, including not wanting to be a financial burden, and willingness to confront opposition in all shapes and forms. Paul expected similar actions and attitudes from the leadership of his associates and fellow-workers.

But, how does Paul define leadership, more directly? Perhaps the Corinthian correspondence has the best answers. First of all, the Corinthians needed to understand that gospel leadership must be defined in terms of both human humility and divine power. Paul put it this way:

When I came to you, brothers and sisters, I did not come proclaiming the mystery of God to you in lofty words or wisdom. For I decided to

know nothing among you except Jesus Christ, and him crucified. And I
came to you in weakness and in fear and in much trembling. My speech
and my proclamation were not with plausible words of wisdom, but
with a demonstration of the Spirit and of power, so that your faith
might rest not on human wisdom but on the power of God (1 Cor. 2:
1–5).

If the power of God, and not just human ability, did not lie behind Paul's
missionary efforts, the enterprise would fail.

Second, Paul consistently defined leadership in terms of servanthood,
much like Jesus did. Just after his call for humility and divine dependence in 1
Corinthians 2, Paul described the nature of gospel leadership this way:

What then is Apollos? What is Paul? Servants through whom you came
to believe, as the Lord assigned to each. I planted, Apollos watered, but
God gave the growth. So neither the one who plants nor the one who
waters is anything, but only God who gives the growth. The one who
plants and the one who waters have a common purpose, and each will
receive wages according to the labor of each. For we are God's servants,
working together; you are God's field, God's building (1 Cor. 3: 5–9).

Again, Paul affirmed the ultimate divine role in gospel leadership. The
gospel leaders, as servants of God, each has a role to play in the gospel mission,
but it is God who gives "the growth." Reward for gospel service depends not on
who is on top, but who carries out his or her role according to the "common
purpose" that is the gospel enterprise. This vision represents a somewhat
upside down expectation for leadership compared to the hierarchy of the
Roman imperial society in which Paul's congregations were imbedded.
Nonetheless, an upside down leadership, with God at the top, and everyone
else equal servants of God's divine purpose, functioned as the *modus operandi*
in Paul's vision of leadership for his congregations and the gospel mission.

Of course, that was not everyone's vision for leadership in Paul's congregations. Some in Corinth, for example, sought more status from their role as
leaders in the Corinthian congregation, to which Paul responded with irony:

Already you have all you want! Already you have become rich! Quite
apart from us you have become kings! Indeed, I wish that you had
become kings, so that we might be kings with you! (1 Cor. 4: 8).

Paul had to mollify their search for glory by citing apostolic suffering:

For I think that God has exhibited us apostles as last of all, as though sentenced to death, because we have become a spectacle to the world, to angels and to mortals. We are fools for the sake of Christ, but you are wise in Christ. We are weak, but you are strong. You are held in honor, but we in disrepute. To the present hour we are hungry and thirsty, we are poorly clothed and beaten and homeless, and we grow weary from the work of our own hands. When reviled, we bless; when persecuted, we endure; when slandered, we speak kindly. We have become like the rubbish of the world, the dregs of all things, to this very rubbish of the world, the dregs of all things, to this very day (1 Cor. 4: 9–13).

Paul used several of these "hardship lists" throughout the correspondence to the Corinthians in order to correct an overly glorified vision of gospel leadership by a core group of leaders in the Corinthian congregation.[7]

Finally, when it was time to commend his leadership, Paul used rather unique criteria for his self-commendation:

Are we beginning to commend ourselves again? Surely we do not need, as some do, letters of recommendation to you or from you, do we? You yourselves are our letter, written on our hearts, to be known and read by all; and you show that you are a letter of Christ, prepared by us, written not with ink but with the Spirit of the living God, not on tablets of stone but on tablets of human hearts. Such is the confidence that we have through Christ toward God. Not that we are competent of ourselves to claim anything as coming from us; our competence is from God, who has made us competent to be ministers of a new covenant, not of letter but of spirit; for the letter kills, but the Spirit gives life (2 Cor. 3: 1–6).

While others in the Roman world depended on commendation letters to support their leadership, Paul depended on the actual existence of a thriving gospel community to demonstrate the authenticity of his ministry. "You yourselves are our letter," he claimed. Further, he once again showed that any competence for his leadership came from divine prerogative and the presence of God's life-giving Spirit.

Thus we must conclude that Paul depended on God for his assignment as an apostle and missionary, that suffering was an integral part of the nature of his leadership on behalf of the gospel communities, and that his love and concern for these communities overruled any personal gains or interests that he, or any gospel leader, might seek from such an assignment. For Paul, gospel leadership was about service, even if that service entailed suffering, hard labor, and criticism from those who misunderstood the nature of the ministry. The ministry may not bring much earthly glory, but satisfaction was derived from knowing one was responding to God's call, serving with God's power, and rewarded with eternal life.

Expectations of associates and co-workers

Paul expected no less from those who served with him and those who assumed leadership roles from among the constituents of his congregations. In all but one of Paul's uncontested letters (Galatians), he commends local leaders and/or his associates to his congregations. These commendation passages, like similar commendations in the Greco–Roman world, provide a window into the qualities Paul expected of his church leaders. They very much parallel what Paul expected of his own leadership.[8]

In commending local church leaders, Paul focused on their hard work and service for the church. To the young, struggling Thessalonian congregation, he wrote:

> But we appeal to you, brothers and sisters, to respect those who labor among you, and have charge of you in the Lord and admonish you; esteem them very highly in love because of their work (1 Thess. 5: 12–13a).

Local church leaders in Thessalonica had proven their leadership skills by means of their hard labor, admonishment and work in the congregation over a period of time. Therefore, they should be recognized for what they are already doing. This is not leadership *ex nihilo*, but leadership recognition that comes from having a track record.

Similarly, when Paul sought out loyal leaders in the turmoil that is the Corinthian congregation, he turned to a proven commodity. Stephanas, and others in his household, had from the very beginning demonstrated their loyalty to Paul and the gospel by means of their service to the gospel community in Corinth:

> Now, brothers and sisters, you know that members of the household of Stephanas were the first converts in Achaia, and they have devoted themselves to the service of the saints; I urge you to put yourselves at the service of such people, and of everyone who works and toils with them. I rejoice at the coming of Stephanas and Fortunatus and

Achaicus, because they have made up for your absence; for they refreshed my spirit as well as yours. So give recognition to such persons (1 Cor. 16: 15–18).

Leadership recognition for Stephanas and the others depended on their devoted service to the gospel community. In addition, their service to Paul and the gospel mission elsewhere ("they refreshed my spirit") also commended them. The gospel community were to serve them because they had served Paul, the community and the cause of the gospel. In fact, anyone who put himself/herself at the service of the church ought to be recognized as a leader in the community.

Paul also commended his immediate associates and other traveling envoys for similar criteria of hard work and service for the community. In addition, he mentioned the risks the associates and envoys took in traveling on behalf of the gospel mission. For example, Epaphroditus had traveled from Philippi to minister to Paul during the latter's imprisonment (Phil. 2: 25–30). Paul's commendation included a reference to Epaphroditus' sacrificial service:

Still, I think it necessary to send to you Epaphroditus – my brother and co-worker and fellow soldier, your messenger and minister to my need; for he has been longing for all of you, and has been distressed because you heard that he was ill. He was indeed so ill that he nearly died. But God had mercy on him, and not only on him but on me also, so that I would not have one sorrow after another. I am the more eager to send him, therefore, in order that you may rejoice at seeing him again, and that I may be less anxious. Welcome him then in the Lord with all joy, and honor such people, because he came close to death for the work of Christ, risking his life to make up for those services that you could not give me (Phil. 2: 25–30).

Epaphroditus' illness demonstrated his commitment to the gospel mission; therefore he deserved leadership recognition ("honor such people"). Moreover, he also showed his love and commitment to the community by being more worried about their concern for him than about the illness itself (2: 26).

In another passage, Paul also commended his closest associate, Timothy, for a similar reason – concern for the gospel community:

I hope in the Lord Jesus to send Timothy to you soon, so that I may be cheered by news of you. I have no one like him who will be genuinely concerned for your welfare. All of them are seeking their own interests, not those of Jesus Christ. But Timothy's worth you know, how like a son with a father he has served with me in the work of the gospel (Phil. 2: 19–22).

Again, besides his concern for the community, Timothy showed loyalty to Paul and service to the Pauline mission; both critical leadership criteria for Paul's closest associates.

In 2 Corinthians, Paul commended a group of envoys who were traveling to Corinth to take care of an important aspect of the Pauline mission – the monetary collection for the church in Jerusalem. The collection team included Titus, one of Paul's closest associates, along with Timothy. Paul writes, "But thanks be to God who put in the heart of Titus the same eagerness for you that I myself have. For he not only accepted our appeal, but since he is more eager than ever, he is going to you of his own accord" (2 Cor. 8: 16–17). Like Timothy, Titus showed singular concern for the well being of the gospel community.

Similarly, the other team members had important leadership qualities grounded in their service to the gospel community. One member was well known among Paul's churches for his preaching skills: "With [Titus] we are sending the brother who is famous among all the churches for his proclaiming the good news" (2 Cor. 8: 18). Another had proven himself to Paul time and again by engagement in the Pauline mission: "And with them we are sending our brother whom we have often tested and found eager in many matters, but who is now more eager than ever because of his great confidence in you" (2 Cor. 8: 22). In short, Paul had confidence in the leadership of all three of his envoys, but especially his closest associate, the only one he mentioned by name in this context: "As for Titus, he is my partner and co-worker in your service; as for our brothers, they are messengers [*apostoloi*] of the churches, the glory of Christ" (2 Cor. 8: 23). In either case, whether immediate associates and co-workers of Paul, or envoys sent by his churches, all these leaders shared a common commitment to the gospel, the gospel community, and the specific expression and activity of it in the Pauline mission.

The Pauline mission included various women leaders whom Paul also commended at critical points in his letters. When the Philippian church needed examples of good leaders who would follow the Pauline injunction to "live your life in a manner worthy of the gospel of Christ" (Phil. 1: 27a), Paul cited Jesus (2: 5–11), himself (2: 17–18), Timothy (2: 19–24) and

Epaphroditus (2: 25–30). However, all of that could be for naught if two key women leaders of the church in Philippi did not heal their leadership rift:

> I urge Euodia and I urge Syntyche to be of the same mind in the Lord. Yes, and I ask you also, my loyal companion, help these women, for they have struggled beside me in the work of the gospel, together with Clement and the rest of my co-workers, whose names are in the book of life.

Paul could not ask the church at Philippi to stand "firm in one spirit, striving side by side with one mind for the faith of the gospel" (1: 27b), if two good examples of that spirit in the past, Euodia and Syntyche, who "have struggled beside [Paul] in the work of the gospel" (4: 3) were not currently seeing eye to eye.[9] Thus Paul commended their past leadership and called for help of another leader to bring about their reconciliation.

Similarly, Paul commended another Christian woman leader to the Romans. Her role was critical to Paul's intentions in writing this letter:

> I commend to you our sister Phoebe, a deacon of the church at Cenchreae, so that you may welcome her in the Lord as is fitting for the saints, and help her in whatever she may require from you, for she has been a benefactor of many and of myself as well (Rom. 16: 1–2).

First of all, Phoebe had exercised a leadership role in a local congregation near Corinth, in the port town of Cenchreae. Paul called her a *diakonos*, the same term he reserved for himself and Apollos in 1 Cor. 3: 5 – "servant" or "minister." Thus, she had that all-important quality in the Pauline mission – service for the gospel community. Second, Paul also referred to her as a "benefactor" or "patron" (*prostatis*) of many, including Paul, in the gospel mission, which probably meant she had provided financial support for the mission.[10]

Thus Phoebe's role had been critical in the Pauline mission on several fronts. She exercised leadership in a local congregation. She had financially supported Paul and the gospel mission as a whole. Therefore, it is significant that Paul sent her with the Romans' letter, because he intended that the Roman house churches, the leaders of several of which he greeted following his commendation of Phoebe (Rom. 16: 3–16), should unite to support Paul's mission to Spain (cf. Rom. 15: 22–24). Phoebe must have had an important advance role to play in Paul's new venture, both to clarify any points of Pauline theology in the letter, and to prepare the Roman Christians to support the Spanish mission.[11] Thus Paul enthusiastically commended her leadership:

"Welcome her in the Lord as is fitting for the saints, and help her in whatever she may require from you."

Paul commended leaders who followed, in some shape or form, many of the lessons he himself had learned from the gospel mission. These lessons included that gospel leadership must entail singular attention to the welfare of gospel communities, especially those in the Pauline mission, but not exclusively. Paul was very much concerned for the well being of the Jerusalem church and organized a collection for them from his own, largely Gentile, churches. In every case, service and hard work mark the good gospel leader.

Paul also wanted his leaders to understand that gospel leadership often must confront much suffering and risk. Certainly, that had been the case in Paul's own ministry. Beside himself, however, the best examples of such willingness to confront opposition and difficulty had been his closest associates. Timothy and Titus, like Paul, had shown keen interest and love in the gospel communities they founded together with Paul. Epaphroditus, a messenger from Philippi to Paul during one of his imprisonments, took all kinds of risks, including a near-death illness, to minister to Paul in one of the latter's most difficult ministry moments.

Finally, Paul expected his leaders to proclaim good news to his communities. Titus could go to Corinth for the collection with "eagerness" (2 Cor. 8: 16) because he had been there before bringing about reconciliation between Paul and the Corinthians (2 Cor 7: 5–16). Phoebe, not only provided monetary support to the Pauline mission, but as a leader in Cenchreae, she no doubt preached the gospel. Thus she was ready to interpret Paul's theological teachings for the Roman churches. Euodia and Syntyche "struggled beside [Paul] in the work of the gospel," which no doubt included proclaiming it in word and deed. The commendations of Phoebe and Euodia and Syntyche also show that Paul, like Jesus, incorporated a diverse group of persons – socially, financially and in terms of gender – into his leadership team.

What precisely was the message Paul and his team shared with such success in the middle years of the first century C.E.? What does such a theological focus say about their leadership? What was the ultimate goal of their leadership?

The goals of Paul's leadership

Most biblical scholarship agrees that Paul rarely expounded on his theology systematically, if at all, in his letters. All of his letters, including what has been perceived as his most famously systematic, the Letter to the Romans, are "contingent" documents based on a "coherent" theology, but expounding the latter is less of a concern than addressing the immediate contextual crisis or situation of his congregations.[12] Thus, Paul was a "praxis theologian," less concerned with a clear, seminal declaration of his core theology, than with ministering to churches in need with whatever theological truth would be best helpful at the moment. Such was the "theological leadership" that he gave his communities.

However, we, of course, catch glimpses of his core theology throughout his writings. Two of these in particular, I think, can help us with lessons for religious leadership in the aftermath of September 11. First, at the conclusion of the biographical defense of his apostolic calling to the Gentiles of Galatia (Gal. 1: 13–2: 14), Paul indicates that the core of his theology entails Christ and the cross:

> I have been crucified with Christ; and it is no longer I who live, but it is Christ who lives in me. And the life I now live in the flesh I live by faith in the Son of God, who loved me and gave himself for me (Gal. 2: 19b-20).

As in Philippians 2: 5–11, Christ becomes a model for our life here on earth. Yet, this life includes something of the will to sacrifice as Christ did, for the cause of the gospel, of bringing good news to those who need it most. A new life in Christ carries with it the call, especially to leaders, to sacrifice so that others might hear and live out that good news.

Another seminal passage in Paul, I think, adds to this sense of mission in his gospel theology. After achieving reconciliation with his Corinthian congregation (as described in 2 Cor. 1–7), Paul proceeds to explain the gospel experience and the subsequent missionary impulse as a "ministry of reconciliation":

> So if anyone is in Christ, there is a new creation: everything old has passed away; see, everything has become new! All this is from God, who reconciled us to himself through Christ, and has given us the ministry of reconciliation; that is, in Christ God was reconciling the world to himself, not counting their trespasses against them, and entrusting the message of reconciliation to us. So we are ambassadors for Christ, since God is making his appeal through us; we entreat you on behalf of Christ, be reconciled to God (2 Cor. 5: 17–20).

Because God has restored right relations between us and our Creator, we too, as "ambassadors for Christ," exercise, in our leadership, the ministry of reconciliation, bringing divided parties into peace.

Paul's letters show that to bring unity in the midst of the discord in many of his communities was central to his leadership skills. In Corinth, he had to heal division over leaders, between rich and poor, and ultimately about his own apostleship. Similarly, in the Galatian churches, questions about his gospel and apostleship brought discord that he had addressed both theologically and biographically. Even in Rome, with house churches that he did not found, he had to heal rifts between Gentile and Jewish constituents in those churches. He writes about the righteous justice of God that brings about personal justification with God, but also "peace" between divided peoples (Rom. 5: 1–5).[13]

Thus what lies at the heart of Paul's leadership activity, and that of his associates, is a firm belief in the gospel of Christ that calls one to accountability before God, and asks one to engage in bringing others into the fold. Further, the implication of such a gospel is that peace and reconciliation should be pursued with one another, both within and outside the gospel community.

Lessons learned from Paul's leadership

Paul's leadership, then, teaches us a variety of factors with regard to religious leadership. First of all, like Paul, religious leaders today need to think through a careful strategy for carrying out their mission. Paul devised an urban ministry strategy, and it worked in terms of establishing key churches at critical junctions throughout the Roman Empire. We must think carefully if we are going to respond responsibly to the crises at hand in the aftermath of September 11. Rash judgments and actions will not serve us well.

Secondly, who will join us in the leadership task is an all-important question. Like Jesus, Paul surrounded himself with a band of associates, his "co-workers." When he commends these leaders, as well as emerging local leaders, to his congregations he cites their track record, which for him must include hard work and sacrifice, *already*, on behalf of the gospel and the gospel community. Their social status, and even gender, traditional qualifying criteria for commendation in imperial society, did not seem to matter as much to Paul as their proven sacrificial service to his congregations. What criteria do we expect of our leaders? Paul did not expect any more than what he expected of himself, and his singular concern for the growth and well-being of his gospel communities drove his ministry and leadership practices. We need religious leaders willing to take a stand and act on it with courage and integrity today, especially in the crisis that we face following the September 11 attacks. Issues of diversity, inclusion, and hearing from voices of all walks of life are part of that firm stance.

Thirdly, we need firm conviction and a sense of mission from our leaders. Paul preached "Jesus Christ and him crucified" (1 Cor. 2: 2) and stood by that message in good times and bad. The cross of Christ was not just an abstract teaching for Paul, but had practical implications. He expected himself and his leaders to live out their theology, and so gospel leadership included a willingness to sacrifice, even their own lives, for the cause of Christ and his people. The core message also included God's reconciling act on behalf of humanity in Christ. If that was the case, how much more should our leadership engage the ministry of reconciliation and healing to divided parties. Perhaps, this is the greatest lesson from Paul's leadership for our own day. The gospel cannot be the gospel without the ministry of peace and reconciliation. We need more religious leaders who practice and promote the art of diplomacy and peacemaking rather than some kind of chauvinistic jingoism that divides rather than unites. Leadership in the Pauline mission included being "ambassadors for Christ" and in Christ God reconciled the world to its Creator. Therefore, a *sine qua non* of gospel leadership is reconciliation. How to achieve reconciliation between divided parties in our communities and our world, no matter how complicated that may seem, and it is, must lie at the heart of our religious leadership activity and proclamation.

Some concluding remarks – Jesus, Paul and leadership post-September 11

Thousands of innocent people lost their lives on September 11, 2001 as a result of criminal acts that call for police action, if not an all-out "war on terrorism." In addition to worldwide police action to bring to justice the perpetrators of this heinous act, the world needs strong, forthright, thoughtful, and compassionate leadership to ensure that something like this does not happen again. Religious leadership from all faiths and denominations must be included among these leaders. What kind of response does the world need from our religious leadership?

The lessons from a New Testament study of the early Christian leaders Jesus and Paul may be helpful in this respect.[14] Jesus showed a singular concern for the poor and oppressed in the context of an oppressive imperial hegemony. To keep those whom nobody else cares about in the forefront of our leadership thought and action must continue to be a major aspect of religious leadership, whether it is the poor and homeless in the South Bronx of New York City or those in Afghanistan in the aftermath of U.S. bombing there after September 11.

Secondly, both Jesus and Paul refused to work alone. Given the complexity of what lies before us in the world forever changed after September 11, we dare not be lone rangers, especially those of us in religious leadership. Dialogue, including dialogue between races, classes, genders, and faiths, must be fostered in order to take right action in the complex matters that lie before us. Religious leaders must show the way in such dialogue.

In line with team approaches to leadership is the need for careful thought and strategies. Paul, in particular, wisely used the resources of the Empire to carry out his mission, even if the mission carried a message that challenged the practices and ideologies of the Empire. All leaders, but religious leaders in particular, must plot together careful action that will promote peace, reconcil-iation, and "good news." Thus, not only is careful strategy needed but also a clear, just mission. Jesus taught his disciples to "love your enemy." Paul taught his churches that God, in Christ, was reconciling the world to Godself, and that, therefore, we need to be instruments of reconciliation. Religious leaders of today must also promote love and reconciliation if they are going to be true to the core values of all religious faith. Even the criminal actions of September 11, as horrific as they were, still call for careful and just action. Bring in the "evil doers," as President Bush called us to do, but in the process let us not forget those values of justice and fair play that we as a nation espouse so loudly, especially when we are not the ones being attacked from outside.

Finally, religious leaders must remember to remain humble in these jingois-tic circumstances that cry out for revenge. When one of Jesus' disciples struck out at his accusers with a sword, Jesus healed the stricken enemy, and declared, "Put your sword back into its place; for all who take the sword will perish by the sword" (Mt. 26: 52). He also went on to rebuke his accusers for their violence (Mt. 26: 55). The message was clear – violence should not be our first reaction every time we are wronged. Hubris rather than sober thought could be behind our actions. Whether or not declaring an all out "war on terrorism" is an overre-action to the September 11 attacks remains to be seen. The point is that religious leaders should weigh in and do so with humility and with a call for humility on all parts, reminding us all of our weaknesses and shortcomings and ultimate dependence on God. The Apostle Paul put it this way:

> Therefore, to keep me from being too elated, a thorn was given me in the flesh, a messenger of Satan to torment me, to keep me from being too elated. Three times I appealed to the Lord about this, that it would leave me, but he said to me, "My grace is sufficient for you, for power is made perfect in weakness." So, I will boast all the more gladly of my

weaknesses, so that the power of Christ may dwell in me. Therefore I am content with weaknesses, insults, hardships, persecutions, and calamities for the sake of Christ; for whenever I am weak, then I am strong (2 Cor. 12: 7–10).

True leaders refuse to hide in the face of calamity and weakness. They do not pursue calamity; they seek improvement in the midst of weakness. Because calamity and worse are inevitable, the challenge lies in how we respond when they come. If a greater cause motivates us, we seek to overcome the calamity and hardship, and we strengthen ourselves for the long haul in spite of our weaknesses. Ultimately, we rely on God to help us through the crisis and guide us in our response. Without such dependence, we can fail miserably. After the crisis brought upon the world by the September 11 attacks, religious leaders are called upon more than ever to show the world how to rely on a higher power than ourselves, "for whenever I am weak, then I am strong."

NOTES

1. See especially John Dominic Crossan, *The Historical Jesus: The Life of a Mediterranean Jewish Peasant* (San Francisco/New York: Harper Collins, 1991), and its popularized version, *Jesus: A Revolutionary Biography* (San Francisco/New York: HarperCollins, 1994). See also Marcus Borg, *Jesus A New Vision: Spirit, Culture and the Life of Discipleship* (San Francisco/New York: HarperCollins, 1987), and its popular version, *Meeting Jesus Again for the First Time: The Historical Jesus & the Heart of Contemporary Faith* (San Francisco/New York: HarperCollins, 1994).
2. See Richard A. Horsley and John S. Hanson, *Bandits, Prophets and Messiahs: Popular Movements at the Time of Jesus* (Minneapolis: Seabury/Winston, 1985), for a description of these and other resistance movements in first-century Palestine.
3. Crossan, *Jesus*, 54–74.
4. For this term and its explanation, see Gerd Theissen, *Sociology of Early Palestinian Christianity*, trans. John Bowden (Philadelphia: Fortress Press, 1978), 8–16.
5. See Plutarco Bonilla, *Los milagros tambien son parabolas* (Miami: Editorial Caribe, 1978), who argues that behind the miracles of healing and exorcism by Jesus and his disciples, lie parabolic action against the powerful political and religious forces of Jesus' day, including the Roman imperial presence and those among Israel's elite who colluded with them.
6. For such a reading of the death of Jesus, see John Dominic Crossan, *Who Killed Jesus?: Exposing the Roots of Anti-Semitism in the Gospel Story of the Death of Jesus* (San Francisco: Harper Collins, 1996), 39–159.

7. See 2 Cor. 4: 8–12, 6: 3–10, 11: 23–30. For Paul's hardship lists as a means of promoting a gospel leadership ultimately dependent on God and not mere human effort, see John T. Fitzgerald, *Cracks in an Earthen Vessel: An Examination of the Catalogues of Hardships in the Corinthian Correspondence*, SBL Dissertation Series 99 (Atlanta: Scholars Press, 1988).

8. For Paul's commendations, see Efrain Agosto, "Paul's Use of Greco-Roman Conventions of Commendation," Ph.D. Dissertation, Boston University (1996). See also my essay, "Commendation in Paul" in J. Paul Sampley, *Paul in His Greco-Roman World: A Handbook* (Valley Forge, PA: Trinity Press International, forthcoming).

9. For this interpretation about the importance of the leadership of Euodia and Syntyche to the gospel witness in Philippi, see Elisabeth Schüssler Fiorenza, *In Memory of Her: A Feminist Theological Reconstruction of Christian Origins* (New York: Crossroad, 1983), 169–170.

10. For the various interpretations of this term in Paul's time, see James Walters, "'Phoebe' and 'Junia(s)' – Rom. 16: 1–2, 7" in Carroll D. Osburn, *Essays on Women in Earliest Christianity*, vol. I (Joplin, MO: College Press, 1993), 167–190.

11. For this possibility, see Robert Jewett, "Paul, Phoebe, and the Spanish Mission," in Jacob Neusner, et.al., eds., *The Social World of Formative Christianity & Judaism: Essays in Tribute to Howard Clark Kee* (Philadelphia: Fortress Press, 1988), 142–161.

12. See the seminal work on this by J. Christiaan Beker, *Paul the Apostle: The Triumph of God in Life and Thought* (Philadelphia: Fortress Press, 1980).

13. On this understanding of the Romans letter, see Elsa Tamez, *The Amnesty of Grace: Justification by Faith from a Latin American Perspective*, trans. Sharon Ringe (Nashville: Abingdon Press, 1993).

14. For many Christians, the New Testament is also an authoritative source for life and action at various levels. For example, orthodox Christians (including many evangelicals and fundamentalists) argue that whatever the Bible says or intends to say, about what we should do, we should obey. This discussion assumes, at the very least, that what we learn from Jesus and Paul about leadership is a valuable *resource* for discussion among all religions, and perhaps action by committed Christians. For many Christians, the lessons on leadership may even be authoritative mandates. I deal with these hermeneutical issues on reading leadership in the New Testament, in a forthcoming book, *Leadership in the New Testament* (St. Louis: Chalice Press). For a broader discussion on "fusing" these two horizons of the past and the present in biblical interpretation, see Anthony Thiselton, *The Two Horizons: New Testament Hermeneutics & Philosophical Description* (Grand Rapids: Wm. B. Eerdmans, 1980).

9

THE BIBLE AND DIALOGUE

Judy Fentress-Williams

"Now the whole earth had one language and the same words."
Genesis 11.1

The destruction of the World Trade Center Towers evokes the story of another edifice of mythic proportion – the tower of Babel. The modern and ancient edifices were constructed to represent the power of their respective cultures and their destruction points to the limitations of humanity. These symbolic towers also serve to remind us of the centrality of dialogue, both in finding theological meaning and in relating to one another.

The argument of this chapter is that the Christian commitment to dialogue is grounded in the very structure of the Hebrew Scriptures. In fact, once one recognizes the dialogic structure that is inherent in the Bible, one can better perceive the theological insights and messages of the text. If the meaning of the text emerges from the dialogue, then it is dialogue with its sensitivity to a variety of voices, languages, and perspectives that is needed as Christians attempt to come to terms with different understandings of the world.

The chapter starts with the tower of Babel. Here I explore the role of language in its capacity to create commonalities and divisions between people. The numerous possibilities inherent in language point to the significance of "dialogic truth" in the Bible. A case study from I Samuel 2–3 provides an example of the truths of the Bible that are produced from its internal dialogue. Finally the chapter reaffirms the fact that a commitment to dialogue is so important in the modern world.

GENESIS 11: 1–9: THE LIMITS OF LANGUAGE

The story of the Tower of Babel not only provides the explanation for the spread of humanity from the Fertile Crescent, but also provides the etiology for different languages. The story is placed at the end of what is known as the primordial history, which contains the stories concerning the origins and nature of the world, God, and humanity. A major theme of the primordial history, the increasing separation between humanity and God, is evident in this account. The goal of the people was to build bricks for a city with a "tower with its top in the heavens." God inspected the construction and responded,

> Look, they are one people, and they have all one
> language; and this is only the beginning of what
> they will do; nothing they propose to do will now
> be impossible for them. Come let us go down,
> and confuse their language there, so that they
> will not understand one another's speech.
>
> Genesis 11:7[1]

If we look at the story allegorically, a strong case can be made that the Tower of Babel is also a story about language and the role it will have in the stories that follow. Even before the languages of the people are confused, the story reveals the possibility of multiple meanings in language. The reason that the people give for building the city and tower is ironically prophetic. They build a tower to keep them from being scattered abroad. What they fear is what they will experience as their words are turned against them.

The people's ability to communicate and be understood by one another empowers them. YHWH responds to the situation by "confusing" the languages of the people. No longer able to communicate with everyone, they migrate towards those who speak their language and form communities based on language. Consistent with the themes of increasing separation between God and humanity, Babel reminds us that part of what it is to be human and distinct from God is to be limited in speech and comprehension. The story is a poignant reminder that "speech binds lives and loosens them, builds society and isolates persons and is both the crown and disgrace of our human existence."[2]

The implications of the allegory are apparent. We form communities with people who sound like us. We are comfortable with people we readily understand, those who speak our language. There are barriers between communities based on language and subsequently, geography. The division of language will forever keep the created beings in a realm separate from that of the deity. Thus we are left at the end of Babel with a language that is not only divided into many different tongues, but also has a multiplicity of meaning within each language. M. M. Bakhtin describes it this way:

> ... regardless of the position and the proximity to me
> of this other human being whom I am contemplating,
> I shall always see and know something that he, from
> his place outside and over against me, cannot see himself:
> parts of his body that are inaccessible to his own gaze
> (his head, his face and its expression) the world behind
> his back ... are accessible to me but not to him. As we
> gaze at each other, two different worlds are reflected in
> the pupils of our eyes ... to annihilate this difference
> completely, it would be necessary to merge into one,
> to become one and the same person.[3]

This philosophy assumes that the individual in isolation has limited perception. The other sees, completes the individual in a way she could not, herself.

These limitations of language immediately confront us when we come to the Bible. The heterogeneity of the text, its literary characteristics and the Bible's status as a theological document present challenges to discerning its meaning. Biblical narrative consists of strands of material that are so remarkably diverse in style, genre and message that there is ongoing debate as to how or whether these components fit together. This heterogeneity militates against a straightforward, singular reading. Historically, biblical criticism has, like the people in the Babel story, divided into camps and formed communities with those who interpret the Bible similarly. As a result, our interpretations of the text focus on one aspect of the text to the exclusion of the rest.

Given the limitations that confront any reader of the Bible, how are we to interpret the Bible? I propose that the literary character of the Bible transforms what we perceive as the babble of different voices into a dialogue that produces theological meaning. This meaning is not fully realized in any single aspect of the text but is found as the words, phrases, and other units of language engage in dialogue with each other. Using a passage from I Samuel, we will observe how individual components work towards meaning through dialogue with other parts of the material. Literature, even sacred literature, is *inherently* dialogic.

TRUTH IN DIALOGUE

For a preliminary definition of how the Bible is dialogic I will turn to Carol Newsom's article, "Bakhtin, The Bible and Dialogic Truth." Here she argues that the issue that prevents theologians and biblical scholars from having a fruitful conversation is that "the type of discourse which is natural to the theologian and which has often been imported into biblical theology is not adequate for engaging the biblical text."[4] At the root of this divide is the tendency of theologians to be driven by a sense of monologic truth, working towards "unity," "coherence," and "systems."[5] Monologic truth as Newsom defines it, has the following characteristics: 1) monologic truth is a "separate thought" or "proposition" – a statement that is true regardless of who says it; 2) this type of truth "tends to gravitate towards a system. It seeks unity;" and 3) "in principle, it can be comprehended by a single consciousness."[6] It is Newsom's contention that in different ways, historical criticism and contemporary literary approaches to the Bible began with "an unchallenged assumption of a monologic sense of truth." In contrast to this definition, dialogic truth "requires a plurality of consciousness ... [which] in principle cannot be fitted within the bounds of a single consciousness." It has an "embodied, almost personal quality" to it, which is in contrast to the abstract notion of monologic truth. Moreover, there is no drift toward the systematic in dialogic truth. "Event" rather than "system" is what gives dialogic truth its unity. It is a dynamic, not a prepositional unity. Finally, "dialogic truth is always open. Bakhtin's term for this has been translated as 'unfinalizability.'" In other words a dialogic approach focuses on the "unresolved and irresolvable questions about the nature of human being."[7] A dialogic approach also assumes that meaning is achieved only when an exchange takes place.

On one level, the dialogue of the Bible is intertextual. One passage refers to another, connecting with earlier or later passages. These elements constitute a conversation within the text, creating an environment that resists closure. On another level the dialogue invites the reader's participation by presenting him with a plethora of clues to be analyzed, thereby preventing him from making the kinds of conclusions that would end the dialogue. This type of reading acknowledges the significance of each utterance in the creation of meaning. However, the peculiarity of the Bible, namely God's presence behind and in the narrative, changes the dynamics of the dialogue. God is behind the narrative to the extent that the Bible is an inspired, theological text. God is in the text as a character that speaks and interacts with other characters. This God, however, is not simply another character. YHWH closes and opens wombs, raises and dethrones kings and sends good and evil spirits. It is the presence of God that transforms the nature of the dialogue.

I Samuel chapters 2 and 3 provide an example of the kinds of challenges the interpreter faces with the heterogeneity of the biblical narrative. Chapter two introduces the genre of poetry into the narrative, and the narrative resumes at the end of Hannah's song. The presence of poetry in the midst of narrative raises questions around the function of the song in the midst of a story. How are we to understand the song, and how does it relate to the larger narrative? An examination of the poem and the narrative in dialogue will provide some interesting insights. Hannah's song in its current position in the narrative makes sense only as it relates to the larger narrative around the rise and fall of Israel. It is also evident that Eli and Samuel's ability to perceive is greatly increased through dialogue. Moreover, it is God who is in dialogue with these characters, sometimes directly and sometimes through another character in the narrative.

I SAMUEL CHAPTERS 2–3: A DIALOGUE OF CONTRAST

Chapter one of I Samuel concludes with Hannah bringing her son to Eli as she had promised the Lord, "for as long as he lives he is lent, שׁאוּל, to the LORD"(vs. 28). The narrative is interrupted with the poetry of Hannah's song in chapter two.[8] Although the location of the psalm is different in various text traditions, it appears the intention was to set the song in the context of dedication and worship at Shiloh. Unlike other psalms set in biblical narrative, the psalm does not directly affect the plot of the story.[9] Moreover, there is scholarly debate over the degree of thematic coherence between the psalm and the narrative. Robert Polzin cites connections between I Samuel 2: 1–10 and II Samuel 22 and on the basis of that connection sees thematic links between the two psalms and the Deuteronomistic history. The reversal theme in Hannah's song speaks to Israel's fate.[10] Peter Miscall, on the other hand sees very little connection between the psalm and the ensuing narrative.[11]

If the psalm does not directly affect the progression of the plot and if the extent to which it shares themes with the larger narrative is debated, what role might the song have in the narrative? The very placement of I Samuel 2: 1–10 at the beginning of Samuel and II Samuel 22 near the end suggests intent on the part of the editor to convey a message. One possibility is that the psalm serves a narrative purpose such as "thematic exposition and characterization."[12] I will make the case that the song's imagery, its parallels to II Samuel 22 and its theme of reversals is not only proleptic, but sets up dialogues with the immediate and larger surrounding narrative. That dialogue causes the reader to focus on the relationship between dialogue and one's ability to perceive in the narrative.

The theme of Hannah's song is consistent and clear. God lifts up the lowly and brings down the mighty. She, the barren, is able to participate in the mighty works of God as he blesses her womb, while the one who has many is "forlorn." The imagery however, is by no means governed by the details of Hannah's story. Apart from the reference to the once barren woman bearing seven (Hannah has six), the psalm contains traditional military imagery (in verse 4) and political allusions in verses 8 and 10.

Using fixed pairs in verses 4–9, the imagery moves back and forth from describing reversals of a "practical" nature, such as the hungry being fed, to much more cosmic examples. In verse 6, God casts into Sheol, and gives death and life. Other examples of God's cosmic power in verses 8b and 10a include descriptions of the LORD setting the world on the pillars of the earth and shattering his enemies. In 10b, the imagery is royal, with the mention of the king and the "the anointed one." The varieties of imagery in the song and the way in which that imagery lends itself to a variety of interpretations supports allegorical readings of the text. For example, Hannah's words, "my horn is raised" (verse 1 in McCarter's translation), is, according to many, a figure of speech "denoting increase of might ... dignity" as the horn is a "symbol of strength."[13] Driver claims it evokes the image of "an animal carrying its head high ... conscious of its strength."[14] The related expression, "cause a horn to sprout" connotes the growth of the horn and can be seen as referring specifically to progeny. On the other hand, the horn can be seen as the distinguishing characteristic of one animal from others.[15] Thus the phrase can be seen as a military image or as one having to do with bearing children. Hannah, the mother of a much-anticipated child, sings the song of victory.[16]

The song in I Samuel 2: 1–10 can also be seen as an "abbreviated" version of II Samuel 22, David's song of thanksgiving. Together the two poems form a poetic inclusio. Whereas Hannah's song anticipates the triumph of the anointed king, in II Samuel 22, the triumphant king looks back on how he has prevailed through YHWH. Because Hannah's song is significantly shorter than David's, the former can be seen as a "proleptic summary" of the latter.[17] What follows is a list of parallel phrases in the two psalms:

I Samuel 2:2 אֵין צוּר כֵּאלֹהֵנוּ "There is no rock like our God."

II Samuel 22:32 מִי צוּר מִבַּלְעֲדֵי אֱלֹהֵנוּ "Who is a rock except our God?"

I Samuel 2:7 יהוה ... מַשְׁפִּיל אַף־מְרוֹמֵם "Yahweh ... makes fall, but also exalts."

II Samuel 22:28 עֵינֶיךָ עַל־רָמִים תַּשְׁפִּיל "Your eyes are on the exalted, you make them fall."

I Samuel 2:8 מֵקִים מֵעָפָר דָּל מֵאַשְׁפֹּת יָרִים אֶבְיוֹן "Raising the poor from the dust, he exalts the needy from the dung pile."

II Samuel 22:28 וְאֶת־עַם עָנִי תּוֹשִׁיעַ "And you save an afflicted people."

I Samuel 2:9 רַגְלֵי חֲסִידָו יִשְׁמֹר "He guards the feet of his faithful ones."

II Samuel 22:26 עִם חָסִיד תִּתְחַסָּד "To the faithful he shows faithfulness."

I Samuel 2:10 עָלָו בַּשָּׁמַיִם יַרְעֵם "Against them (or the Most High) thunders in heaven."

II Samuel 22:14 יַרְעֵם מִן־שָׁמַיִם יהוה "Yahweh thunders from heaven."

I Samuel 2:10 יִתֶּן־עֹז לְמַלְכּוֹ "He gives power to his king."

II Samuel 22:51 מַגְדִּיל יְשׁוּעוֹת מַלְכּוֹ "Magnifying the victories of his king." [18]

In addition to the dialogue between Hannah's song and I Samuel 22, there is a dialogue within I Samuel 2:1–10. Robert Polzin identifies at least three voices in the internal dialogue of the song/prayer: the voice of Hannah, that of the triumphant King David, and the Deuteronomist in what Bakhtin referred to as a "polyphonic composition." This is a dialogue that is "both harmonious and dissonant, transparent yet opaque, looking backward and forward, full of thematic variations on themes already met or soon to be encountered." [19] This variety of voices in I Samuel 2:1–10 gives the song a more general application than II Samuel 22, which takes the form of an individual thanksgiving. [20]

Another dynamic that is present is the immediate and polemic contrast between those that God is lifting up and those that God brings down. The uplifting of the lowly does not happen in a vacuum. It takes place in the presence of the mighty being brought down. God is just as involved with what happens to the mighty as God is involved with the fate of the lowly. The focal point of all this movement is the LORD, this God of the cosmos who is over the fate of the impoverished and the fate of the exalted ones. An allegorical reading of this song and its royal imagery predicts the fate of not only Saul but also David, and the entire monarchy.

McCarter picks up on the Deuteronomistic tone of the song and describes it as an "affirmation of the relationship between divine justice and the human condition."[21] The song is clearly Deuteronomistic in tone. Noth assigns verses 2, 3, and 4 to the Deuteronomist, verses which exalt God and depict YHWH as the one who weighs actions.[22] The polemic is firmly established in the imagery of the song and implicitly carries with it the simplicity of the Deuteronomist theology that certain behavior warrants blessings and certain behavior warrants curses.

This contrast between the ones God has chosen to exalt and those God has chosen to bring down continues throughout the chapter in its narrative portion that forms a dialogue with the preceding material. The insertion of poetry into a narrative calls attention to the significance of the content of the passage. Although the Hebrew Bible mixes prose and poetry, Hannah's song belongs to a category of poetry that would be classified by form as a psalm placed in a narrative context. A number of these psalms (Hannah's song included) occupy "thematically climactic and structurally crucial positions" within the narrative.[23] Hannah's song looks back on a recent victory while looking forward to the events surrounding the advent of the monarchy. At the conclusion of Hannah's song, the narrative is formed around the same Deuteronomistic themes with a series of contrasts, briefly outlined as they appear in chapter two:

Samuel in service to Eli (verse 11)
Eli's sons' sins in priestly office (12–17)
Samuel and his family (18–21)
Eli confronts his sons (22–25)
Samuel grows in stature and favor (26)
Oracle against Eli and his house (27–36)

Verse 11 begins the narrative section with a report of Samuel serving YHWH under Eli's supervision. The following six verses (12–17) detail the sins of Eli's young sons surrounding sacrifice which is in contrast to verses 18–21 which tell us of Samuel who was "in the service of the LORD," wearing a linen ephod.[24] The section makes reference to his family in the context of the annual sacrifice at which time Hannah delivers a new robe, which she makes for her son each year. We are also told that because of her offering of her son, God blesses Hannah with five additional children. In verse 22, the narrative returns to Eli and his attempt to correct his sons. He warns them of the severity of their sins around cultic activity. His words can be seen as a forewarning to the monarchy and to Israel: If a man sins against a man, the LORD may pardon him; but if a man offends against God, who can obtain pardon for him? (vs. 25). Verse 25 relates that Eli's sons disregarded his warning with a curious explanation, "for the LORD was resolved that they should die." Now the cosmic power of the God who brings down and lifts up in Hannah's song comes to mind in the reading of these words, but with it comes the question that will haunt us throughout the Deuteronomistic History. Is repentance unobtainable for certain characters in the larger narrative, because God decides not to make it available?[25] With this mention of God's intention the narrative introduces an element that is far more complex than anything we find in the song.

The contrast of young Samuel with these worthless, בני בליעל, young men is heightened with the immediate contrast of והנער, making reference to Samuel who grew "both in stature and in favor with the LORD and with the people" (vs. 26). After a passage detailing not only the fact that Eli's sons have displeased God, but that their sins are known among the people, who have made this known to Eli, we read of Samuel, who is achieving just the opposite effect among the people and with the LORD. The polemic of contrast continues, but now it is not nearly as simple or as neat as it was in the song. In this narrative is the disturbing addition that Eli's sons did not listen to him because of God's designs.

Verse 26 finds itself sandwiched within an ongoing condemnation of the house of Eli. In verses 27–36, the text continues its account of the fall of Eli's sons. A man of God delivers a word of condemnation to Eli, condemning him for "honor[ing] your sons more than me by fattening yourselves on the choicest parts of every offering of my people Israel?" (vs. 29). Here the words of the prophet recount both how God chose the tribe of Levi "to go up to my altar, to offer incense, to wear an ephod before me" (vs. 28), and that Eli's house, because of their sin, will now be brought down:

> See, a time is coming when I will cut off your strength
> and the strength of your ancestor's family, so that no
> one in your family will live to old age. (vs. 31)

In the condemnation, the polemic contrasts observed in Hannah's song resurface:

> Then in distress you will look with a greedy eye on
> all the prosperity that shall be bestowed upon Israel;
> (vs. 32 a)

> Everyone who is left in your family shall come to
> implore him [the new faithful priest] for a piece
> of silver or a loaf of bread, and shall say, Please
> put me in one of the priest's places, that I may eat
> a morsel of bread. (vs. 36)

In Hannah's song, she, the protagonist, is the lowly one who is exalted while it is her rival who is brought down. Her experience provides a lens through which we initially understand the song. The narrative provides the example of a priest who has come full circle. His story is communicated from the mouth of Hannah and is understood in dialogue with her story. The lowly was lifted up and that same one is then brought down. Thus the polemic described in the song of the low being made high is not only an external dynamic involving an insider and an outsider. It is also an internal one, carrying the possibility that one's disregard for God's laws will cause them to be brought down, just as their obedience to God allowed them to be lifted up.

The dialogue of contrasts in the song is simple in its Deuteronomistic message. If you fall into a designated category (lowly, hungry or barren) you will be lifted up. If you happen to fit into the opposite category, you will be brought down low. While the song provides an operating framework for the remaining narrative, it is the dialogue with the narrative that underscores the extent to which this framework is dynamic and complex. The narrative raises the questions of God's motives in the raising up and taking down of individuals and it raises the question of what happens to the lowly after they are elevated. Taken in isolation, the dialogue of reversals in the song is more of a diatribe than a dialogue, as it does not contain the opportunity for dialogue that is available in the narrative. Where the prose is subtle, the song conveys its message "with blunt and forceful commentary."[26] The song/prayer is not consciously directed to a readership but to YHWH, which makes the reader more of an observer than a participant.

What is described in poetic compact language takes on different form and nuances in the realm of prose. Even though as Kugel rightly points out, there is a terseness to biblical narrative that gives it the appearance of the extension of poetry, there still remains a difference between the way poetry and narrative communicate. The song of Hannah with its variety of imagery looks forward not only with imagery but also by making reference to specific events and/or characters that have nothing to do with Hannah's experience. The song begins with Hannah's situation and very quickly moves beyond it to encompass the cosmic dimension whereas the narrative remains with a specific situation, alluding to other events such as the "anointed" in verse 10. As the narrative provides the details around the simple dynamic described in the song, other questions arise; for example, what is Eli's role in his son's demise and what is God's role in the demise of the house of Eli?

That the dynamic of reversals conveyed in the poetry becomes more complex in the narrative can be seen in the introduction of perception in chapter three. As was the case in the previous chapter, the narrative uses the dynamic of contrast. Chapter two ends with the words of condemnation for the house of Eli from the mouth of the "man of God." Chapter three begins with the recurring message, "Now the boy Samuel was ministering to the LORD under Eli." Young Samuel, who is learning to hear the voice of God, is contrasted with Eli, whose behavior demonstrates his lack of ability to perceive (hear and see) God.

Chapter three makes numerous references to perception – who sees, who hears and who understands. Here is a list of the references:

3:1 The word, דבר of the LORD was "rare"
there were not many visions חזון

3:2 Eli's eyes עינו were weak so he could barely see לראות

3:3 The lamp נר of God had not yet gone out

3:4 God calls ויקרא Samuel

3:5 Samuel answers Eli, Eli sends him back to bed

3:6 God calls קרא again. Samuel goes to Eli and Eli sends him back.

3:7 Narrator tells us that Samuel did not yet know ידע the LORD and the word דבריהוה of the LORD had not been revealed יגלה to him

3:8 God calls קרא a third time and Samuel went to Eli. This time Eli understood קביד it was the LORD who was calling him

3:9 He instructs the boy on how to respond, "Speak דבר LORD for your servant is listening שמע"

3:10 God calls, ויקרא and this time Samuel gives the correct response

3:11 God delivers a message, which begins with a command about perception, "See, הנה I am about to do something דבר that will make the ears of everyone who hears שמעו it tingle ..."

3:15 Samuel is afraid to tell or make known מהגיר the vision המראה to Eli

3:16 Now it is Eli who calls ויקרא,. Samuel

3:17 Eli threatens to curse Samuel if he hides מכחד anything of God's message דבר from him (forms of נגד appear in this verse five times)

3:18 Samuel tells ויגד, or makes known to Eli, everything כל־הדברים, hiding כחד nothing from him

3:19 The LORD is with Samuel and none of his words מכל־דבריו fall to the
   ground
3:20 He is recognized/understood וידע as a prophet
3:21 The LORD continues to appear להראה at Shiloh where he reveals נגלה
   himself to Samuel by his (the Lord's) word בדבר

The chapter concludes with the obvious reversal of the regular appearance
of the LORD, which is in contrast to the rarity of this event in the beginning of
the chapter. Eli's time as priest is quickly winding down while Samuel is the
one who hears from the LORD with reliability (none of his words fall to the
ground), and at this point in the narrative he is established both as prophet
and one with priestly duties.

The references to perception offer a number of possibilities for interpretation. The end of Eli's time of service to God is marked by his inability to see.
Eli was unable to perceive that Hannah was praying when she came to the
temple and mistook her for being drunk. He wrongly chides her for being a
"worthless woman" בת־בליעל, and is unable to discipline his sons who are in
fact worthless בני בליעל. When God calls Samuel and he mistakes God's voice
for that of Eli, it is understood as he did not yet know the LORD. However, Eli
who should have been able to perceive is slow to recognize that the one calling
Samuel is God, just as he is slow to recognize Hannah's intentions and his son's
sins. Eli's difficulty with perception is of interest in light of Bakhtin's understanding that individuals in isolation have limited perception. In the case of
the call of Samuel, it is the repeated appearance of the young boy that assists
Eli in understanding that the voice he hears is that of God. Eli's lack of perception can be attributed, on the one hand, to a dimness that affects not only his
eyes but also his heart. On the other hand, Eli's difficulty in perception
supports the idea that the other sees what the individual cannot – Eli and
Samuel help each other to perceive. The narrative supports this interpretation,
for in spite of the fact that it takes him a while to understand, it is Eli who
instructs the young Samuel in how to respond to the LORD.

The message that God has for Samuel is a word of condemnation that
echoes in some regards the word of the LORD that came to Eli from the man
of God in chapter 2:27 ff. The first word of condemnation makes reference to
Eli and his line being cut off from their position of serving God but there is
also reference made to those who will remain from the line. The second word
of condemnation that comes to Samuel is much briefer and acknowledges the
first. This second word of condemnation against the house of Eli which comes

directly from God carries with it the additional message that "the iniquity of Eli's house shall not be expiated by sacrifice or offering forever" (vs.14). The second condemnation forms a dialogue of increasing doom with the first. In keeping with the polemics of the song and the narrative, Eli's demise occurs within the context of Samuel's rise; more specifically Eli assists Samuel in learning the voice of the LORD and Samuel delivers the final word of condemnation to Eli. As the narrative points out in the case of Eli, the same one who is lifted up can be brought down. Eli's example raises a question about anyone who is lifted up, namely, will they like Eli find themselves on the other end of God's cosmic work? It is noteworthy that God would choose Samuel, whom we later come to trust as one whose words come true, to deliver the final condemnation against Eli as his first prophecy.

Samuel's first prophecy serves a very interesting literary and theological function here. His words are uttered about a situation of which he most likely is not fully aware. We do not know what Samuel knew about the man of God who spoke to Eli earlier. What we do know is that his first prophetic word is not God's first word on this matter of Eli's house. Similarly, Hannah's song speaks to events far beyond the scope of her personal experience. She is, unknowingly, a prophetic voice for the entire Deuteronomistic History. The very nature of the prophetic word as shown in this section is dialogic and for that reason extends far beyond the individual who speaks it. Moreover, the speaker does not have to be aware of the power of the prophetic word in order for it to be effective. The word simply has an integrity of its own that is not separate from the speaker but goes far beyond the experience of the speaker because it is dialogic. That the word of YHWH – the word that determines the fate of individuals and nations – comes from the mouths of those considered weak in their society, women and young boys, forms its own "dialogue of contrast."

Another dialogic contrast is seen in the wordplay at the beginning and end of chapter three. When Samuel is called, the text informs us that "Samuel did not yet know, יָדַע, the Lord; the word of the Lord had not yet been revealed, יִגָּלֶה, unto him"(vs. 7). This situation has changed by the end of the chapter. Now that Samuel has been called, there is a new reality. "All Israel, from Dan to Beersheba, knew וַיֵּדַע that Samuel was a trustworthy prophet of the LORD"(vs. 20). This reversal has implications for all Israel; "The LORD continued to appear at Shiloh, for the LORD revealed himself נִגְלָה to Samuel at Shiloh with the word of the LORD" (vs. 21).[27] That the root for "reveal" גלה also means to go or take into exile is noteworthy. With the beginning of this

new period in Israel's history that will lead to the establishment of the monarchy, there is in the vocabulary the specter of the exile. Thus Samuel's new role
as prophet marks the advent of the monarchy and the conclusion of the
monarchy in exile.

The theological implications of this dialogue of contrast include the
following: first, the contrast between poetry and narrative lead us to consider
carefully how perception is affected by dialogue. The subtleties of narrative
cause us to see the poetry in a different, more nuanced way. It is the narrative
around Eli and his sons that reveals the same one who is lifted up can be
brought down. Second, in the narrative that contrasts Samuel and Eli's sons
we have the opportunity to observe how perception, the ability to hear and
understand God, works. The ability to perceive comes from God and can only
be understood as God reveals meaning. On some occasions, as is the case with
Samuel in chapter three, the understanding can be revealed through
dialogue.[28] As Eli's story indicates, one's ability to perceive can "grow dim."
One's ability to perceive is directly related to one's obedience to the deity. At
the center of the contrasts and reversals is YHWH. As Hannah's song states, "It
is the LORD."

CONCLUSION

The analysis of I Samuel chapters two and three provides a number of examples of the ways the Bible engages in dialogue. The dialogical nature of the text
makes it impossible for a reader to discern the many levels of theological
meaning if they read certain aspects of the text to the exclusion of others.
Effective biblical interpretation goes against the primordial event of division
of language. The variations in voice and perspective exist not to compete but
to converse in their movement towards meaning. It is through listening for the
conversation that takes place across genre, voice and time that we begin to see
beyond that which our individual perspective affords us.

What is the purpose of the dialogue? Stephen Prickett's discussion of
metaphor is helpful in describing what the Bible achieves in its dialogism. He
defines metaphor as the uniting of two separate concepts. As they are brought
together, they are both changed. For example, in the children's tune, "row, row,
row your boat," the final line is, "life is but a dream." In reality, life is not a
dream and a dream isn't real life, but the metaphor by uniting the terms
creates a new reality that exists only within the confines of the metaphor.[29] The
dynamic of metaphor is analogous to the dialogue that occurs within a text or

between texts. Metaphor is a *dialogue* between two separate realities that creates a new reality, or meaning. Similarly, the Bible unites, on one level, a variety of human perspectives over time. On another level, the Bible brings together the divine with the ways of humanity. These two realms are in many senses separate; however in the metaphorical language of the text, the two are united and thereby changed. It is for this reason that the Bible must use the language of metaphor – its language betrays what it is doing, namely bringing together at least two different realities. Metaphor interacts with the dialogic nature of the text. The dialogue of the Bible continues beyond any given metaphor, or moment. Thus biblical narrative connects one moment with other events across time and thereby moves the reader through time. In addition to the dialogue of uniting the divine with the human, there is an additional dynamic that occurs when the reader engages the text. When the reader comes to the Bible, she is brought together with this text and in this interaction between the reader and the text, two separate entities operate dialogically, that by definition is transformative for the reader. This is the goal of biblical narrative, to transform the reader. However, that transformation can only occur if the reader is willing to enter into dialogue with the text, and in some instances other readers.

To what extent does the metaphorical activity that we see in the Bible inform our current situation apart from the way we read the text? I will offer two suggestions. First, the events of September 11 are a violent metaphor. One in which a number of different cultural and religious perspectives collided. If the goal of metaphor is to bring two different entities together for the transformation of both, we should be thoughtful and intentional about our response. Many Americans are asking questions about Islam and the Muslim World and thinking about the world beyond our borders and interests for the first time. This dialogue should not be taken on simply to achieve our own ends, but to broaden our perspective. The United States has been engaged in a dialogue that began long before September 11 and we now have an opportunity to reflect upon our history of interactions with the rest of the world. We should also consider what it means to be good stewards of the many resources and privileges with which we have been blessed.

The second suggestion is for those of us who comprise the leadership of the Christian tradition. The story of I Samuel makes clear that a leader's worth is directly connected to one's ability to hear God's voice. Eli took his role for granted and had difficulty hearing from God. The story in I Samuel 2 and 3 reminds us that the prophetic voice is not in the expected places. God spoke through the once barren Hannah and the boy Samuel. Consequently, Eli heard from God when he took seriously what his society deemed "the least of these." Not only does the prophetic voice come from unexpected places, but as was the case with Eli in I Samuel, it may not be what we want to hear. The dynamic in this narrative is clear – those who God has elevated run the risk of suffering a reversal. This seems to happen to those who lose the ability to find God's message as it is conveyed from unexpected sources.

NOTES

1. Here and throughout the chapter I use the New Revised Standard Version of the Bible.
2. Michel Fishbane, *Biblical Text and Texture* (Oxford, England: Oneworld Publications, 1998), 36.
3. M. M. Bakhtin, *Art and Answerability: Early Philosophical Essays by M.M. Bakhtin*, ed. Michael Holquist and Vadim Liapunov, trans. Vadim Liapunov (Austin: University of Texas Press, 1990), 22–23.
4. Carol Newsom, "Bakhtin, the Bible and Dialogic Truth," *Journal of Religion*, 76, 1996: 291.
5. Newsom's assessment of theologians being driven by a monologic sense of truth is helpful, but her distinction between biblical scholars and theologians leaves the impression that biblical scholars are free from this need to work towards unity. This is clearly not the case. Much of biblical scholarship, both diachronic and literary is arguably driven by a sense of monologic meaning.
6. Newsom, "Bakhtin, the Bible and Dialogic Truth," 292.
7. Ibid., 301.
8. Also referred to as a prayer or psalm.
9. In the Masoretic text, the song is set in the context of Hannah's worship following her dedication of Samuel. The text reads, וישתחו שם ליהוה ותתפלל חנה ותאמר. The Vatican Codex of the Septuagint omits all the intervening material except, "and she said," making the psalms a continuation of the dedicatory speech. A fragment from Samuel from Qumran (4QSam a), sets the song after Hannah's worship, but the setting is more ambiguous than in the MT. The text reads, [... ותעזב ע הו שם ותשתחו ליהוה ...] James Watts, *Psalms and Story: Inset Poetry in Hebrew Narrative* (Sheffield: Sheffield Academic Press, 1992), 20–21.
10. Robert Polzin, *Samuel and the Deuteronomist* (Bloomington and Indianapolis: Indiana University Press, 1989), 36–39.
11. Peter Miscall, *I Samuel, A Literary Reading* (Bloomington and Indianapolis: Indiana University Press, 1986), 15.
12. James Watts, *Psalm and Story: Inset Hymns in Hebrew Narrative* (Sheffield, England: JSOT Press, 1992), 28.

13. P. Kyle McCarter, *I Samuel*, The Anchor Bible Series, vol. 8 (New York: Doubleday, 1980), 71.
14. Samuel R. Driver, *Notes on the Hebrew Text of the Books of Samuel* (Oxford: Clarendon Press, 1913), 23.
15. McCarter, *I Samuel*, 71.
16. James Watts points out that it is "traditional and appropriate … for an Israelite woman to be singing … a victory song like I Samuel 2.1–10." Looking to Miriam's song in Exodus 15 and Deborah's song in Judges 5 he concludes, "Hannah's jubilation finds voice in a song typical of Israelite women." *Psalm and Story*, 30.
17. Polzin, *Samuel and the Deuteronomist*, 31–33.
18. Watts, *Psalm and Story*, 24.
19. Polzin, *Samuel and the Deuteronomist*, 31.
20. I Samuel 2:1–10 is designated a victory song in the form of a hymn while II Samuel 22 is classified as an individual (royal) thanksgiving (Watts, 26).
21. McCarter, *I Samuel*, 74.
22. Martin Noth, *The Deuteronomistic History* (Sheffield, England: JSOT Press, 1984), 91.
23. James Watts, *Psalm and Story*, 11.
24. The reference to the linen ephod may be an intentional connection to David in II Samuel 6:14.
25. This is the dynamic in the text that David Gunn draws on to make his argument in *The Fate of King Saul* (Sheffield: JSOT Press, 1980).
26. James Watts, *Psalm and Story*, 32.
27. Uriel Simon, *Reading Prophetic Narrative* (Bloomington and Indianapolis: Indiana University Press, 1997), 72.
28. This is also the case in the exchange between Eli and Hannah in I Samuel 1 and in the exchange between Saul, Samuel, and the Witch of Endor in I Samuel 28.
29. Stephen Prickett, *Words and the Word* (Cambridge: Cambridge University Press, 1986), 222.

10

9.11: CONTRASTING REACTIONS AND THE CHALLENGE OF DIALOGUE

Ian Markham

The task of this chapter is to start reflecting theologically on the significance of the terrorism that was perpetrated on America on September 11, 2001. It is no more than a "start" because we do not know how events will develop. But it is a "start" made in the conviction that some theological (and the rest of the book is embarking on the same task in respect to other forms, namely social, political) reflection is needed sooner rather than later. All the contributors to this book are persuaded that unreflective action could be, literally, catastrophic for the world. Dialogue has been chosen because the event of September 11 has shown both the difficulty of dialogue (in that different faith traditions interpret the event differently) and at the same time the manifest need for dialogue.

Dialogue has many goals. At its simplest it is an alternative to violence or force – a way of enabling the potential parties to handle their differences that does not lead to bloodshed or death. However, for my purposes, I am assuming a more exalted goal, namely that the participants arrive at a clearer understanding of the nature of the world – in all its social, political, and cultural complexity – and the relationship of God to that world.[1] (In many respects it is close to the view of dialogue assumed by Judy Fentress-Williams in her chapter on the Bible and Dialogue.) Dialogue is Socratic in purpose, not in the sense that the truth is a rediscovery of what is already there, but that the goal of dialogue is a better understanding of the truth. Or as David Lochhead puts it: "The Platonic legacy points us to the possibility that dialogue may be a condition of truth, a way of knowing truth that is not possessed by any one of the dialogical partners alone."[2] This goal of dialogue moves beyond the goal of simply listening and understanding the other.[3] This is clearly important but very limited. The quest for the truth is part of the privilege of being human. And given that many of the hostilities between communities and cultures are grounded in a particular world perspective the goal of clarifying (or, at least, partially illuminating) "what happened" or "what is the case" is important. Therefore the task of ascertaining "what exactly happened on September 11" goes to the heart of the dialogical enterprise.

This chapter divides into three sections. The first explores the relationship between events such as that of September 11 and theological reflection. It attempts to answer the question: what has theology got to do with this tragedy? The second section looks at four different vantage points of the September 11 event. The purpose of this section is to illustrate the differing set of assumptions underpinning these interpretations. The third section offers an analysis of these four interpretations and attempts to identify precisely why dialogue is such a challenge.

"EVENTS" AND THEOLOGY

It is proper that Theology has an interest in everything that happens. The God we worship sustains everything that is; therefore there is, ultimately, a theological interpretation of everything that happens in life. Certain occasions in history, however, are bound to be more significant than others. These historically significant occasions I am calling "events".[4] The relationship between events and theology is a complex one. By events, I mean here moments of catastrophic change for a nation – for example wars, assassinations, and natural disasters. By theology, I mean the task of interpreting the event from within a worldview (or, as we shall see later, a better term may be "world perspective") that takes the transcendent seriously. The complexity of the relation between the two arises because it is difficult to see whether the event has any long-term significance. Apart from the level of perhaps theodicy or the related attempt to explain the event from the vantage point of providence, most happenings in this rapidly changing world prove to be fairly ephemeral even if they seem shattering at the time. The issue, then, is when does an event prove significant to shape a (or even the) theological conversation?

Within the history of Christian theology, certain events have proved *pivotal* in the light of their effects. The First World War is recognized as a key event in the history of Christian theology. Karl Barth famously described the day that he saw his teachers of theology sign a declaration supporting the war aims of the Kaiser as a black day indeed for theology.[5] And since then, many historians have insisted that the nineteenth-century liberal theology of Harnack et al died in the trenches of the Somme. The plausibility for this claim arises from the surrounding narrative and subsequent effects: at the end of the nineteenth century many Europeans believed in "progress" and were confident about the basic goodness of people. For the continent to then embark on a vicious and, in many respects, futile war completly undermined the European self-perception, producing either a rejection of religion or a reaction into the kind of assertion of divine priority found in the teaching of Karl Barth. For Judaism, the Holocaust is an equally pivotal event. For example, Richard Rubinstein, the Jewish scholar, has argued that Holocaust was a defining moment for Judaism: it was the moment when the providential God of the Hebrew Bible became implausible and Judaism had to recognize that only the Jewish people themselves can ensure their own survival.[6]

Other events prove more *tangential*. Leaving aside its political effects, the assassination of Martin Luther King had an impact on the emergence of a more radical black theology, but was not itself defining. A radical black theology predated this moment: the combination of slavery and a continuing civil rights battle are sufficient conditions to create a theological radicalizing of the African American community. On the other hand, the assassination of a great and "moderate" visionary did provide an impetus for the writing of James Cone.

Then there are some events that appear significant at the time, but ultimately prove *ephemeral*. Much was written and felt at the time of the tragic death of Diana, Princess of Wales, of the iconic significance of her death and the evident need for religious symbolism to help people interpret that life. It might yet be too soon to say, but it seems that her death provoked a deeply profound reaction that did not give rise to a more substantial theological mood. It was a matter of deeply felt emotion which lacked any theological grappling point in the dominant British culture, so deeply secularized in its thought-forms and assumptions.

Now whether the event of September 11, 2001 proves *pivotal, tangential,* or ultimately *ephemeral* for theological reflection in the religious traditions of Islam, Christianity, and Judaism, whether in the U.S. or elsewhere, is at present difficult to determine. Only time will tell. In my judgment, it is likely that this event will prove significant and will be at least a "tangential" influence on certain theological developments. Perhaps it might even be pivotal. For this to happen a plausible narrative that captures a before and after – comparable in form to Karl Barth's interpretation of the First World War – will need to emerge. And there is a narrative that does suggest itself; one that, ironically, is much like Barth's interpretation. It is this: September 11 demonstrated the illusion of the view that secular, liberal democracy is the major, dominant ideology in the world. Prior to September 11, there was a sense that, given that the 1989 Eastern European Revolution had removed the last main competitor to liberal market-orientated democracy, there are no ideological competitors to the social organization and structure exemplified or typified by the United States. Fukuyama's talk of the "end of history" had some plausibility.[7] And Richard John Neuhaus gave eloquent expression to this sense in his book *Doing Well Doing Good*.[8] But after September 11, we are reminded that the Islamic world is not persuaded of the appropriateness of secular, liberal democracy as purveyed in the United States. Within our global village, "revivalist" forms of Islam are increasingly making their presence felt. These revivalist forms of Islam are competition ready and willing to flex its not inconsiderable ideological and military power. An antecedent of this action was the *fatwa* issued by the then Iranian ruler Ayatollah Khomeini on the novel by Salman Rushdie: it was an overt challenge to the Western presumption in favor of the freedom of expression. With September 11, the Islamic challenge was brought right to the heart of American civil, political, and economic life.

Rightly or wrongly (and probably it is more wrong than right), this event creates a new global dynamic; it is an Islamic revivalism against an ostensibly impregnable global capitalism. Theology is going to be shaped by this event for two reasons: first, it is a religious challenge to a secular economic world perspective; but second, the secular economic world perspective emerged from a Christian culture. Although capitalism is not Christianity, we have an Islamic challenge to both Christianity and capitalism. Theology is a key discourse in both understanding the challenge and helping to construct a response to it. It is the constructive response to the challenge that makes dialogue so essential. This will now become the focus of the chapter.

Primarily the term dialogue has a set of verbal and prepositional associations. Dialogue, for obvious reasons – because it is what the word means, creates an image of people "talking" with each other. Although dialogue on this level is vitally important, it obscures a key difficulty. Parties to such a dialogue always bring an existing "world perspective", made up of the social, cultural, economic, gender, and ethnic assumptions that make people think what they do. Such half-conscious life underpins dialogue. It is made up of the axioms, assumptions, and cultural history that form the given framework of our conscious analysis of the world. The real disagreements between communities are grounded in this realm. The problem with "dialogue" is that it rarely reaches this set of background beliefs or seeks to bring them to awareness.

To illustrate how important these conflicting world perspectives can be I propose now to analyze four contrasting interpretations to the World Trade Center attacks. The first is the interpretation underpinning the speech of President Bush to the Joint Session of Congress on September 20, 2001. This I shall suggest is the "mainstream U.S. interpretation". The second is a pro-Israel, Jewish interpretation. The third is a pro-Arab, Palestinian interpretation. These three have religious aspects, but are also broadly cultural. The fourth is an overtly religious interpretation, the position of Jerry Falwell, which we may see as illustrative of Christian fundamentalism.

For the purposes of the exercise I do not intend to pass any judgments on these different positions. My task is descriptive, although, as with all description, aspects of my own world perspective are bound to show through!

POSITION ONE: THE MAINSTREAM U.S. INTERPRETATION

In his speech to the Joint Session of Congress, President Bush said the following: "Americans are asking, why do they hate us? They hate what we see right here in this chamber – a democratically elected government. Their leaders are self-appointed. They hate our freedoms – our freedom of religion, our freedom of speech, our freedom to vote and assemble and disagree with each other. They want to overthrow existing governments in many Muslim countries . . . They want to drive Christians and Jews out of vast regions of Asia and Africa . . . These terrorists kill not merely to end lives, but to disrupt and end a way of life. With every atrocity, they hope that America grows fearful, retreating from the world and forsaking our friends. They stand against us, because we stand in their way. We are not deceived by their pretenses to piety. We have seen their kind before. They are the heirs of all the murderous ideologies of the twentieth century."[9]

For Bush, and I would suggest, most Americans, it is a puzzling question "why do they hate us?" The main answer given and one presented very effectively in the special edition of the *West Wing*, is that the United States is committed to pluralism in a way that alternative societies are not. There is in the United States freedom to pursue different visions of the Common Good; there is no obligation to affirm simply one vision of the Common Good. This pluralism, enshrined in the Constitution by the separation of Church and State, conflicts with any strong ideology, whether religious or not, that wants one view of the Common Good to triumph.

Underlying this self-perception is a broader narrative that has been analyzed in the literature at considerable length and seems to involve the following components. First, as Robert Bellah pointed out in his analysis of civil religion in the United States, there is a narrative of an immigrant people finding a promised land and creating the most remarkable nation on earth. Coupled with this, there is the remarkable Constitution, the commitment to certain fundamental freedoms, enshrined in law and protected by the separation of powers. "Progress", "freedom", and "advanced" are all key words in the U.S. self-perception. Second, the United States has intervened decisively in two world wars, thereby preventing Europe from falling under totalitarian regimes. President Bush alludes explicitly to the fact that Americans have fought and defeated totalitarian ideologies before, and therefore Islamic revivalist ideologies will be fought and defeated as well. Third, the United States has a fundamental vocation to use its power and wealth as an agent for good (as defined in terms of values already mentioned) in the world. After the Second World War, the Marshall Plan enabled Europe to rebuild itself, making it a prosperous and successful part of the world. And even when it comes to Afghanistan, the President notes that "after all, we are currently its largest source of humanitarian aid."[10]

Of course, there is an awareness that there is a darker side to U.S. history. But even here, these aspects of the American past are accommodated in terms of the society's own growing pains and increasing comprehensiveness. So the Founding Fathers did not appreciate the importance of accepting the African American as an equal partner in the American story, but President Lincoln (with his Gettysburg Address) and Martin Luther King (with his campaign for civil rights) have gone a considerable distance in rectifying that error. Or disasters in Vietnam (or an ambivalent foreign policy in the Middle East) are often interpreted as understandable errors: on Vietnam the understandable fear was the expansion of Communism, which drove the United States to invest many thousands of lives in fighting.

Hatred of the United States is therefore a hatred of goodness. Hence the strong language in his speech that "Every nation, in every region, now has a decision to make. Either you are with us, or you are with the terrorists."[11] We are in the midst of a battle against good and evil.

POSITION TWO: THE PRO-ISRAEL, JEWISH POSITION

Anti-semitism is a continuing serious difficulty, especially for any Jewish person. Christian anti-semitism has taken a variety of forms. From Augustine's "Jewish people bear the mark of Cain" to the charge of deicide attached to the cruxifixion of Jesus, displacement and persecution have been features of Jewish life for centuries.[12] Naturally the most dramatic illustration of this persecution was the Holocaust. The slaughter of six million men, women, and children between the years 1939 and 1944 at the heart of European Christendom has inevitably dominated the Jewish self-perception. Hitler's project of attempting to destroy Judaism nearly succeeded. The total number of Jews today runs to a mere 14,890,000 – just 0.3 percent of the world's population.[13]

One hope that lay behind Zionism was that the persecution would diminish. European Jews learnt the hard way that hundreds of years of settlement in a country did not mean that they were accepted. Herzl hoped that with a land of their own and the related symbols of national identity, the Jewish people would be just one more nation of many nations in this world.[14]

We all know now that the State of Israel has not achieved this. Indeed it has probably done the opposite. The State created a new form of anti-semitism, namely an Islamic form. It is generally agreed by historians of religion that relations between Islam and Judaism have been much more cordial than relations between Christianity and Judaism. The prophet Muhammad clearly entrenched respect for the "People of the Book", and Jews generally flourished (certainly survived) under Islamic rule. Since the emergence of the State of Israel, however, and especially since 1967, relations between Jews and Muslims have been under considerable strain.

From the Jewish perspective, the extent of the antagonism is puzzling. Jewish commentators make much of the fact that once the State of Israel was established in 1948, it has been the Arab states in the region that have attempted to "drive the Jewish people into the sea." Indeed the four wars in the region since the founding of Israel are all seen to have been initiated by the Arab neighbors. Security is the major issue in Israeli politics. From a Jewish perception there is ample evidence that the world cannot be trusted: the responsibility of the Jewish state is to protect itself as the condition of survival.

The "law of return" (i.e. the legal entitlement of all Jews that they can settle in Israel) means that there is at least one safe place for the Jew in this turbulent world. If everywhere else in the world becomes unsafe for the Jew, then at least there is a homeland. From this perspective, then, the survival of a people depends on the survival of the State of Israel.

For a Jew, the anti-semitism of the Christian and Islamic world is the challenge. And, from this perspective, the events of September 11 illustrate decisively the problem of Islamic antagonism. Islam has given birth to highly distinctive forms of terrorism. With the possible exception of Japanese kamikaze pilots, a terrorist being willing to maximize the impact by committing suicide along with his victims places him (almost always – rarely a 'her') in a unique position.

Three themes have dominated the Jewish interpretation of events. The first is to affirm the American assertion that all forms of terrorism are intolerable. So Heskel M. Haddad, President of the World Organization for Jews from Arab Countries, wrote in the *New York Times* that:

> Our goal should not be to eliminate Osama bin Laden but rather to eliminate all terrorism. We should focus on all countries that advocate terrorism or harbor and support terrorists . . . We should learn to emulate Israel and its fight with terrorists and its measures to counter hijacking and terrorism, and not ally ourselves with Yasir Arafat or Syria or Iran, no matter how tempting their appeal may be.[15]

This is interesting: it destroys the "concept" of freedom fighter, which proved so significant in South Africa. The argument here is this: terrorism targets the innocent and uses deeply destructive methods of furthering the cause. Therefore, however just the cause, terrorism is an illegitimate means of advancing it. The Israeli Prime Minister Ariel Sharon made this argument explicitly when he said: "Acts of terror against Israeli citizens are no different from bin Laden's terror against American citizens. Terror is terror and murder is murder. There is no forgiveness for terror and no compromise with terror."[16] Sharon's point therefore flows into the second theme, which is to link the "terrorism" of Bin Laden with the opponents of Israel. Sharon did, initially, describe Arafat as Israel's Bin Laden, even if, more recently, he made a strong distinction between the legitimate aspiration of the Palestinians and terrorism. The point is that from a Jewish perspective a connection does seem legitimate. This is for several reasons. There is the similarity between events in Israel and in the United States, or, as Joseph Alpher puts it: "Despite the vast difference of scale, the similarity between the suicide attacks on the World Trade Center and on Tel Aviv's Dolphinarium or Jerusalem's Sbarro restaurant will be self-evident to most Americans."[17] In addition, it is considered illegitimate to blame Israel for the breakdown in the peace process, partly because suicide bombings were a feature of Israeli life even when the process was flourishing and partly because there is a deeper "civilizational clash between militant Islam and the Western democracies."[18]

Underpinning this observation is the suggestion that at root the key difference here is a commitment to pluralism at least in the sense of the toleration of diverse political parties and freedom of the press etc. The Israeli State and the United States are both committed to pluralism: the problem with the terrorists responsible for the destruction of the World Trade Center is that they are not. From a Jewish perspective, there is a feeling that this difficulty with pluralism extends to all forms of Arab nationalism.

The third theme is the deeply ironic sense that the attack on America is justifying continuing antagonism towards Israel that has anti-semitic overtones. Jonathan Rosen draws parallels between this moment and Hitler's Germany; he writes:

> I am not being chased down alleyways and called a Christ killer ... But in recent weeks I have been reminded, in ways too plentiful to ignore, about the role Jews play in the fantasy life of the world. Jews were not the cause of World War II, but they were at the metaphysical center of that conflict nonetheless, since the Holocaust was part of Hitler's agenda and key motivation of his campaign. Jews are not the cause of World War III, if that's what we are facing, but they have been placed at the center of it in mysterious and disturbing ways.[19]

Rosen believes that the preposterous claim that "American support for five million Jews in Israel is to blame for September 11" is not only empirically false (plenty of Islamic militants were plotting against America when the peace process was at its height) but illustrates how European anti-semitism continues to infect reporting and analysis of global affairs. Even "the Mideast crisis needs to be solved" for Rosen carries sinister overtones; he writes:

> [S]ince most of the players in the Middle East do not accept the existence of Israel, since "solving the Mideast crisis" would for them entail a modern version of Hitler's final solution, the phrase takes on weird and even sinister overtones when it is blandly employed by well-intentioned governments calling for a speedy solution. And this Orwellian transfor-

mation of language is one of the most exasperating and disorienting aspects of the campaign against Israel. It has turned the word "peace" into a euphemism for war.[20]

The point is simple: it takes an anti-semitic mind to blame September 11 "on the Jews". The truth is that there is a dangerous form of Islamic revivalism that needs to be confronted. In this both Israel and America can and should stand together.

POSITION THREE: THE PRO-ARAB, PALESTINIAN POSITION

Given the thousands of innocent victims, there are very few commentators who are suggesting that the Americans "deserved" the terrorism. Bin Laden is obviously the exception: and it is possible to draw attention to the nature of the targets – the Pentagon as a symbol of U.S. military power and the World Trade Center as a symbol of U.S. capitalism – and suggest it was appropriate to attack these two highly destructive agencies. However, the more widespread interpretation in the Arab world stresses that the environment that created the terrorism is one that the United States must accept some responsibility for.

This is undoubtedly the line taken by many Arab states; however, in addition, we find examples of it amongst the European powers. Even the British Foreign Secretary, Jack Straw, found himself provoking the anger of the Israeli government, when he told the Iranian press: "I understand that one of the factors which helps breed terrorism is the anger which many people in the region feel at events over the years in Palestine."[21] And in his subsequent statement, clarifying his position to the Israeli government, Straw stated: "There is never any excuse for terrorism. At the same time, there is an obvious need to understand the environment in which terrorism breeds. That is why the whole of the international community is so concerned to see a lasting peace in the Middle East."[22]

The important element in the Arab anger with the West is the seeming indifference the West shows over the Palestinian refugees. This problem has its roots in the creation of the State of Israel in 1948. At its inception, some 700,000 Palestinians were displaced.[23] As the Yom Kippur war broke out in 1967, the problem was further exacerbated: some 300,000 people were moved from the West Bank and Gaza Strip (some of these were moving for the second time). In June 1995, there were approximately 991,577 people in camps, with a further 2,181,064 registered refugees not in camps, many living in Jordan.

It is impossible to calculate the extent of the human misery these figures represent. There are now three generations of refugee families in these camps. And seven years of peace negotiations, since the Oslo Accords in 1993, have not made a material difference to these families: instead conditions have deteriorated. There has been no full surrender of land occupied by Israel in 1967, the control of clean water remains problematic, and Jewish settlements have expanded. In addition every time there is a security alert in Israel, the Israelis restrict the movement of Palestinians between the "islands" that are ostensibly controlled by the Palestinian National Authority.

Underpinning this vast human tragedy (that statistically remains constant), there is, of course, a broader narrative. Ninety percent of Palestinians are Sunni Muslims, the other 10 percent are Christian. From an Arab, Islamic perspective, in 1918 there was a Jewish population of 2 percent, then with the urging of the British the figure grew to 5.5 percent in 1935, and 6 percent in 1947. So from this vantage point, the United Nations Partition plan was manifestly unjust; it gave 52 percent of the land to create a Jewish state and the rest would be an Arab state.

In view of this it is not surprising that the creation of Israel provoked the subsequent wars, including the first one in 1948. Each time Israel occupied more territory (1956, 1967, 1973). Israel and its American ally ignored the repeated calls of the United Nation in Resolution 242 that Israeli armed forces should withdraw from "territories of recent conflict."

Now given this background, the growing sense of despair needs to be confronted. On a variety of levels there are difficulties: politically, there is no progress; as a result, economically, there is increasing poverty; and therefore, culturally there is growing hostility to the perceived causes of their predicament. Terrorist groups are able to grow when all alternative political options seem to be unavailable.

Three other causes of resentment towards the United States need to be noted. The first is global capitalism, which is seen as impoverishing poorer Islamic states. The second is the continued sanctions and bombing of Iraq. And the third is the presence of U.S. troops on Saudi soil. On the first, there is a cultural war between American multinationals and indigenous cultures. The combination of American English as the global language, the arrival of fast food, and the celebration of a pluralism that seems to extend too far (into advocating alternative lifestyles) create a challenge to any people attempting to retain their own cultural identity. Add to this the difficulty that the cultural oppressors have very little sensitivity to the problems they are creating, then the resentment can be significant. On the issue of Iraq, there is the suffering of a people coupled with the illegitimate goal that the only acceptable way forward, so it seems to the Allies, is for Saddam Hussein to lose power. The harshness with which Iraq is treated is in marked contrast to the generosity and support that Israel receives. The third is the hardest for the Western mindset to understand. In much the same way as the West misjudged the impact of the publishing of a novel that had a distinctively ambiguous portrayal of the prophet and his wives, so the West finds it difficult to appreciate that there are limits to acceptable action even when protecting Western oil interests in Kuwait. Mecca and Medina are sacred places: these places are located in Saudi Arabia; therefore it is wrong for that country to be violated.

POSITION FOUR: CHRISTIAN FUNDAMENTALISM

The final position I want to present is that of Pat Robertson and Jerry Falwell, in effect the Christian Fundamentalist interpretation of events. Unlike the other three, where the focus is cultural, though, especially in cases two and three, with strong religious aspects, this is, ostensibly, a purely religious interpretation of the event. Pat Robertson and Jerry Falwell are both major figures on the so-called Fundamentalist right in American religious and political circles. Although the hostile press coverage provoked an apology from Falwell, the sentiments expressed are still worth examining. For my purposes they serve as an important reminder of two truths: first, Christianity traditionally has offered some sort of explanation of events in terms of the providence of God, which is the framework for Falwell's comments; second, it is worth remembering that interfaith dialogue in all traditions needs to deal with their most conservative members. After all, conservative adherents make up the majority of believers and also pose the problem for co-existence, toleration, and dialogue.

The comments were made on a television program called "The 700 Club" and broadcast two days after the terrorism, on 13 September. Pat Robertson was the interviewer. There are two interesting aspects to the interview. The first was that Falwell identified the suffering of America with the suffering of Israel. So Falwell starts by drawing an analogy between Hitler and the Islamic fundamentalists:

> December 7, 1941, when we entered the war against Japan, Germany, Italy. Hitler's goal was to destroy the Jews among other things, and

conquer the world. And these Islamic fundamentalists, these radical terrorists, these Middle Eastern monsters are committed to destroying the Jewish nation, driving her into the Mediterranean, conquering the world. And we are the great Satan. We are the ultimate goal. I talked this morning with Tom Rose publisher of the *Jerusalem Post*, an orthodox Jew, and he said, "Now America knows in a horrible way what Israel's been facing for 53 years at the hands of Arafat and other terrorists and radicals and barbarians."

Falwell's interpretation of these events overlaps with the second of my four positions. The motives here are primarily theological and well documented. Despite the purely modern political context of their comments, the Jewish nation has an important role in the eschatological narrative of much of the American evangelicalism. In particular, the numerous promises made to the people of Israel in the Hebrew Bible are believed still to be valid, in addition to seeing "true Christians" as heirs of God's biblical promises. Hence, one component to Falwell's interpretation of events is the affirmation of many of the arguments that shape the Jewish response to the event.

The second element is the "blame" placed for the terrorism on certain liberalizing tendencies in American life. There is an unspoken question underpinning the narrative, which is this: why did God permit the tragedy to inflict America? This question about God's purposes is an entirely proper theological question. It is a question that emerges from the eighth century BCE prophets of ancient Israel. As the Babylonians swept in to take the Jewish people into exile in the sixth century BCE, so the prophets had provided an interpretation of why exactly God permitted this suffering and humiliation. The explanation provided tended to focus on the failure of the Jewish people to observe the requirements of the Torah. It is a comparable explanation that Falwell provides for the terrorism of September 11. Naturally, this does not mean that "Islamic fundamentalists" are not responsible nor that they are not "wicked", but it provides an explanation as to why God permitted the tragedy. Falwell's explanation is to identify the "sins" of modern America. The exchange with Robertson runs as follows:

> *Falwell:* [W]hat we saw on Tuesday, as terrible as it is, could be minuscule if, in fact . . . God continues to lift the curtain and allow the enemies of America to give us probably what we deserve.
> *Robertson:* Jerry, that's my feeling . . .

Falwell: The ACLU's got to take a lot of blame for this.

Robertson: Well, yes.

Falwell: And I know that I'll hear from them for this. But, throwing God out successfully with the help of the federal court system, throwing God out of the public square, out of the schools. The abortionists have got to bear some burden for this because God will not be mocked. And when we destroy 40 million little innocent babies, we make God mad. I really believe that the pagans, and the abortionists, and the feminists, and the gays and the lesbians who are actively trying to make that an alternative lifestyle, the ACLU, People For the American Way, all of them who have tried to secularize America. I point the finger in their face and say "you helped this happen".

Robertson: Well, I totally concur, and the problem is we have adopted that agenda at the highest levels of our government.

The task of listing the sins of a nation is obviously tricky. For Falwell, the sins are those performed by the secularists, abortionists, pagans, liberals, and homosexuals. For those of a more left-leaning, Democrat persuasion, the proponents of sin might be big business or those who damage the environment. The point is that for many religious people in the world: God allowed this to happen to America. For Falwell, the cause is the failure of the American people to recognize God in the public realm and to permit legislation that leads to the slaughter of the unborn. For Muslims, perhaps with the sympathies outlined in position three, God permitted this to happen as a judgment for the sins of U.S. foreign policy.

A sense of providence is at the heart of all traditional forms of religions.[24] The vast majority of believers in all the major religious traditions have this sense: Falwell and Robertson articulated it from one particular perspective. The question underpinning their analysis is entirely appropriate: why did God allow the terrorism to occur?

ANALYSIS OF THE FOUR DISCOURSES

The word "dialogue" has a strong verbal and propositional emphasis. A dialogue occurs when people converse. The point of our present exercise is to demonstrate that the verbal exchanges are in fact the least interesting aspect of a meeting of two world perspectives. If representatives of these four traditions were placed in a room, then the verbal exchanges would hide much more than they would reveal. For underpinning each sentence is a cultural narrative, a total worldview, an economic vantage point, as well as the gender agenda. When a Jewish person refers to "security", it needs to be interpreted in terms of the recent genocide attempt on all Jewish people; when an evangelical attacks "abortionists", this needs to be interpreted in terms of an evangelical interpretation of the moral traditions derived from Scripture. Failure to uncover these basic points of view means that communication does not occur; the difficulty involved in making such links brings out the impossibility of such dialogue.

Let us explicate further the complexity of genuine communication. First, we have the linguistic differences; second, the cultural and historical narrative; third, the world perspective and especially the internal explanations offered for disagreement; and fourth, gender and economic aspects.

On the first, the significance of the language barrier is easily overlooked for those of us who speak English. It is a key theme in Alasdair MacIntyre's critique of liberal modernity that we imagine it is so easy to communicate in the international language of English. This illusion is one of the most fundamental errors of modernity.[25] MacIntyre emphasizes the considerable (and sometimes insurmountable) difficulties involved in translation. For him, there simply are numerous languages, truly distinct, not just in obvious ways but in the mental assumptions and patterns which they embody. Even a given nation has different languages in use for different communities, and the English of the sixteenth century was not the same as that of today, even for the English themselves. Hence, translation of a particular text will not include all the explanatory beliefs that make the text fully intelligible. This means that when two traditions meet there will be certain concepts that are untranslatable. Understanding will only come through learning the dialogue partner's tongue as a second first language (becoming bilingual so that the second language is known as intimately as the first). A person thus equipped will understand the explanatory purpose of the language from within.[26]

Although it is true that a translated text can provide a partial understanding of the text to a person in another language tradition, MacIntyre is right to stress the connection between language and ways of thinking and therefore the need to learn the other's language as well as one knows one's own.

The language difference is the first most visible level that needs to be tackled. The second is that of cultural and historical narrative. We arrive at all conversations with a sense of location determined by a past that is largely given – both national or cultural and personal. In much the same way that no one "opts" into the language that is learnt from birth, so one does not opt into the parental culture that surrounds us. This parental culture provides the "assumptions" that become part of our framework for thinking about the world. Our conscious life is much less important than the assumptions underpinning that life, and they will be formed and re-formed through the events and circumstances that affect us. So, for example, the American commitment to the "rights of the individual" is now so entrenched in American culture that it is simply assumed to be "true"; for a Hindu such assumptions are not only questionable but also barely understandable.[27]

The cultural and historical narrative is an enormous area. Extended discussion of it is impossible. Suffice to note, it is difficult to assess but obviously important to be aware of the following: the island of England, Scotland, and Wales has not (so the English "myth" goes) been successfully invaded since 1066, yet it took resolute defense of that island during the blitz in the 1940s for survival to succeed.[28] This fact is not part of the conscious life of an English person, but perhaps it partly explains the willingness of the British to support American action in the current emergency. Britain's imperial past, with the mythology of the white man's burden, no doubt also contributes to a certain fellow feeling. The Jewish person's awareness of the holocaust, or the Palestinian awareness of the displacement and refugee status of an entire people, or the Afghanistan experience of endless internal strife and continuing poverty are all shaping the lives of people living now. We are in a very real sense defined by our past, even if a certain kind and level of education may help us in part to transcend it.

After language and our historical-cultural location, we arrive at our world perspective. A world perspective is not simply the conscious belief system that shapes a person's self-understanding, but the whole dynamic of being human in a particular time and place, which includes the factors already identified (language and historical-cultural location) as well as the economic, gender, and sexuality factors. In its conscious aspect, we find a world perspective has two explanatory functions.[29] The first concerns the positive features of human life and experience; so, for example, the Christian tradition attempts to explain the apparent purpose, design, and moral obligation we experience. These are positive features of the world in that they are phenomena that can be cited as evidence for the world perspective. The second concerns the negative features of human life and experience; for the Christian world perspective this would include the fact of evil, and more importantly for our present purpose, the existence of discordant elements, such as groups that disagree. What exactly would be classified as a negative or positive feature would vary from world perspective to world perspective, but the important point is that each world perspective must, if it is going to be successful, provide some sort of explanation for those features that appear to count against itself. One of the most important explanations a world perspective must provide will be for the existence of traditions that disagree. In other words, each world perspective must supply an explanation of disagreement.

A good illustration of a world perspective supplying this internal explanation of the existence of different traditions that disagree is found in the world of Thomas Aquinas in the thirteenth century. Thomism has immense explanatory power in Western Christianity and has been in many respects both popular and successful. Aquinas's system of natural theology was intended to show how Christian tradition could explain the positive features of human life and existence. One of the problems for Aquinas is the existence of other religions. The *Summa Contra Gentiles* was written as a source book for missionaries involved in converting Muslims and Jews. In his account of unbelief (i.e. from a Christian standpoint) Aquinas shows how his system can explain the existence of other religions. He explains carefully the different sorts of infidelities. There are the Jews who reject the Old Testament's foreshadowing as now fulfilled in the revelation of Christ; there are the Muslims who choose to fight against the revelation; and there are the Christian heretics who rebel against the truth despite growing up with it. The problem in all three cases is simply human sinfulness. This is part of his explanation for these alternative traditions, the other part being the doctrine of predestination. Aquinas writes, "Some people God rejects. We have seen already that predestination is part of providence, and that its working allows failures in the things in its charge. Since by divine providence human beings are ordained to eternal life, it also belongs to divine providence to allow some to fall short of this goal."[30] So within the Thomist system there is a two-fold explanation for different world perspectives – for those that disagree. The first is human sinfulness; and the second is the doctrine of predestination. Muslims are both sinful and not chosen. This internal explanation functions mainly in respect of other traditions in their entirety rather than with an eye on individuals.

Commitment to a world perspective is both made possible and justified by this internal explanation of the negative features of human life and experience. This internal explanation provides the necessary device that entitles one to be committed. Commitment to a world perspective is partly shown by the attitude one has to different traditions that disagree. Given also that world perspectives emerge from a particular historical-cultural location, one can also see how these internal explanations of alternative world perspectives are devices that enable a community to retain its identity against other communities. They are a means by which commitment is justified.

Other world perspectives that provide closed explanations can be found in the more doctrinaire forms of politics: for example, where disagreements are interpreted solely in terms of class interests. This crude, closed type of explanation is a mark of the fanatic. From the terrorist responsible for the events of September 11 to the revolutionary Marxist, the same closed account can be seen. Dialogue between two religious, political, or cultural groupings with such a closed explanation for disagreements is virtually impossible. It is not that neither will listen to the other, but that each is interpreting the disagreement according to its own world perspective, which has already provided the explanation of why people disagree with it. The irony here is that the explanation that they will be giving each other probably will be very similar; each believes that the other is resisting the truth because of the other's sinfulness.

Some of the examples used here have been taken from very "reactionary" forms of religion or religious culture, and although such religion provides an excellent example of closed accounts of disagreement, it is wrong to assume that the same tendency cannot be seen in more "liberal" forms of religion and politics. Some evidence has arisen that many institutions in the American academy require a political orthodoxy that makes it difficult for conservatives (both politically and theologically) to contribute to the debate. "Political correctness" is underpinned by an internal explanation for disagreement that dismisses all those who disagree with liberal relativist assumptions as racist, sexist bigots. All closed explanations of disagreement lead to intolerance within that world perspective. This is true of both the intolerant fundamentalists and the liberals, perhaps more so in the latter case because narrowness of viewpoint is the very negation of what liberals believe in.

As a result of the Enlightenment, many are less persuaded by these "closed" accounts, especially for religious disagreements. Instead such people tend to operate with an "open" account for disagreement. An "open account" concedes that there may be truth in different world perspectives that disagree. It is open because it recognizes the tentative nature of human knowledge and because it recommends tolerance as a necessary means of ascertaining the truth about the world. It is liberal, because it captures a thread most liberals have had in common – that the world is open to a variety of interpretations and that God intended it to be so. Open accounts of disagreements capture the complexity of the world, assess the evidence with care, and make enormous demands in terms of intellectual consistency and tolerance of diversity.

These two different types of explanation – closed and open – for disagreement enable us to understand why dialogue is so difficult. The possibility of dialogue depends on an open account of disagreement, at least as a starting position. Two people with closed accounts of disagreement will produce the most intractable dispute. Two people with open accounts of disagreement have the most potential for progress, because both parties assume that there must be an element of truth or at least of fascinating interest in the other's world perspective. Two people with differing accounts of disagreement will often result in one person interpreting the interest as evidence that conversion is possible, and the other puzzled as to why there is so little understanding of his or her own position.

Before moving to the final consideration that shapes the dialogue, it is important to stress that some sort of explanation for disagreement is important and that occasionally a "closed" account can be true. I have a closed account of disagreement for the racist: I do not believe there is any truth in the racist world perspective and tend to explain the view point as a result of a tragically narrow experience of the world and strong "tribal" allegiances. When it comes to dialogue, we need to identify the account of disagreement that is operating on both sides and explore its appropriateness.

Finally, dialogue flounders because of the different economic, ethnic, sexual, and gender divides. This in many respects requires a chapter in its own right: so to make it manageable I shall provide two illustrations of this group of factors. First, as feminists are right to point out: both the terrorist action and the subsequent retaliation against Afghanistan are led by men: women in both cases are some of the victims. And second, the charge of hypocrisy in that Americans have been indifferent to the suffering of the people of (for example) Iraq or the Palestinian camps yet require sympathy and support during their own very limited (even though intolerable) suffering is one of the key factors in the antagonism that the U.S. faces.

THE SCIENCE OF DIALOGUE

It would be the counsel of despair not to find some means of rising to the challenge of dialogue. The alternative would be a Nietzschian vision of a world where the competing demands are managed by the exercise of power with a view to minimizing the damage that different cultural stories and world perspectives can inflict on society. In short this is the ruthless secular alternative.

It is incumbent upon those of us who identify with a religious world perspective to illustrate that it is possible to "dialogue" such that religion then plays a constructive role in our society. To do this, it is necessary to move beyond the sentimentality of dialogue to the science of dialogue.

For many dialogue is confined to "talking" to each other; for this, it is suggested that it is important to be "open" to each other. So Leonard Swidler writes, "By dialogue is meant a conversation on a common subject between two or more persons with differing views. The primary goal of dialogue is for each participant to learn from the other."[31] So Swidler offers the following basic ground rules of inter-religious dialogue: first, participants must be honest; second, they should assume the same integrity in the other; third, each should define themselves; fourth, all should avoid presuming on the areas of disagreement; and lastly, Swidler writes, "although interreligious dialogue must occur with some kind of 'corporate' dimension to it … it is also fundamentally true that it is only persons who can enter into dialogue."[32] The problem with this model of dialogue is that we end up with abstract individuals, disentangled from communities that make sense of their world perspective, who are invited to get acquainted with each other. It operates in a world of sentimentality, where the real cultural, social, economic, gender issues are evaded. It becomes "surface" dialogue and fails to reach down to the underlying dynamics that are really shaping our views. The science of dialogue is a call to locate the conversation more firmly in the traditions, narratives, and contexts that make us real. It is not scientific in that it is attempting to arrive at a theory grounded upon observation that correctly anticipates subsequent results. Rather it is scientific in attitude. Although this might be continuing to feed a caricature of science that Thomas Kuhn and others have undermined, the idea is that dialogue needs to be much more ruthless and demanding. It must move beyond the polite exchange of views involving largely Western affluent and liberal participants, with a focus around understanding different beliefs and supporting shared ethical values. The science of dialogue attends to the communal narrative underpinning the world perspective; it is aware of the internal explanation for disagreement that is operating; it detects and recognizes the significant gender, economic, and ethnic differences.

These four interpretations of September 11 need to be heard. They need representatives that can articulate each position with clarity. The science of dialogue is to take the strongest versions of these positions and start unpacking the complexity; it is as we encounter the complexity that we can start to identify ways forward that transcend the entrenched alternatives.

CONCLUSION

September 11 is an event that is forcing the religious and secular communities to take dialogue more seriously. First, we need to dialogue with the deeply held religious convictions that, however misguided, clearly underpinned the motives of those involved in the attack. Second and more significantly, we need to dialogue between those who are arriving at markedly different and contrasting interpretations of the attack. The reason why this is so important is because these different interpretations will justify subsequent action. And the best illustration of this is the continuing gap between Jewish/Israeli perceptions and Palestinian ones. Third, we need dialogue to reach beyond the simply sentimental and become much more willing to locate and contextualize the respective narratives.

"Dialogue or die" might seem dramatic, but increasingly the case can be made that these are our alternatives. As we realize how difficult dialogue is, it becomes possible then to rise to the challenge of dialogue.[33]

NOTES

1. My colleague, Jack Ammerman, argues that this "cognitive" goal for dialogue ends up setting up a needlessly high standard. Instead the goal of dialogue should be changed behavior. I am sympathetic to the view that many people can for all sorts of non-rational reasons adjust their behavior without a "clearer understanding of the world". However, one completely proper and necessary aspect of the dialogue, which after all will focus on the capacity of language to communicate effectively, is to illuminate the truth through conversation.
2. David Lochhead, *The Dialogical Imperative. A Christian Reflection on Interfaith Encounter* (New York: Orbis Books, 1988), 48.
3. See an eloquent statement of this goal of dialogue in Leonard Swidler's short chapter called 'Interreligious Dialogue' in Richard W. Rousseau, ed., *Interreligious Dialogue* (Scranton, PA: Ridge Row Press, 1981).
4. My colleague Worth Loomis suggested that the paradigm event for American History is probably the American Civil War. For a good discussion of the impact of this event on the history of ideas, see Louis Menand, *The Metaphysical Club. A Story of Ideas in America* (New York: Farrar, Straus and Giroux, 2001).

5. For an excellent treatment of the influence of the war on Karl Barth see Timothy J. Gorringe, *Karl Barth. Against Hegemony* (Oxford: Oxford University Press, 1999), 35ff.

6. For Richard Rubenstein see R. L. Rubenstein and John K. Roth, eds., *Approaches to Auschwitz. The Legacy of the Holocaust* (London: SCM Press, 1987).

7. For Francis Fukuyama see *The End of History and the Last Man* (New York: Avon Press, 1992).

8. See Richard John Neuhaus, *Doing Well Doing Good* (New York: Doubleday, 1991)

9. President Bush, 'Address to a Joint Session of Congress and the American People', September 20, 2001. Text taken from http: //www.whitehouse.gov

10. Ibid.

11. Ibid.

12. For a good history of Christian anti-semitism see Dan Cohn Sherbok, *The Crucified Jew* (London: Harper Collins, 1992).

13. See Ian Markham, ed., *A World Religions Reader* (Oxford: Blackwell, 2000), 372.

14. See Theodor Herzl, *The Jewish State* (New York: American Zionist Emergency Council, 1946).

15. Letter in the *New York Times* September 23, 2001. Jeffrey H. Tigay raises another dimension to this point in his letter to the *New York Times*, in which he attacks the decision of the U.S. government to support the creation of a Palestinian state: he writes, "Even before Sept 11, announcing such a plan after a year of Palestinian terrorism would have been seen as a reward for terrorism. For the government to leak these plans now damages our credibility – not only in the eyes of the terrorists, but also in the eyes of the American people, who will see that the United States is prepared to reward terrorism if it is persistent enough." The argument here works on the premise terrorism is such an illegitimate way of attaining any goal that it is important that the goal is never realized.

16. Ariel Sharon, Special Parliamentary Session of the Knesset as quoted in "Israel's pivotal role" by Flore de Preneuf as published in Salon.com News, see http: //www.salon.com/news/feature

17. Joseph Alpher, "Stronger Alliance, Limited Options" in *The Jerusalem Report Magazine* as available on http://www.jrep.com/Israel/Article. Alpher is a former Mossad official and former Director of the Jaffee Center for Strategic Studies.

18. Ibid.

19. Jonathan Rosen, 'The Uncomfortable Question of Anti-Semitism' in the *New York Times Magazine,* November 4, 2001, 48.

20. Ibid., p.50.

21. As reported in the *New York Times*, "Muddle over Arafat-Peres Meetings Is Frustrating for Bush" in September 25, 2001.

22. Ibid.

23. It is difficult to establish the precise numbers. The United Nations Conciliation Commission in 1949 suggested 726,000 people. See http://www.arts.mcgill.ca/MEPP/PRRN/proverview.html.

24. For the Abrahamic traditions, providence is simply the action of God in history. For Hinduism and Buddhism, the equivalent interpretation involves *karma* (the moral law of cause and effect in the universe).

25. See Alasdair MacIntyre, *Whose Justice? Which Rationality?* (London: Duckworth, 1988), 385f.

26. For a fuller discussion of MacIntyre and his views of language and translation see my *Truth and the Reality of God* (Edinburgh: T&T Clark, 1998), chap. 3.

27. This point is developed in my 'The Politics of Inclusivity' in *Humanitas. The Journal of the George Bell Institute*, 2 (2), April 2001, 139–56.

28. This myth disregards the successful invasion of England in 1688; this is wholly suppressed in the national mind.

29. This description of the purpose of a world perspective and the internal explanation for disagreements was first developed in my article "World Perspectives and Arguments: Disagreements about Disagreement", *The Heythrop Journal*, 30, 1989, 1–12. The theme was also developed in my *Plurality and Christian Ethics* (Cambridge: Cambridge University Press 1994).

30. Thomas Aquinas, *Summa Theologiae*, vol. 32, 2a2ae question 10, article 8. Translated by Thomas Gilby (London: Eyre and Spottiswood, 1975).

31. Leonard Swidler, "Ground Rules for Interreligious Dialogue." In Richard W. Rousseau, *Interreligious Dialogue* (Scanton, PA: Ridge Row Press, 1981), 9.

32. Ibid., p.11.

33. This paper was originally delivered at a Collegial Sharing before my colleagues at Hartford Seminary. It was much improved as a result of their comments, especially those of Heidi Gehman, Jack Ammerman, and Worth Loomis. I am also grateful to Professor Leslie Houlden and Dr. Shannon Ledbetter who read and made suggestions on an earlier draft.

PART III

BROADER ISSUES

11

RECORDING THE MOMENT: MOVING FROM A COLLECTION MODEL TO A DOCUMENTATION MODEL

Jack W. Ammerman

INTRODUCTION

"No great man lives in vain" writes Thomas Carlyle, Scottish essayist and historian. "The history of the world is but the biography of great men."[1] Until recently, this view of history dominated not only the field, but guided the types of materials collected as source material. Chris Foges writes, "historical source material was to be found at battle-grounds, in Papal proclamations, in temples and palaces, and in the doings and sayings of those great men."[2] Those not playing leadership roles were ignored in the writing of history, and, not surprisingly, in the types of source materials collected to document it.

A tension between what Foges calls the "aristocratic" and the "democratic"[3] approach to history has existed for centuries, but the aristocratic view long dominated. Since the Second World War, however, historians' interest in the ordinary has grown. The social and political changes of the 1960s intensified the focus on marginal groups that had long been hidden from history. As interest in minorities grew, historians began exploring a new past by looking at the daily lives of ordinary people. Emerging disciplines of study shed light on the life and mores of all aspects of society as sociologists, anthropologists, and folklorists turned their attention to non-documentary forms of evidence.

As non-documentary evidence has increased in importance for the study of history, the dialogic nature of this larger body of evidence has become apparent. Stories from various perspectives provide multiple layers for interpreting events. Greater discernment is possible when events are interpreted in light of official documents as well as this non-documentary evidence. Historians now recognize that determining what happened is in fact an exercise in dialogue among these various bodies of evidence.

Biblical scholars recognize the dialogical nature of scripture as well. Discerning the many theological levels in scripture is impossible when portions of the text are read in exclusion from others. In her essay elsewhere in this book, Judy Fentress-Williams suggests that the "variations in voice and perspective exist not to compete but to converse in their movement toward meaning."[4]

In his contribution to this volume, Ian Markham suggests that the "science of dialogue is a call to locate the conversation more firmly in the traditions, narratives, and contexts that make us real."[5] Here Markham echoes Fentress-Williams in affirming both the importance of dialogue for theological reflection and that it is the place where these variations in voice and perspective engage each other. Through that engagement, the participants arrive at a better understanding of truth.

Markham focuses particularly on the complexity of the dialogical relationship between theology and events. Recognizing that some events have greater significance for theological reflection than others, Markham classifies some events "pivotal," others "tangential," and still others "ephemeral." While he uses this classification to point out the difficulty in deciding the significance for theological reflection of any event, librarians face a similar dilemma. Deciding what materials to collect, and equally important, what not to collect requires the librarian to develop some means of determining what materials will be most valuable in adding depth and focus to the library's collection.

It is not surprising that scholars have been forced "to come out of the libraries, out of the government records, and out of ivory towers to find information [that represents these various voices]."[6] Libraries have been slow to change traditional collecting patterns to reflect these changes in scholarly research. Traditional collection development policies frequently focus on commercial publishers that use well established marketing and delivery channels. The non-documentary evidence that has become so important to scholars is frequently created and distributed outside of those structures. Usually classified as "ephemera" by librarians, its ephemeral nature is, in part, a consequence of traditional library collecting patterns. Even when the trace evidence of ordinary daily living is collected by libraries, it frequently ends up in a vertical file with little (if any) indexing to make the material accessible to researchers. Librarians, however, typically do not collect materials they deem unimportant, so they use the term differently than Markham. This classification is generally not a judgment of the lack of importance of the material, but a consequence of the non-standard collecting and maintenance efforts required to add it to the library's collection.

That collection decisions might be event-driven is a rather unusual notion among theological librarians. Collection policies are developed that provide a framework within which collection decisions are made. The goal is to work within that framework to make collection decisions over a long period of time that result in a strong, well focused collection. Making collection decisions in response to a single event, even one as momentous as the September 11 tragedy, may seem like setting aside the policy to make *ad hoc* decisions.

So it is not surprising that theological libraries might be slow to imagine documenting a national tragedy. In a recent E-mail query,[7] a group of theological librarians were asked if their libraries had in any way planned to, or attempted to, document the September 11 attack on the World Trade Center and Pentagon or its aftermath. The responses to this informal query indicated that few libraries had acted to document any aspect of the tragedy. Apart from those libraries that were attempting to collect published materials about Islam, terrorism and bio-terrorism in order to help their library users better understand those subjects, only two responded positively indicating that they were attempting to collect materials to document the event. One collected materials to document the prayer and worship services offered along with the special support offered to students. Another attempted to document how the denomination that supports the seminary had responded to the crisis. While one should be cautious in reading too much into such a small number of responses, the limited response suggests that few theological libraries are attempting to document the event.

What should a theological library be collecting? Many are small with limited resources. Often the primary collection development goal is to support the curriculum of the school. The curriculum is frequently defined narrowly, however, to refer to only those courses that are taught by the faculty. The Association for Theological Schools in the United States and Canada, however, asserts in its standards for accreditation "[t]he theological curriculum, comprehensively understood, embraces all those activities and experiences provided by the school to enable students to achieve the intended goals."[8] This easily includes the student's engagement with library resources.

If "the over-arching goal [of the curriculum] is the development of theological understanding,"[9] then the theological library's acquisition policies and practices should result in a collection that allows and encourages library users to recognize and engage the variations in voice and perspective present in the world. An aptitude for theological reflection and deepening spiritual awareness demands a dialogical engagement with the texts one studies, as well as other readers of those texts who hold varying perspectives. As Fentress-Williams suggests, such dialogical engagement becomes transformative.

One might go on to say that theological reflection should not be limited to traditionally published texts. The events of our lives, including national disasters, provide substance for our theological reflection. This is not to suggest theological libraries should abandon their collection development policies. Rather, it is to suggest that those policies must insure that materials collected can in fact provide documentation for the many voices and perspectives that exist. The risk always exists that a book purchased by a library will not be used. Just as that risk does not prevent the library from purchasing books, it should not prevent the library from collecting non-documentary evidence.

What should a theological library collect to document a national tragedy? No single answer will fit all libraries. Collection decisions for non-documentary evidence should not blur the focus of the library's collection. Rather, it should add depth and clarity to that focus. The decisions about what to collect should include an assessment of what is already being collected by other libraries and organizations. Following is a brief list of those documentation projects that have emerged as of this writing. It is surely not comprehensive, but represents the major projects that are planned or underway.

DOCUMENTING THE SEPTEMBER 11 TRAGEDY

A number of projects to document the September 11 tragedy have begun. Not surprisingly, New York City and the state of New York are heavily engaged in documenting what has happened as a result of the attack on the World Trade Center. These efforts are typical of governmental or aristocratic approaches to documenting an event. Governor George Pataki instructed all state agencies involved in disaster recovery efforts to contact the New York State Archives to ensure that their records are assessed and scheduled appropriately.[10] These records will measure how the state and local governments have responded to the tragedy, but they will not tell the whole story.

In addition to these efforts to document governmental responses, some are trying to document the more individual and spontaneous responses to the disaster. Several efforts are underway to collect personal remembrances in either written or oral form. The New York Historical Society has invited state residents to submit remembrances. The New York State Library's Manuscripts and Special Collections division is collecting written reminiscences and images of the tragedy. Perhaps one of the largest efforts has been mounted by the American Folklife Center at the Library of Congress. The Center has invited folklorists across the nation to document on audio tape the thoughts and feelings expressed by citizens following the September 11 attacks.[11] These recordings will be added to the Center's collection.

Agencies beyond the sites of the September 11 attacks have attempted to cooperate with the American Folklife Center's effort. The Iowa Department of Cultural Affairs, for example, has invited Iowans to "share their personal experiences and feelings of September 11, 2001, by reciting their stories on audio tape."[12] The State Historical Society provided taping facilities to assist state residents in recording their experiences.

Davia Nelson and Nikki Silva, two independent radio producers in California have begun developing what they call a Sonic Monument "documenting both the routines of daily life at the World Trade Center before the attacks and the events of September 11."[13] They are initially collecting voice-mail messages but also hope to collect sounds from dictation tapes, tourist videos made before September 11, training films used by World Trade Center tenants, audio recordings of financial transactions or any other "shards of sound that capture the expressions, exchanges, and humanity that defined the buildings."[14]

Museums are natural leaders in documenting such events in that their primary focus is the collection and preservation of artifacts. Several New York museums are actively collecting materials related to the September 11 attack on the World Trade Center that are appropriate to their collections. The South Street Seaport Museum, which documents the maritime community in New York Harbor and its own local neighborhood, is collecting oral histories, photographs, videos, and any appropriate artifacts that illuminate the maritime community's response to the crisis. The Museum of Comic and Cartoon Art is collecting lithographs, publishers' proofs, copies, and other prints of comic and cartoon art inspired by the events of September 11, 2001. The New York Fire Museum is collecting digital and photographic images of and stories about the rescue effort and images of memorials that mourners in New York City and elsewhere created in honor of firefighters lost in the tragedy.[15]

E-mail and the World Wide Web became primary vehicles for many to express their responses to the September 11 tragedy. In the days immediately following September 11, observed Matthew Mirapaul, "every conceivable corner of the Internet [was] jammed with reactions to the attacks."[16] Yet the World Wide Web is by its very nature ephemeral. Webmasters quickly learn that few people revisit a web site to read the same content. As weeks pass, the content that quickly emerged after September 11 is being replaced by new content. To preserve some of the web content that emerged, the Library of Congress collaborated with webArchivist.org and archive.org to create a digital archive for September 11 related web content. The publicly accessible archive September11.archive.org "is an attempt to corral the Net's wildly diverse contents into a central research repository."[17]

The transitory nature of ephemera makes collecting them no less important. Spontaneous shrines created in response to disaster are "communal and spontaneous performances of grief. … [They] are a way for people to work out a personal connection to an otherwise numbing catastrophe and [bring] comfort to thousands and thousands of people during this disaster."[18] Unlike memorials that are often designed with permanence in mind, these shrines are designed for an immediate audience. Permanence is not a design factor. When left unprotected from the weather, they rapidly deteriorate.

CityLore, the New York Center for Urban Folk Culture, is photographing impromptu shrines or other public expressions of grief.[19] The Somerset Historical Society collects tributes left at the site of the crash of United Airlines Flight 93 near Shanksville, Pennsylvania. Barbara Black, the curator of the Historical Society gathers and catalogs items left by visitors. Included in the items she collects are "cards and notes left with people's feelings about the crash … stuffed animals, and banners."[20]

The Internet provides a virtual forum for the creation of Cybershrines. Common after the death of Diana, Princess of Wales and more recently after the death of race car driver, Dale Earnhardt, "Cybershrines were also a common response to the collapse of the Texas A&M University bonfire, the crash of the airplane carrying members of the Oklahoma State University basketball team, and the recent spate of American school shootings, as well as the assassination of Yitzhak Rabin in Jerusalem."[21] Cybershrines, web pages containing condolences, virtual candles, and montages of images and sounds, flooded the Internet after the September 11 tragedy.

Whether virtual or physical, these spontaneous shrines perform multiple roles. They offer the creator of the shrine an opportunity to make a ritual offering. The folk art creations become public expressions of deeply felt emotions. They also become pilgrimage sites, and are, therefore, "sacred shrines rather than secular memorials."[22] Transitory though they may be, they are significant expressions of feelings and spirituality.

Design is not the only factor affecting their lack of permanence. Some materials disappear as a result of suppression. Among the web pages archived by September11.archive.org are those that have been taken offline because they are from jihad-themed sites. If not archived immediately, these pages would probably have been lost forever.

The Asian Division of the Library of Congress has a collection of ephemeral material "relating to the Tiananmen Square massacre and uprising in 1989 – pamphlets, flyers, materials, which if not collected by a great library, would disappear or vanish into a private collection. The history of what happened in Tiananmen in 1989 is a little better known because the Library of Congress has brought together that kind of fleeting material, material which the [Chinese government] would be very glad to see disappear completely."[23]

EPHEMERA IN LIBRARIES

Collecting ephemera is not a new pursuit. For centuries, people have collected everyday documents such as postcards, broadsides and posters. Many of these collections are private such as one created by artist Chris Sullivan. He began collecting notes that he found left on telephone poles, ads for handymen, and notes left on cars parked illegally in driveways. He has organized this collection that he calls "The Journal of Public Domain" as an effort to "tell the story of life in the city."[24]

While Sullivan's collection has actually been on public display, many of these private collections remain so poorly cataloged and publicized that they are unknown, much less accessible to scholars. Until recently, few libraries have focused resources either on collecting or cataloging collections of ephemera. Emerging among librarians, however, is a new interest in such collections. The University of Virginia's Rare Book School offered for the first time a course entitled "Printed Ephemera" in 2001. The course description indicates that "underpinning this course is the view that ephemera deserve serious attention from cultural, social, and business historians, from design and printing historians, and from those with curatorial responsibilities for collections of paper-based materials."[25]

Collecting and organizing ephemera was the topic of a discussion at the fifty-fifth Annual Conference of the American Theological Library Association in June 2001. Individually printed sermons were popular particularly in eighteenth and nineteenth-century England. A number of theological libraries have large collections that are either uncataloged or undercataloged. Sermons have proven to be significant primary documentation for scholars interested in rhetoric, social history, homiletics, and history of biblical interpretation. "There was considerable interest expressed in finding ways to upgrade the cataloging records for the sermons in bibliographic databases, work through the backlog of uncataloged sermons in libraries, share/exchange duplicate sermons, and digitize a body of sermons to facilitate access."[26]

COLLECTING WITH A RESEARCHER'S EYE

While librarians and scholars have both rediscovered the importance of ephemeral items, they approach collecting ephemera in very different ways. Researchers most often gather data with a very focused agenda. A researcher formulates a hypothesis or a specific subject emerges that captures her interest. She develops a protocol to gather data to test the hypothesis or learn more about the subject. The model for collecting data flows from the research agenda.

Bill Ellis, a folklorist, studies jokes that emerge out of tragedy. In the wake of the September 11 tragedy, he proposed a model for collecting World Trade Center jokes.[27] He expects jokes to flow in waves, following a latency period during which humor seems inappropriate. The jokes that emerge will make use of dominant visual images from the tragedy, and E-mail will be a primary vehicle for the communication of these jokes. Based on his model, he has constructed a data gathering strategy that will allow him to gather the data he needs for his research.

Like Ellis, other scholars develop models that aid them in gathering the data to advance their research. Out of her previous work, Sylvia Grider provides guidance for collecting and maintaining spontaneous shrines. Richard Stone gathers junk mail as a means of studying popular culture in Australia.[28] Each of these scholars approaches the collection of ephemera from the perspective of her or his research agenda.

Librarians, on the other hand, collect materials with the hope that they will be used by more than one researcher. Rarely do they begin collecting ephemera with a single research agenda in mind. More frequently, they stumble into it. Occasionally a collection begins when someone donates a private collection to the library. Perhaps as frequently, a librarian recognizes that the library has unintentionally accumulated a number of items that because of their format require a similar kind of care or storage. These ephemeral materials are organized by format rather than by subject. Occasionally a concerted effort is made to collect similar items. But for the librarian, there is less often a clear understanding of who might use these materials, or for what purpose they might be used. Rarely is a research protocol developed to guide the collection. Rather, the library is more likely to collect through donations from other collectors, or on the basis of what items can be easily acquired.

Without a clear focus on what is to be documented, the thought of attempting to collect ephemeral materials to document a national tragedy can be daunting for a library. One theological librarian responding to the query about documenting the September 11 events indicated that his library had not attempted to collect anything because there was "so much to collect." This statement is in fact true, but it also reflects the perspective of a librarian as opposed to a social scientist collecting data for research.

Librarians have developed great expertise in selecting and acquiring materials published through standard publication channels. With publishers' catalogs, Cataloging In Process records, tables of contents and indexes, a book selector can easily determine whether an individual book fits the criteria for inclusion in the collection. Librarians can even arrange with a book distributor to send books fitting a pre-defined profile for the book selector to review.

Ephemera, on the other hand, lack these easy tools which aid selection. Collecting is more difficult, requiring more initiative on the part of the librarian. Most of the standard tools that serve librarians in the acquisition of published materials simply do not work for ephemera. Consequently, librarians tend to collect materials in formats that are easy to collect and process. From this perspective, librarians tend to be collectors as compared to social science researchers who attempt to gather data in a much more focused manner to document their study.

A MODEL FOR DOCUMENTING A NATIONAL TRAGEDY

One always hopes that a strategy for documenting a tragedy will never be needed, but the reality is that tragedy does happen, whether on a local or national scale. It would be helpful if libraries had time to carefully deliberate about what should be collected. As we have seen, some materials disappear so quickly that they are missed if deliberation requires an extended period of time. Developing a model for making collection decisions at times of a tragedy may improve the chances of collecting ephemeral materials. Following are suggestions for how to approach a documentation project.

Work collaboratively

Attempting to document comprehensively any tragedy on a national scale and mostly on a local scale is simply beyond the scope of any one library. Existing collection development priorities can not be easily set aside. Collaboration is not only helpful, it is essential. In New York, a coalition of repositories is working to collect and preserve documentary evidence of the attack on the World Trade Center. The World Trade Center Documentation Task Force is coordinating information and encouraging collaborative efforts among New York agencies and institutions.[29] Libraries usually participate in both formal and informal groups and associations that could collaboratively design efforts to document a tragedy. The group can function in many ways. It could take an active role to coordinate the efforts or seek external funding, or it could simply be a mechanism by which member libraries communicate their efforts in order to avoid duplication. Within academic institutions, collaboration could take place between the library and faculty members in order to design data gathering projects that could benefit both.

Clearly articulate what you want to document

This is perhaps the most difficult part of the decision process for a library. It forces the library to move beyond traditional collecting patterns that are often driven by the format and availability of materials. It perhaps shifts the focus of the library from collector to researcher. What questions or research agenda drive the collecting project? Certainly existing collection development policies should provide a framework for thinking about what to document, but they may not always provide the focus that is essential in determining what to collect.

Academic and research libraries are perhaps best positioned to approach this question, but even public and special libraries might find ways to collaborate with scholars in the design of a documentation project. Formal or informal conversations between scholars and librarians might help the library to focus its efforts. Rarely will a library want to develop a single research agenda that will guide its collection. Consulting with scholars from multiple fields may enable the library to collect materials in such a way as to meet the research agendas of multiple local scholars. Librarians at Texas A&M University, for example, would probably want to talk with Sylvia Grider from the Anthropology Department about what she thinks should be documented based on her work following the collapse of the bonfire at the University. One would expect her to identify things about the disaster that might benefit her own research in addition to strengthening the library's collection. But librarians may also want to talk with scholars from other fields to gain a broader understanding of how the materials they collect might be used by scholars from multiple academic disciplines.

Such conversations can assist not only in identifying what to document, but also the types of materials that are likely to provide the best documentary evidence. Scholars with data-gathering expertise can assist in designing a methodology for collecting the materials. They can also assist in helping the library know how to catalog the materials to make them most accessible to a researcher. The result is a collection of materials that are clearly focused to document a specific aspect of the disaster and usable by the research community.

Define a manageable strategy for gathering, cataloging and preserving the materials

Ultimately, a documentation project has to be manageable within the resources available to the library. When collecting ephemera, this can be a challenge. It may be difficult to predict the volume of materials that will emerge. A library may need to begin collecting before the final details of a documentation project are finalized; however, materials collected are of little value if there will be insufficient resources to catalog, preserve, and store them. Certainly external funding can be solicited, particularly when working collaboratively with other institutions and scholars. The likelihood of securing this funding before the library needs to begin collecting is not high. At some point, institutional resources will be required. A well designed project clearly identifies the available institutional support and projects at least a rough estimate of when it might become available.

It is helpful to design documentation projects that can be scaled up both in size and over time. If institutional resources limit the amount of collecting that can be done, the project might be scaled to a more manageable size. A researcher might suggest collecting random samples of material, or collecting for a shorter period. Collecting might be done at selected times rather than continuously. Bill Ellis projected that World Trade Center jokes will probably come in waves.[30] Defining a project that would collect jokes during those waves rather than continuously might be a way of scaling back the project.

A project might also be designed with several phases. The first would be the collection phase. Institutional resources could be directed to that effort, delaying the cataloging until fewer institutional resources were required for collecting. By allowing the project to extend over a longer time period, limited institutional resources may be less strained.

DOCUMENTING THE RESPONSE OF FAITH COMMUNITIES TO A NATIONAL DISASTER

In June 2001 a group of theological librarians gathered to discuss possibilities of collecting and cataloging individually printed sermons.[31] Such items, popular in eighteenth- and nineteenth-century England, have proven to be helpful resources in a number of disciplines. Folklorists have used them to study the use of oral narratives in Kenya.[32] One historian has used sermons to study the history of giving and fund-raising in eighteenth-century England.[33] Thanksgiving sermons and funeral sermons are routinely used to explore everything from family values[34] to civil religion.

The discussion, which initially focused on early printed sermons, expanded to include strategies for collecting contemporary sermons published on web sites or photocopied and made available on literature tables in a variety of congregations. The collection might be developed in such a way as to automate much of the collecting and indexing process, thus minimizing the ongoing administrative overhead cost for the library.

Such a collection model is not without its problems. Many ministers, particularly in Pentecostal and evangelical denominations, simply do not produce a full manuscript of their sermons. Even those who do may not print or post the sermons to a web site. Such a collection model would probably not result in a collection that a social scientist would consider to be truly represen- tative. While the discussion has stimulated an ongoing conversation about collecting and indexing sermons, no formal plan for collecting sermons emerged.

As a part of an ongoing planning process, Hartford Seminary Library began exploring with the Seminary faculty the types of primary resources the Library should acquire and maintain. One of the emphases of Hartford Seminary's Hartford Institute for Religion Research (HIRR) is the study of local faith communities. HIRR sociologists routinely observe, interview, and survey faith communities in gathering data for their research. In July, a conversation with the Congregational Studies Project Team[35] provided an opportunity to focus on the materials that will best serve those scholars and students interested in studying congregations. Suggestions included worship bulletins, sermons, newsletters, and other literature distributed to congregation members. Even with these interesting collection possibilities, it was clear that these researchers had difficulty thinking like librarians. The conversation was structured to think about an ongoing collection of materials divorced from any particular research agenda, which, while helpful, did not ultimately result in an effort to begin collecting materials.

Two months later, disaster struck. One would not have to work in a seminary community to notice the expressions of faith and spirituality that emerged in response to the September 11 attacks. In the days immediately following, vigils, prayers, and participation in public worship events increased. The Gallup Organization discovered that 47 percent of respondents to the Gallup Poll on September 21–22, 2001 indicated they had attended a worship service in the past seven days, which would have included the weekend immediately following the September 11, 2001 attack on the World Trade Center and the Pentagon.[36]

The Library began exploring the kinds of efforts that were being made to document the September 11 tragedy. As related above, many attempts were launched to document the events from institutional perspectives. State archives and agencies were collecting materials. There were interesting projects to collect the reflections of individuals. Oral histories, poems, E-mail messages and spontaneous shrines were being collected. What did not appear to be documented was the response of faith communities in public worship.

A sermon collection project began to emerge as a possibility for two reasons. First, it would be consistent with the kinds of documentary evidence that could be used by scholars studying congregations as well as historians and researchers from other fields. It would allow scholars to study how congregations deal with pain, suffering, and evil from various disciplines including sociology, history, theology, biblical studies, and homiletics. In addition, it would be a valuable effort to document a kind of civic response to the national tragedy. The increase in worship attendance turned out to be short-lived. By November, the number of respondents indicating worship attendance in the previous seven days had returned to the average 42 percent where it has hovered for many years.[37] Nancy Ammerman suggested that we were probably seeing the Christmas/Easter crowd at worship on the weekend of September 16. She indicated that worship attendance on major Christian holidays like Easter and Christmas by those who do not otherwise attend is related to one's concept of what it means to be a good citizen. She proposed that the increase in worship attendance on September 16, 2001 was probably a result of those who felt it important to show their citizenship by attending worship.[38] Collecting sermons preached on that weekend could be a way to document, at least through the sermon, what ministers wanted these "good citizens" to hear.

The challenge is to design the collection to increase its value to potential users. Despite early conversations with sociologists of religion, the collection began very much as a librarian might begin it. An announcement was made to enlist Seminary faculty and staff in collecting sermons from congregations they attended. Clergy were invited to submit sermons primarily on the basis of existing relationships with the Library. At its beginning, no intentional design was implemented to insure a representative sample.

The collection has grown more slowly than originally planned. The available time for collecting sermons has not been as great as desired. More initiative on the part of the Library will be required to provide a substantial collection.

Cataloging has been delayed on the sermons. Before cataloging begins, the Library intends to consult with other libraries as well as scholars who might use the collection. Past practice has cataloged such collections at the collection level rather than the item level. For print materials, this made the collections difficult to use. If the Library were to create a digital archive, it is possible that full-text searching could be implemented. If this were the case, item level cataloging might not be essential. Insuring accessibility is the goal for the collection. The Library will work with its users to determine what level of cataloging is important for the collection.

Sermons have been collected in a variety of formats including print, digital files, and audiotape. Permanent storage of these diverse formats is still being considered. As mentioned, one option under consideration is a digital archive that allows full-text searching. The Library needs to decide whether to select a common format for the sermons, or whether to continue to store them in multiple formats. An additional issue for consideration is whether sermons in audio format should be transcribed, in order to facilitate full-text searching.

The early stage of development of this collection means it can still be shaped to better meet the needs of the researchers. The Library plans to continue its conversation with researchers both informally and formally. In addition to ongoing faculty conversations, it hopes to sponsor a more formal consultation in which historians and sociologists will be invited to assist the Library in shaping the collection.

CONCLUSION

Twice in this chapter I have asked what theology libraries should collect to document an event like the September 11 tragedy. The obvious assumption behind that question is that they should be collecting something. One of the primary assumptions behind this volume is that events like the September 11 tragedy are worthy of reflection from a number of academic disciplines. If such an event goes undocumented, what will be the evidence upon which scholars base their reflection? The task of reflection is relatively easy less than one year after the event. In ten years, or 100 years, it will be much more difficult without the documentation. The same can be said of collecting the materials that document the event.

This is particularly true of the ephemera that give voice to stories and perspectives that are not reflected in official documents. The window of time for collecting ephemera is often narrow. Working collaboratively to design collection projects and to develop means to make collections of ephemera more accessible results in rich collections capable of supporting the scholarly research and theological reflection advocated in this volume.

As the other authors in this volume both affirm and demonstrate, theological discernment and the development of a deeper understanding of our world through disciplined reflection and research demand a dialogical engagement with the complexity of our world. Developing a library collection that provides the potential for such dialogue requires that multiple voices and perspectives be represented. Simply collecting materials using traditional library models may not be sufficient to insure a collection capable of engaging the library user in dialogue with the complexity of our world. Building such a collection is both our challenge and responsibility.

NOTES

1. Thomas Carlyle, "The Hero as Divinity." In *On Heroes, Hero Worship, and the Heroic in History* (Project Gutenberg, 1841).
2. Chris Foges, "Far from Ephemeral. (Study of Graphic Ephemera by the Centre for Ephemera Studies, University of Reading)," *Print*, 53(2), 1999.
3. Ibid.

4. Judy Fentress-Williams, chapter 9 in this vol.
5. Ian S. Markham, chapter 10 in this vol.
6. Foges, "Far from Ephemeral."
7. This admittedly informal and unscientific query was sent to ATLANTIS (an electronic discussion list for theological librarians). With close to 400 subscribers, ATLANTIS is hosted by the American Theological Library Association and primarily serves its members. Librarians were asked if their libraries had developed a plan for collecting materials to document the September 11 tragedy and/or its aftermath, if so, what they were trying to document, what was being collected, and who was involved in the decision. Six responses were received.
8. The Association of Theological Schools in the United States and Canada, "Section 4: The Theological Curriculum," In *ATS Accreditation Standards* (Pittsburgh: The Association of Theological Schools in the United States and Canada, 2002).
9. Ibid.
10. New York State Historical Records Advisory Board, 2001, *Documenting the Tragedy: Organizational Documentation Projects* [Web Site] accessed November 25, 2001); available from http://www.nyshrab.org/WTC/projects.html.
11. "Library of Congress Documents Reactions to September 11, 2001, Tragedy for Posterity," *News from the Library of Congress*, September 26, 2001.
12. *Iowa Department of Cultural Affairs; The American Spirit Project*, [Web Site] (Iowa Department of Cultural Affairs, 2001, accessed December 12, 2001); available from http: //www.culturalaffairs.org/americanspirit.htm.
13. Todd Lappin, "Preserving the Voices of the Twin Towers," *New York Times*, October 11, 2001.
14. Ibid.
15. *Documenting the Tragedy: Organizational Documentation Projects* (accessed November 21, 2001). The New York State Historical Records Advisory Board maintains a helpful list of ongoing documentation projects developed by organizations in New York.
16. Matthew Mirapaul, "Arts Online; How the Net Is Documenting a Watershed Moment," *New York Times*, October 15, 2001.
17. Ibid.
18. Sylvia Grider, "Preliminary Observations Regarding the Spontaneous Shrines Following the Terrorist Attacks of September 11, 2001," *New Directions in Folklore*, 5 (2001).
19. *City Lore*, [Web site] (City Lore, 2001, accessed December 11, 2001); available from http: //www.citylore.org/.
20. Barbara Black, "Noah Adams Interviews Barbara Black, Curator of the Somerset County Historical Society." In *All Things Considered*; December 11 (Washington, DC: 2001).
21. Grider, "Preliminary Observations".

22. Ibid.
23. James J. O'Donnell, "Library of Congress Staff Briefing," ed. Library of Congress (Washington, DC: Library of Congress, 2000) as reported by Gail Fineberg, "Panel Chair Briefs Staff on NAS Report," in *Bicentennial Conference on Bibliographic Control for the New Millennium; Confronting the Challenges of Networked Resources and the Web* (Library of Congress Cataloging Directorate, 2000).
24. Ana Marie Cox, "Paper Trail," *Mother Jones*, 24 (4), 1999.
25. Rare Book School, *R B S History Course Offerings* [Web Site] (Virginia: University of Virginia, 2001, accessed December 13, 2001); available from http://www.virginia.edu/oldbooks/bulletin/history.html#ephemera.
26. M. Patrick Graham, "The Printed Sermon." In Margret Tacke Collins, ed., *Fifty-Fifth Annual Conference of the American Theological Library Association* (Durham, North Carolina: American Theological Library Association, 2001).
27. Bill Ellis, "A Model for Collecting and Interpreting World Trade Center Jokes," *New Directions in Folklore*, 5, 2001.
28. Richard Stone, "Junk Mail: Printed Ephemera and Preservation of the Everyday," *Journal of Australian Studies*, September, 1998.
29. *Documenting the Tragedy: Organizational Documentation Projects* (accessed November 21, 2001).
30. Ellis, "A Model for Collecting."
31. Graham, "The Printed Sermon."
32. Ezekiel B. Alembi, "Telling Tales: The Use of Oral Narratives in Religious Sermons in Kenya," *Folklore*, 13, 2000.
33. Donna T. Andrew, "On Reading Charity Sermons: Eighteenth-Century Anglican Solicitation and Exhortation," *Journal of Ecclesiastical History*, 43 (4), 1992.
34. Eileen T. Dugan, "The Funeral Sermon as a Key to Familial Values in Early Modern Nordlingen," *Sixteenth Century Journal*, 20 (4), 1989.
35. The Congregational Studies Project Team is an informal coalition of scholars and researchers who share an interest in congregations. Additional information is available from http://www.hirr.hartsem.edu/about/about_cs_project_team.html.
36. Gallup Organization, *Gallup Poll: Religion Indicators* [Web site] (The Gallup Organization, 2001, accessed December 2, 2001); available from http://www.gallup.com/poll/indicators/indreligion.asp.
37. Ibid.
38. Nancy T. Ammerman, "Conversation About Church Attendance," (Hartford: 2001).

12

INTERNAL SECURITY AND CIVIL LIBERTIES: MORAL DILEMMAS AND DEBATES

Heidi Hadsell

INTRODUCTION: SECURITY MEASURES

As a result of the terrorist attacks of September 11, while the United States carries out its military campaign in Afghanistan and its diplomatic campaign in Europe and elsewhere, it also is acting to insure its internal security. Some of the measures taken towards internal security are relatively simple, straightforward, and also non-controversial. Such measures include increased airport security, and the transference of the task of airport baggage checks from private firms to the federal government. Other measures reach more deeply into established laws and practices of the U.S. society, and pertain more closely to the U.S. system of justice and to the understanding of civil liberties as established by the American Constitution and its Amendments. These measures, the full implications of which are still not understood, provoke partisan political controversy, legal controversy, and also ethical debate. This chapter focuses on some of the ethical questions related to the security measures put in place from September 11 through December. First there is a brief description of the major security measures taken, then a consideration of the typical reactions to these measures, and finally a focus on some of the emerging ethical questions provoked by these measures.

A journalist writing in the *New York Times* described the security measures taken since September 11 in the following manner:

> In bold and unilateral strokes, the Bush administration has in recent weeks reshaped the American legal system to fight terrorism in ways

unthinkable before September 11, from monitoring the conversations of suspected terrorists and their lawyers to creating special military tribunals to prosecute terrorists without the usual Anglo-Saxon niceties.

Public complaints were slow to come, and official scrutiny was scant at first. But a bipartisan chorus of skeptics and outright critics has now built to a political force that must be reckoned with.[1]

What are the measures to which he refers? And why such consternation? Briefly and in rough chronological order the internal security measures established since September 11 can be documented as listed below.

The Office of Homeland Security established

On September 30, the office of Homeland Security was created. This was the unit that was entrusted with preventing terrorist infiltration in the United States and with the special duty to ensure that the airlines are safe.

President Bush signed the "Patriot Act" into law

The anti-terrorism bill, known as the "Patriot Act", whose full name is: "The Uniting and Strengthening America by Providing Appropriate Tools Required to Intercept and Obstruct Terrorism Act of 2001" was passed by the House of Representatives 357–66 on October 24, and passed in the Senate by a vote of 96–1 on October 25, and was signed by President Bush on October 26. Major elements of this act include: first, any non-citizen who endorses terrorist activities or belongs to a group which does can be either deported or refused entry at the border to the United States. Second, terrorist activity has been broadened in meaning to include non-citizens who use "dangerous devices," or who raise money for terrorist groups. And third, any non-citizen who the U.S. Attorney General certifies on "reasonable grounds to believe" as endangering national security can be detained, and held indefinitely, although the Justice Department has to bring criminal or deportation charges against him or her within seven days. Such incarcerations can be secret, and criminal proceedings are bound by gag orders. Fourth, the rules on surveillance have also changed. It is now easier for law enforcement agencies to watch both citizens and non citizens – since they now have been given increased powers of surveillance including new wire tapping powers which, among other things, now include cell phones. Surveillance rules now also include an expanded use of foreign intelligence information by law enforcement agencies.

In recognition of the special nature of this act which was provoked by the events of September 11, the "Patriot Act" includes a sunset law of December 31, 2003.

Detentions of suspected terrorists

Detentions of people suspected of being related in some way to the events of September 11 began immediately on or after the 11th, and every day until November 3 the Department of Justice issued a tally of arrests by which time 1,147 people had been detained. The Department of Justice then stopped issuing the daily tally. At no time were the names of the majority of the people arrested made public. According to the Justice Department, a small number of the persons detained have been detained as material witnesses, many have been detained for immigration violations, and then there are those detained on a number of other charges. As of the first week of December 2001, some 500 names of those detained had still not been disclosed, and stories in the press were increasing of hardworking, law-abiding people arrested and detained for weeks without being charged of any crime.

The media is asked to restrain itself

Since September 11 the media has been asked several times by the State Department, on a voluntary basis, to limit the content of some of their news reports. Specifically, the media was asked not to run video tapes of Osama bin Laden, because the State Department feared they could contain secret encrypted messages which would aid the enemy. More recently the media was given a tape of Osama bin Laden by government officials who, in this case, seemed not to fear encrypted messages. Journalists have complained about being kept away from battlefields in Afghanistan, to such an extent that it has sometimes compromised their ability to report the news.

Eavesdropping

Attorney General John Ashcroft issued orders on November 8 allowing federal prison authorities to eavesdrop on attorney–client conversations involving people suspected of posing a direct threat to national security.

Military tribunals

On November 13 President Bush signed an order which makes a provision for military tribunals to try any non-citizen of the Unites States who is charged with terrorism. Under the provisions of this order, it is finally the President himself who determines who to try in military courts. Not only does this mean that the evidence that led to the charges against the person on trial will not be made public, which is one of the explicitly stated goals of this measure, it also means that the person thus charged has no right to a public trial, no right to a trial by jury, and no right to confront the evidence. No such similar procedure has been announced for citizens of the United States charged with terrorism.

It is worth noting, however, that on December 11, 2001, the U.S. Government announced that a French citizen of Moroccan ancestry, suspected as an accomplice to the terrorist acts of September 11, who has been in custody since mid-August, will be brought to trial in U.S. civil courts, rather than a military tribunal.

Immigration tightens up

As indicated above, hundreds of people have been arrested since September 11 and are being held on immigration violations as well as a number of other charges not directly related to the terrorist attacks. A number of measures to tighten immigration procedures have been taken, including new border agreements with Canada, and the requirement that airlines from certain countries send ahead passenger manifests for planes arriving in the United States. It is now reportedly harder for people from certain countries considered to be friendly to terrorists to obtain a visa to enter the U.S.

A new regulation on the detention of immigrants was issued on October 26 by Attorney General John Ashcroft for the Immigration and Naturalization Service (INS). This new regulation allows the INS to disregard any release order issued by an immigration judge in cases where the agency says it believes that a non-citizen is a danger to the community or a flight risk.

On November 13 the Justice Department asked law enforcement agencies across the country to identify and question some 5,000 Muslim men, ages 18–33, who entered the country with legal temporary visas in the last several years. It asked local police forces, and colleges and universities, where many of these men are enrolled, to cooperate in the interview process. Universities and colleges have also been asked to identify to law enforcement officials those students who are here in the United States on student visas, who are not attending class or who have dropped out of the institution.

One illustration of this pressure on students occurred on December 15. Ten people from the Middle East in the United States on student visas were arrested in San Diego for violating the terms of their visas. Immigration officials characterized this action as the beginning of a "major crack-down on foreigners who violated the terms of student visas."[2]

Expanded rights to infiltrate religious groups and gatherings

The government's plans to expand the legal ability of law enforcement agencies to infiltrate and to eavesdrop on gatherings of religious groups across the United States has been reported in a number of respected newspapers. (I have been unable to find sufficient information to ascertain whether this is rumor or fact.)

With the exception of the anti-terrorism bill know as the Patriot Act of October 25, the U.S. Congress has largely played the role of bystander in each of these measures, not having been invited to debate or to vote on these issues.

In the three months following September 11, the entire country was put on alert three times against imminent attacks, each for a number of days. For none of these alerts has the federal authority in charge been able to specify when or where or by what means the terrorists might act, or even who the terrorists might be.

REACTIONS TO THESE INTERNAL SECURITY MEASURES

The Media, Congress, and U.S. Allies

While the Patriot Act passed with a large majority in the House and with only one dissenting voice in the Senate, the more recent decisions taken by the government, especially the Presidential order that established the military tribunals for non-citizens suspected of terrorism, which thus effectively denies even U.S. residents who are not citizens the rights associated with civil trials, have met with increasing questions and concerns. The concerns about the violation of some of the civil rights guaranteed by the U.S. Constitution, the upsetting of the delicately balanced separate powers of the U.S. government, and the centralization of decision-making and power in the Presidency are well expressed by this editorial in the *New York Times* on Friday, November 16, 2001 called "A Travesty of Justice":

> President Bush's plan to use secret military tribunals to try terrorists is a dangerous idea, made even worse by the fact that it is so superficially attractive. In his effort to defend America from terrorists, Mr. Bush is eroding the very values and principles he seeks to protect, including the rule of law.

The administration's action is the latest in a troubling series of attempts since Sept. 11 to do an end run around the Constitution. It comes on the heels of an announcement that the Justice Department intends to wiretap conversations between some prisoners and their lawyers. The administration also continues to hold hundreds of detainees without revealing their identities, the charges being brought against them or even the reasons for such secrecy...

But by ruling that terrorists fall outside the norms of civilian and military justice, Mr. Bush has taken it upon himself to establish a prosecutorial channel that answers only to him. The decision is an insult to the exquisite balancing of executive, legislative and judicial powers that the framers incorporated into the Constitution... In the place of fair trials and due process he has substituted a crude and unaccountable system that any dictator would admire.

Alberto R. Gonzales, counsel to President Bush, in an article in the *New York Times* entitled: "Martial Justice, Full and Fair,"[3] responded to this kind of criticism:

Military commissions do not undermine the constitutional values of civil liberties or separation of powers; they protect them by ensuring that the United States may wage war against external enemies and defeat them. To defend the nation, President Bush has rightly sought to employ every lawful means at his disposal. Military commissions are one such means, and their judicious use will help keep Americans safe and free.

The response of the President, the Attorney General and others in the Bush administration to critics is demonstrated by this quote. Invariably the administration responds with some form of the argument that America is facing a crisis, a war, and one must do everything possible to defeat the enemy, that such measures are necessary, constitutional, and in accordance with precedents.

The measures taken to date, as well as the arguments put forward by government authorities to defend them, have met with considerable popular approval, so much so that it is probably politically unwise for elected officials who wish to be re-elected, to voice objections very loudly. Those few in Congress who do complain about aspects of the new measures or about being sidelined in their role as law-makers, or who raise questions about the constitutionality of these measures, by and large, do so with little fanfare.

The high levels of popularity enjoyed by the Bush administration, including approval ratings for the Attorney General John Ashcroft, make it easy for

Bush, Ashcroft, and others to dismiss those who question the constitutionality and morality of some of the measures that they have introduced, and to characterize those that do ask questions and voice concerns as small and radical groups of civil libertarians who, on the extreme left and right, are far from the mainstream of the U.S. population. Sometimes the administration has gone further than this as when John Ashcroft recently declared that those who do not support these measures "aid and abet" the enemy. He said: "To those who scare peaceloving people with phantoms of lost liberty, my message is this: your tactics only aid terrorists."[4]

The open support and enthusiasm for the Patriot Act on the part of the American public was followed by widespread but fairly quiet acquiescence regarding measures such as that of the establishment of the military tribunals for non-citizens suspected of terrorism. This apparent unanimity of support began to give way slightly by mid-December, a trend which was noted by an increasing number of journalists. An article published in the *New York Times* on December 12 is representative. It was published under the heading of "Public is Wary but Supportive on Rights Curbs". "Americans are willing to grant the government wide latitude in pursuing suspected terrorists but are wary of some of the Bush administration's recent counter-terrorism proposals and worried about the potential impact on civil liberties."

The international community began to react as well. Spain for example has made no secret of its refusal to cooperate with the United States by sending suspected terrorists for trial in the United States unless the latter guarantees that those suspects will not be tried by military courts. Similarly, France has announced its intention not to cooperate as long as there is the threat that persons extradited from France to the United States could face the death penalty.

This kind of reaction on the part of some American allies lends weight to those who argue that the military tribunals will have the opposite effect to that intended, because their use will provoke the allies into non-cooperation with the United States. The military tribunals also leave the United States open to the charge of yet one more type of American exceptionalism, since the U.S. seems to have no intention of using the International Court in the Hague.

THE ETHICAL DEBATE

The terrorist attacks demonstrated dramatically and tragically both the depth and breadth of terrorist possibilities and the extent of personal vulnerability inside the United States. The attacks greatly frightened the American people who are accustomed to thinking of themselves as invulnerable to such attacks, despite recent evidence to the contrary. Clearly it was critically important that government offices and departments respond quickly with a review of all the different aspects of internal security and that they take the necessary measures to insure the safety of citizens.

The "Patriot Bill", with its emphasis on the re-examination and updating of surveillance methods, the broadening of the term "terrorist" (a term which remains too vague), the provision for new powers to detain and expel non-citizens suspected of terrorist sentiments or activities, aimed at making up for what was experienced as a general lack of preparedness. The administration had to be seen to be taking the basic steps necessary to insure public safety. The sunset clause of December 31, 2003 that was built into the act, insured that if the steps were insufficient, or conversely too draconian, they would automatically be re-evaluated by Congress or expire. The fact that large bi-partisan majorities passed the bill was reassuring. Indeed few objections were raised at the time or later. The consensus seemed to be that, given the necessary trade offs between security and civil liberties, a good balance had been struck. Some measures were necessary and those taken, while they did limit elements of the civil liberties of all, they did not overly infringe on the rights either of citizens of the United States or non-citizen residents.

While the Patriot Act continues to enjoy considerable support, increasingly questions are being raised and comments made about many of the other internal security measures. Some of the questions relate to how each measure was passed, with objections raised at the small or even non-existent role that Congress has played since the passing of the Patriot Act. Other objections relate to the way non-citizens are being increasingly targeted and given separate treatment from citizens in terms of rights. Further there is concern about the secrecy that seems pervasive, from the gag rules in trials, to the government's introduction of measures against threats about which it cannot provide data. The concentration of power in Presidential hands is another fear of some. Each measure is different with correspondingly different responses. These are considered next.

MILITARY TRIBUNALS

The Presidential decree regarding military tribunals was by definition not an act of congress. There was thus no debate about the measure before it became law. This fact is one of the moral objections to the military tribunals. In addition the law stipulates that it is the President himself who decides which non-citizens suspected of terrorist activity will be tried in military tribunals. Thus not only does this give the President a new source of power, but, perhaps more importantly, debate is once again, not an option.

The measure, aimed as it is at all non-citizen residents of the United States, encompasses some twenty million people who are in the country legally, many of whom have been resident for many, many years and who contribute to the society in countless ways. There are moral issues that revolve around the separation between citizens of the United States and non-citizen residents. We live and work in the same communities, legal residents contribute greatly to the economic and cultural life of the U.S.; why then set them aside for this treatment? And why suppose implicitly that citizens are not or cannot be involved in terrorist activities? Is it not the case that citizens can also be terrorists? Indeed we have tragic and ample evidence that this can be the case. Why then the different legal treatment between citizens and non-citizens?

Another set of moral questions has to do with concerns about what happens to community, to trust, cooperation, to enjoyment of community when portions of it are separated out as suspect and treated differently? Here the memory of the camps for the Japanese Americans during the Second World War should give us pause for thought. In recent years many public figures have expressed their shame at their war-time support for the Japanese internment camps and their regret that Japanese citizens were not more fully trusted as integral members of their communities. The U.S. government, it seems, is currently making a similar mistake as it now begins to treat non-citizens, especially those from certain countries, with similar suspicion and a potential suspension of basic rights that in principle apply to all. What then, critics ask, have we learned morally from the internment of the Japanese during the War? At what point should or will this rupture of community become a common concern?

Terrorists exist, and probably within the United States, and they do have accomplices. Both the terrorists and their accomplices do need to be identified and brought to trial. But even for those who are guilty, or may be guilty, of terrorist acts, as heinous as their crimes are or may be, is it morally acceptable to treat them in a way that sets them apart, as if they are a different species? Should they rather be treated not differently, but as people who are entitled to the protection of the very laws that were created and perfected over the years to protect precisely those such as the terrorist suspects.

TOLERANCE

There is considerable irony in the fact that the terrorists, whose freedoms were sharply curtailed by their own governments in their countries of origin, took full advantage of the civil liberties enjoyed in the United States, including the freedom to practice religion. They used these freedoms, freedoms not available in many countries of the world, of movement, of religion, of financial transfers and so forth, in order to plan and carry out their attacks. Indeed given the legal restrictions in many of their countries of origin, had they remained there, it is likely that it would have been impossible to have planned and executed their attacks against the United States. Just as they used U.S. technology against U.S. targets, the terrorists used U.S. civil liberties against the country that had guaranteed them.

These attacks represent a considerable challenge to the ethos of tolerance in the North American society. This nature of the challenge is new because of the violent manner with which it is faced by the terrorist acts. The fact that the liberties of a tolerant society are enjoyed both by those who would ensure the liberties of others, and by those who would abuse them is not a new challenge. This is a moral conundrum which asserts itself with some regularity in a variety of ways in North American history. Should one advocate and practice tolerance towards those who one knows will use the legal rights and values of tolerance against its practitioners and the system itself? Can one morally do otherwise?

The freedom of religion in the United States is a highly valued civil right. How absolute that right is when it is abused by those who would violate other valued civil rights in the name of their religion, or for the sake of the practice of their religion, is a question that is open for on-going moral discussion and legal decisions. U.S. courts, for example, have often demonstrated their willingness to violate the freedom of religion of Christian Science parents for the right of the state to protect the right to life of the child whose parents do not want conventional medical treatment for the child.

IMMIGRATION

While no new dramatic laws are yet in place regarding immigration, it is clear that inside the United States and at the borders the unwritten rules have changed. The U.S. has announced that it will be slow to grant visas for young men from a number of countries considered to harbor terrorists and encourage terrorism. The recent crackdowns on student visa violations are new.

Colleges and universities, many of whom have considerable international student populations, are concerned about the changing immigration practices. They are also concerned about their moral and legal roles in the interviewing of targeted international students, or in advising the authorities of visa violations. Academic institutions are used to guarding their student records with great care. Now they worry about changing that practice and about the effect their participation in new procedures may have on student trust, on student community, and on student enrollment.

Immigration laws and practices are issues about which lively, informed debate is badly needed. Immigration law changed dramatically in 1965 when the U.S. started admitting an unprecedented number of immigrants. Interestingly, the 1965 immigration law is the source of much of the religious pluralism suddenly so evident in the United States today. Immigration priorities have in recent years clearly been oriented toward the accommodation of business, manufacturing, and agricultural interests which are strong advocates of ever new sources of plentiful, cheap labor. If the intention and practice of immigration law is to change, there should be a substantive, national debate.

There are always those in moments of crisis, such as the period since September 11, who will advocate the importance of the unlimited power of government to act quickly to deal with threats to safety. The military dictatorships of the Southern Cone of Latin America in the 1960s and 1970s counted on the majority of their populations making just this kind of calculation. In fact the ideology, developed in Latin America with the help of the U.S. military, used to justify the suppression of civil liberties for the sake of public security was called the "Doctrine of National Security." It was a doctrine which appealed to people's fear of unknown internal enemies related to, and aided by, external enemies (Communists), seeking to undermine the beliefs and way of life of South American countries, and which therefore justified unprecedented military and police power and the curtailment of civil liberties within each country.

There are also always those who will just as fiercely advocate vigorous defense of the full range of civil liberties. These are to be valued as the hard won accumulation of centuries of struggle, even if these rights may be used by those seeking to harm others or the system of government itself. This position is one that values civil liberties to such an extent that it is willing to risk national safety in order to protect them. Thus during the Viet Nam war, those who were against the war asserted their right to dissent even while the nation was at war, much to the fury of those on the other side. They also asserted the need to control the government's authoritarian impulses even in moments of crisis, and the importance of healthy national debate.

On balance we have, as a nation, learned a number of things that we forget at our peril. Whether it be the experiences I cite here – the Japanese internment; the experience with the Doctrine of National Security in the Southern Cone; and the experience of the Viet Nam war; – or the many, many other common experiences that one could cite. Our moral thought is in part shaped by and informed by these experiences and their contemporary parallels and analogies. In fact, one could argue that one national moral imperative is to remember what we have already learned.

THE RELIGIOUS RESPONSE

Over the months since September 11 one searches in vain for substantive public responses to the issues of internal security and civil liberties, on the part of the many religious communities in North America. Many religious communities moved quickly in their pastoral responses to the tragedy of September 11, and some were quick to express their hopes for a measured and reasonable U.S. military response in Afghanistan. A number of religious communities have underlined the need for justice, not revenge, in response to the attacks on September 11. But in regard to the issues of internal security and civil liberties, religious communities, whether Christian, Muslim, or Jewish, have not been vocal or visible. Consequently, members of religious communities are, by and large, left to think through these issues largely without aid from their religious leaders.

In Christianity at least three broad themes emerge as one moves towards the formation of a Christian ethical response to the questions and dilemmas posed by the tensions between internal security and civil liberties. The themes are Christian orientation towards the stranger; Christian understandings of human sin; and the Christian relationship to political authorities. I will discuss each in turn.

Hospitality to the stranger

The question of the stranger is and has been a central moral theme in Christianity. It is a theme that one confronts repeatedly in both the Hebrew Bible and in the New Testament. In these texts repeatedly, and in varieties of ways, faithfulness to God is viewed through the lens of the relationship to the alien or the stranger. Time and time again the faithfulness of an individual or of a whole community is either tested by its treatment of the alien in its midst or assessed according to the treatment of the stranger.

Central to the Christian faith is the understanding that love of God and love of neighbor go together, they are essentially inseparable. In the New Testament book of *Luke* the author records Jesus telling the story of someone who has been robbed and left at the side of the road. Twice people from his own tribe pass him by without stopping to help. The third person who passes stops to help. This third person however is a Samaritan, someone who is from outside the tribe of Israel. As Jesus finishes telling this story he asks his interlocutors: "which of these three, do you think, was a neighbor to the man who fell into the hands of the robbers?" The man replied "The one who showed him mercy." Jesus said to him, "Go and do likewise." (Luke 10: 36–37)

In this story as elsewhere Jesus teaches that the love of neighbor includes the love of the stranger. The stranger *is* the neighbor, regardless of the differences, such as tribe or kinship, prescribed by social convention. In stories such as this and in those of Jesus' own actions, the stranger, the alien, the outcast, the poor, are reached out to, embraced, included. This inclusion, this hospitality to the stranger, this willingness to see through social convention and established practices in order to serve the stranger and the ability to perceive that the stranger is indeed the neighbor is a central requirement of faith. This treatment of the stranger is suggestive today as communities across the country ponder the questions of strangers in their midst – especially those who are Muslim.

Suddenly to treat those who have been literally our neighbors for decades as strangers, and to separate them from the rest of the community as if they automatically bear the guilt of others who speak their language, hail from their country of origin, or practice the same religion, is an act of fear and intolerance which Christians would do well to question. Christian love of the other, the stranger, is as an active concern for open hospitality and justice. The inclusive norms of hospitality towards those that, because of their nation of origin and religion, many treat as "suspicious" should be followed even more carefully than usual. The fact that this is a nation composed almost entirely of immigrants adds weight to the importance of an ongoing ethic of inclusive hospitality for the millions who have done nothing wrong and find themselves caught in this conflict.

Clearly it is the case that there may be some among us, or from outside of the boundaries of the United States, who are guilty of crimes related to terrorism. Even for these people, however heinous their crimes may be, if the established norms of justice in practice in this country are to be violated, the reason and the justification for this must be very clear indeed. The moral burden to demonstrate urgent necessity is clearly on those who advocate suspension of rights. The Christian understanding of love is one that advocates justice and which takes as ongoing the active concern for humane conditions for all imprisoned, and just and fair legal treatment of those who have been arrested.

Human sin

The second broad theme helpful as we think about civil liberties is that of human sin. In the Christian tradition sin is understood as part of the human condition and thus part of each human being regardless of who or where he or she is. This understanding of sin is one that thus inevitably includes the self, the groups to which one belongs, and even the nation to which one belongs. The ubiquitous presence of sin among humanity is an understanding of sin which may encourage one to be quicker at self-critique, and slower to exclude even the terrorists and their sympathizers from the ranks of humanity, than has been the general public stance in the last few months.

The distribution of sin among all of humanity is also an understanding, which should enable one to think less exclusively in terms of "us" and "them". This ability to think outside the easy stereotypes, and thus more cautiously and carefully in ways which do not attribute only good to one side, and only evil to the other, is not popular at times of war when people want quick and easy answers and want also to be assured that theirs is the righteous cause. And indeed it has not been popular during this time of conflict, either with citizens or their leaders. But while perhaps not appreciated in such times of fear and conflict, the refusal to demonize even one's enemies is a necessary and important contribution to the debate, and one that Christians, among others, could offer.

The theologian Reinhold Niebuhr describes sin as (in part) the temptation of people who are in fact full of limitations, to see themselves as without limits, and, thus accordingly, to see the "other" as the carrier of all sin and limitation. This temptation to view the self and the groups to which one belongs as good and the other as evil is particularly true of social groups according to Niebuhr. Individuals are more likely to be capable of complex thought than the groups to which they belong. But be it as individuals or groups Niebuhr writes: "But man is destined, both by the imperfection of his knowledge and by his desire to overcome his finiteness, to make absolute claims for his partial and finite values. He tries, in short, to make himself God."[5]

Elsewhere Niebuhr makes the same point in a way that seems as if he were speaking directly both to the people of the United States and to the terrorists who attacked it: "Nothing short of the knowledge of the true God will save them from the impiety of making themselves God and the cruelty of seeing their fellow men as devils because they are involved in the same pretension."[6] The Protestant theologian Paul Tillich, who knew war even more directly than Reinhold Niebuhr, also emphasizes the importance of careful and subtle thought and a realistic awareness of limits especially in times of international conflict and security fears at home. In writing about this theme he sometimes uses the image of "saying yes and saying no."

> Yes alone is the arrogance which claims that its limited truth is the ultimate, but which reveals by its fanatical self-affirmation how many hidden No's are present in its ground. No alone is the resignation which denies any ultimate truth but which shows by its self-complacent irony against the biting power of every word of truth how strong the Yes to itself is that underlies its ever-repeated No.
>
> Truth as well as life unite Yes and No, and only the courage which accepts the infinite tension between Yes and No can have abundant life and ultimate truth. How is such a courage possible? It is possible because there is a Yes above the Yes and a No above the No of life and of truth. But it is a truth which is not our own.[7]

Autonomy

Finally, it is important at times such as these for Christians to think through their many relationships with the state to which they belong and its governing authorities. Western history is replete with examples of the wide range of possibilities in this relationship, ranging from Christian legitimation of and unquestioning support of the State regardless of what it does, to Christian resistance to governmental authorities, at least on the part of some groups, over matters of conscience such as that of slavery. Tillich, who lived in Nazi Germany and then the United States during the Second World War, is careful to admonish Christians that "this truth which is not our own" referred to above, is not the truth of the civil authorities of the states to which we belong. Thus Tillich believes it is important not to identify too closely as a Christian individual or group with any given state, but rather to guard a relative autonomy and independence of thought and values. Here also it is important to say both "yes" and "no."

Such Christian leaders as Martin Luther King also demonstrated the importance of maintaining a loyal but critical distance from governments and authorities. This distance enables one to raise questions, to think for oneself as a person of faith, to see things from fresh angles. This distance also ensures against the temptation of religious authorities to lend their legitimacy and authority uncritically to the civil authorities. While loyalty is important, especially at times of war, one way religious authorities can be loyal is to ensure the requirements of justice, through such things as demanding that the civil authorities act with the greatest possible transparency in decision-making; that the authorities give substantive reasons for the decisions made; and also to seek assurance from the proper authorities that the measures taken are directly responsive specifically to security needs and not to other agendas or fears or prejudices.

Like the people they represent, democratic governments are not always wise, they can make serious mistakes especially in times of war, mistakes that might be prevented in a context of open discussion and debate. At the very least, open discussion invites the full range of opinion in the society, and it may act helpfully to brake government action that otherwise would proceed too quickly or move in the wrong direction.

Patriotic zeal and religious faithfulness are not the same thing and cannot be conflated. "God bless America" is a supplication, a plea or a prayer of an insecure people seeking to discern and do God's will. But both the arrogance of power and the hysteria of fear turn "God Bless America" into a statement of special righteousness and privilege. This leads to the mistaken and dangerous conclusion that God is "on our side." This facile and simplistic conclusion is one to which Christians should say a resounding "No," even as we affirm our need for protection.

While the ethical reflection of theologians such as Tillich and Niebuhr do not solve the specific moral problems related to questions of civil liberties and internal security, they do suggest a tone, an attitude, which while respectful of the need to ensure internal security, and to bring to trial the guilty, seeks to be fair minded and dispassionate, welcoming of the stranger, which seeks equal justice for neighbor and stranger and which is ever aware of its own limitations.

It is likely that even agreeing on a common approach, Christians will not always agree among themselves or with others, on where the lines should be drawn in the tension between civil liberties and internal cohesion or security. Indeed the lines can be and are drawn in different ways in different societies, at different moments in history. Even among democracies in the West the lines can be and are drawn very differently. While agreement is probably impossible, debate about where to draw the lines is possible and very important. In fact it is in part though vigorous and public debate that Christians can live out their care for justice to the stranger, and also continue to contribute to the ongoing vocation of the United States, a land of immigrants, as a place of refuge, and a space of democratic rights for just such debate.

Public debate, equal treatment of all, the checks and balances of democratic government are, as it turns out, the best kinds of measures available to encourage responsible leadership and careful decisions. One concludes therefore that the morally best, if not the most efficient way to fight terrorism, and thus to ensure internal security, is in the end through the use of the practices and laws of democracy as hammered out over the last several centuries. It seems fitting that since it is the case that terrorists can use the practices and liberties of democracy against that democracy itself, so too can that democracy use its own practices and liberties against the terrorists.

NOTES

1. Todd S. Purdum, "Ashcroft's About-Face on the Detainees," *New York Times*, November 26, 2001.
2. "10 Arrested in Visa Cases in San Diego," *New York Times*, December 11, 2001.
3. *New York Times*, November 30, 2001.
4. "A Nation Challenged: The Senate Hearing; Ashcroft Defends Anti-terror Plan; Says Criticism May Aid U.S. Foes," *New York Times*, December 6, 2001.
5. Niebuhr, Reinhold, *An Interpretation of Christian Ethics* (New York: Meridian Books, 1956): 82.
6. Ibid., 213.
7. See Tillich, Paul, "Yes and No." In Paul Tillich, *The New Being*, (New York: Charles Scribner and Sons, 1955): 102.

BIBLIOGRAPHY

CHAPTER ONE

Niebuhr, H. Richard, *The Responsible Self: An Essay in Christian Moral Philosophy* (San Francisco: Harper and Row Publishers, 1963).

Niebuhr, H. Richard, "War as Crucifixion." *Christian Century* 60 (April 28, 1943).

CHAPTER TWO

Abu Zayd, Nasr Hamid, *Mafhum al-nass: dirasa fi 'ulum al-qur'an* (Casablanca: al-Markaz al-Thaqafi al-'Arabi, 1988).

Abu-Rabi', Ibrahim M., *Intellectual Origins of Islamic Resurgence in the Modern Arab World* (Albany: State University of New York Press, 1996).

Adonis ['Ali Ahmad Sa'id], "Reflections on the Manifestations of Intellectual Backwardness in Arab Society." In *CEMAM Reports* (Beirut: St. Joseph University, 1974), and *al-Thabit wa'l mutahawwil*, 3 vols (Beirut: Dar al-'Awdah, 1983).

Ahmad, Khurshid, "Islam and Democracy: Some Conceptual and Contemporary Dimensions." *Muslim World*, 90 (1&2), Spring 2000.

Ahmed, Akbar, *Jinnah, Pakistan and Islamic Identity: The Search for Saladin* (London: Routledge, 1997).

Akbar, M. J., *Nehru: the Making of India* (London: Viking, 1988).

Akhdar, al-'Afif, "Min naqd al-sama' ila naqd al-ard" in F. Lenin, *Nusus hawla al-mawqif mina al-din*, tr. Muhammad al-Kabbe (Beirut: Dar al-Tali'ah, 1972).

Alavi, Hamza, "Pakistan and Islam: Ethnicity and Ideology." In Fred Halliday and Hamza Alavi, eds., *State and Ideology in the Middle East and Pakistan* (New York: Monthly Review Press, 1998).

Ali, Tariq, *Can Pakistan Survive? The Death of a State* (London: Penguin, 1983).

Alili, Rochdy, *Qu'est-ce que l'islam?* (Paris: La Découverte, 1996).

Anderson, Benedict, *Imagined Communities* (London: Verso, 1991).

——, *The Spectre of Comparisons: Nationalism, Southeast Asia and the World* (London: Verso, 1998).

Arkoun, Muhammed,"History as an Ideology of Legitimation: A Comparative Approach in Islamic and European Contexts." In Gema M. Munoz, ed., *Islam, Modernism, and the West* (London: I. B. Tauris, 1999).

Asad, Talal, *Genealogies of Religion: Discipline and Reasons of Power in Christianity and Islam* (Baltimore: Johns Hopkins Press, 1993).

Asfur, Jabir, *Hawamish 'ala daftar al-tanwir* (Cairo: Dar Su'ad al-Sabah, 1994).

Ayubi, Nazih, *Political Islam* (London: Routledge, 1994).

Azm, Sadiq Jalal, *Naqd al-fikr al-dini* (Beirut: Dar al-Tali'ah, 1969).

——, *al-Naqd al-dhati ba'da al-hazimah* (Beirut: Dar al-Tali'ah, 1969).

——, "Sur l'islam, la laïcité et l'Occident." *Le Monde Diplomatique*, September 1999.

Barakat, Halim, *The Arab World: Society, Culture, and Change* (Berkeley: University of California Press, 1993).

Barsamian, David, *Iqbal Ahmad: Confronting Empire* (Cambridge: South End Press, 2000).

Beddoes, Julie, *London Review of Books*, 23 (23), November 29, 2001.

Benjamin, Walter, "Critique of Violence." In Peter Demetz, ed., *Reflections: Walter Benjamin* (New York: Harcourt, 1978).

Bennabi, Malek, *Islam in History and Society*, tr. Asma Rashid (Islamabad: Islamic Research Institute, 1988).

Berman, Marshall, *All That is Solid Melts into Air: The Experience of Modernity* (London: Penguin, 1982).

Bishri, Tariq, *al-Hiwar al-islami al-'ilmani* (Cairo: Dar al-Shuruq, 1996).

Bouhdiba, Abdelwahab, "Place et fonction de l'imaginaire dans la société arabo-musulmane." In *Culture et société* (Tunis: Université de Tunis, 1978).

Brahimi, Abdelhamid, *Stratégie de développement pour l'Algérie* (Paris: Economica, 1991).

Brown, L. Carl, *Tunisia: The Politics of Modernization* (New York: Praeger, 1964).

Burgat, François, ed., *L'Islamisme au Maghreb: La Voix du sud* (Paris: Karthala, 1988).

Charfi, 'Abd al-Majid, *Tahdith al-fikr al-islami* (Casablanca: Nashr al-Fennek, 1998).

Chatterjee, Partha, *The Nation and Its Fragments: Colonial and Postcolonial Histories* in *The Partha Chatterjee Omnibus* (New Delhi: Oxford University Press, 1999).

Chaudhuri, K. N., *Trade and Civilization in the Indian Ocean: An Economic History from the Rise of Islam to 1750* (Cambridge: Cambridge University Press, 1985).

Cooley, John K., *Unholy Wars: Afghanistan, America and International Terrorism* (London: Pluto Press, 2000).

Davis, Anthony, "How the Taliban became a Military Power." In William Maley, ed., *Fundamentalism Reborn: Afghanistan and the Taliban* (New York: New York University Press, 1998).

Gellner, Ernest, *Muslim Society* (Cambridge: Cambridge University Press, 1981).

Ghannoushi, Rashid, *al-Huriyyat al-'ammah fi'l dawlah al-islamiyyah* (Markaz Dirasat al-Wihdah al-'Arabiyyah, 1993).

——, *On Secularism and Civil Society* [Arabic] (London: al-Markaz al-Magharibi li'l Buhuth, 1999).

Gibb, Hamilton, *The Travels of Ibn Battuta*, three volumes (New Delhi: Munshiram, 1993).

Girard, Rene, *Violence and the Sacred* (Baltimore: the Johns Hopkins University Press, 1979), and *Things Hidden since the Foundation of the World* (Stanford: Stanford University Press, 1987).

Goodson, Larry P., *Afghanistan's Endless War: State Failure, Regional Politics, and the Rise of the Taliban* (Seattle: University of Washington Press, 2001).

Hammami, Rema and Martina Rieker, "Feminist Orientalism and Orientalist Marxism." *New Left Review*, 170, July–August 1988.

Harvey, David, *The Condition of Postmodernity* (Oxford: Basil Blackwell, 1989).

Hasan, Mushirul, *Legacy of a Divided Nation: India's Muslims since Independence* (Boulder: Westview Press, 1997).

Hefner, Robert, *Civil Society: Muslims and Democratization in Indonesia* (Princeton: Princeton University Press, 2000).

Heyd, Uriel, "The Ottoman Ulema and Westernization in the Time of Selim III and Mahmud II." In Albert Hourani, Philip Khoury and Mary Wilson, eds., *The Modern Middle East: A Reader* (Berkeley: University of California Press, 1993).

Huwaydi, Fahmi, *al-Maqalat al-mahdhurah* (Cairo: Dar al-Shuruq, 1998).

Ibn Khaldun, *The Muqaddimah: An Introduction to History*, three volumes, tr. Franz Rosenthal (New York: Pantheon Books, 1958).

Ibrahim, Sa'd al-Din, "al-Mufakkir wa'l amir: tajsir al-fajwah bayana sani'i al-qarar wa'l mufakirrin al-'arab." In al-Tahir Labib, *al-Intellijensia al-'arabiyyah* (Tunis: al-Dar al-'Arabiyyah li'l Kitab, n.d.).

Ibrahimi, 'Abd al-Hamid, *al-Maghreb al-'arabi fi muftaraq al-turuq fi dhil al-tahawwulat al-duwaliyyah* (Beirut: Markaz Dirasat al-Wihdah al-'Arabiyyah, 1996).

'Imarah, Muhammad, *al-Dawlah al-islamiyyah bayna al-'ilmaniyyah wa'l sultah al-madaniyyah* (Cairo: Dar al-Shuruq, 1988).

Jabiri, Muhammad 'Abid, "al-Mujtama' al-madani: tasa'ulat wa afaq." In 'Abdallah Hammoudi, *Wa'y al-Mujtama' bi dhatihi: 'an al-mujtama' al-madani fi'l maghrib al-'arabi* (Casablanca: Dar Tubqal, 1998).

Jarrah, Nuri, *al-firdaws al-dami: wahid wa thalathin yawman fi'l jaza'ir [The Bleeding Paradise: 31 Days in Algeria]* (London: Riad al-Rayyes Books, 2000).

Kahin, George, *Nationalism and Revolution in Indonesia* (Ithaca: Cornell University Press, 1952).

Kakar, M. Hassan, *Afghanistan: The Soviet Invasion and the Afghan Response, 1979–1982* (Berkeley: University of California Press, 1995).

Kenz, Ali, "al-Islam wa'l hawiyyah: Mulahadhat li'l bahth." In Markaz Dirasat al-Wihdah al-'Arabiyyah, *al-Din fi'l mujtama' al-'arabi* (Beirut: Markaz Dirasat al-Wihdah al-'Arabiyyah, 1990).

——, *Algerian Reflections on Arab Crises*, tr. Robert W. Stooky (Austin: Texas: University of Texas Press, 1991).

Khan, Bashir Ahmad, "The Ahl-i-Hadith: A Socio-Religious Reform Movement in Kashmir." *The Muslim World*, 90 (1&2), Spring 2000.

Kolakowski, L., *Main Currents of Marxism*, vol. III (Oxford: Oxford University Press, 1978).

Laroui, Abdallah, *L'idéologie arabe contemporaine* (Paris: Maspero, 1970).

——, *The Crisis of the Arab Intelligentsia: Traditionalism or Historicism?* (Berkeley: University of California Press, 1976).

Laski, Harold J., *Liberty in the Modern State* (Harmondsworth: Penguin Books, 1938).

Mahmud, Zaki Najib, *Tajdid al-fikr al-'arabi* (Cairo: Dar al-Shuruq, 1978).

Malik, Jamal, *Colonialization of Islam: Dissolution of Traditional Institutions in Pakistan* (New Delhi: Manohar, 1996).

Massignon, Louis, *Essay on the Technical Language of Islamic Mysticism*, tr. Benjamin Clark (Notre Dame: University of Notre Dame Press, 1997).

Matinuddin, Kamal, *The Taliban Phenomenon: Afghanistan 1994–1997* (Karachi: Oxford University Press, 1999).

Mustafa, Yusra, "Azmat al-muthaqaf al-'aqlani." In Mahmud Amin al-'Alim, *Qadayah Fikriyyah, al-Fikr al-'Arabi 'ala masharif al-qarn al-wahid wa'l 'ishrun* (Cairo: Dar Qadayah Fikriyyah, 1995).

Nizami, Khaliq Ahmad, *History of the Aligarah Muslim University* (New Delhi: Idarah-I Adabiyat-I Delli, 1995).

Noer, Deliar, *The Modernist Muslim Movement in Indonesia, 1900–1942* (Kuala Lumpur: Oxford University Press, 1978).

Qureshi, Ishtiaq Husain, *Education in Pakistan* (Karachi: Ma'aref, 1975).

Racine, Jean-Luc, "Pakistan: Quel islam pour quelle nation? *Le Monde Diplomatique*, December 2001.

Rahman, Fazlur, *Islam and Modernity: Transformation of an Intellectual Tradition* (Chicago: University of Chicago Press, 1982).

Ramonet, Ignacio, "Nouvel ordre, rébellions, nationalismes: Un monde à reconstruire." *Le Monde Diplomatique*, May 1992.

Rashid, Ahmed, *Taliban: Militant Islam, Oil and Fundamentalism in South Asia* (New Haven: Yale University Press, 2001).

Roethke, Theodore, "The Far Field." In *The Collected Poems of Theodore Roethke* (New York: Doubleday, 1975).

Rosenthal, Franz, "The Stranger in Medieval Islam." *Arabica: Journal of Arabic and Islamic Studies*, XLIV (1), January 1997.

Sa'id, Rif'at, "al-Islam al-siyasi: mina al-tatarruf ila mazind mina al-tatarruf." In *Qadayah Fikriyyah*, vol. viii, 1989.

Shafiq, Munir, *Fi al-hadathah wa'l khitab al-hadathi* (Casablanca: al-Markaz al-Thaqafi al-'Arabi, 1999).

Shukri, Ghali, *al-Nahdah wa'l suqut fi'l fikr al-misri al-hadith* (Beirut: Dar al-Tal'iah, 1982).

——, "Misr: firdaws khayru al-umam." In *Qadayah Fikriyyah*, vols 13–14, 1989.

——, *Mudhakarat thaqafah tahtadir* (Cairo: al-Hay'ah al-Misriyyah al-'Ammah, 1995).

——, *Diktatoriyat al-takhalluf al-'arabi* (Cairo: al-Hay'ah al-Misriyyah al-'Ammah li'l Kitab, 1994).

Sullivan, Andrew, "This is a Religious War." *New York Times Magazine*, October 7, 2001.

Tizini, Tayyib, "Nahwa 'ilmaniyyah takun madkhalan li mashru' 'arabi nahdawi jadid." *Al-Tariq*, 55 (6), 1996.

Toffler, Alvin, *Future Shock* (New York: New York University Press, 1970).

Vassiliev, Alexi, *The History of Saudi Arabia* (New York: New York University Press, 2000).

Wannas, Munassif, "al-Din wa'l dawla fi Tunis: 1956–1987." In Markaz Dirasat al-Wihdah al-'Arabiyyah, *al-Din fi'l mujtama' al-'arabi* (Beirut: Markaz Dirasat al-Wihdah al-'Arabiyyah, 1990).

Warraq, al-Haj, "Sina'at al-wahm: al-asbab al-ijtima'iyyah li dhahirat al-hawas al-dini fi'l sudan." In *Qadayah Fikriyyah*, vol. viii, 1989.

Williams, Raymond, "Means of Communication as Means of Production." In his *Problems in Materialism and Culture: Selected Essays* (London: Verso, 1997).

Wink, André, *Al-Hind: The Making of the Indo-Islamic World*, 2 vols (New Delhi: Oxford University Press, 1996).

Zakariyya, Fouad, *al-Sahwah al-islamiyyah fi mizan al-'aql* (Cairo: Dar al-Fikr li'l Dirasat wa'l Nashr wa'l Tawzi', 1989).

——, "al-Falsafah wa'l din fi'l mujtama' al-'arabi al-mu'asir." In Markaz Dirasat al-Wihdah al-'Arabiyyah, *al-Falsafah fi'l watan al-'arabi al-mu'asir* (Beirut: Markaz Dirasat al-Wihdah al-'Arabiyyah, 1985).

——, "al-'Ilmaniyyah darurah hadariyyah".

Zaki, Ramzi, *Wada'an li'l tabaqah al-mutawasitah* (Cairo: Dar al-Mustaqbal al-'Arabi, 1998).

Zghal, Abdelkader "al-Istratijiyya al-jadidah li harakat al-itijah al-islami: munawara an al-ta'bir 'an al-thaqafah al-siyasiyyah al-tunisiyyah." In Markaz Dirasat al-Wihdah al-'Arabiyyah, *al-Din fi'l mujtama' al-'arabi* (Beirut: Markaz Dirasat al-Wihdah al-'Arabiyyah, 1990).

——, Le retour de sacré et la nouvelle demande idéologique de jeunes scolarises: Le cas de la Tunisie." *Le Maghreb Musulman,* 1979.

Ziring, Lawrence, *Pakistan in the Twentieth Century: A Political History* (Karachi: Oxford University Press, 1997).

Zurayk, Q., *al-Mualafat al-kamilah li'l doktor Qustantine Zurayk,* 4 vols (Beirut: Markaz Dirasat al-Wihdah al-'Arabiyyah, 1995).

CHAPTER THREE

"American Baptist Men Disaster Relief Teams Participate in New York City Clean-Up" [internet]. American Baptist News Service, October 22, 2001 [cited November 26, 2001]. Available from http://www.abc-usa.org/news/102201.htm.

Ammerman, Nancy T., "Congregation and Community" (New Brunswick, NJ: Rutgers University Press, 1997).

——, "Doing Good in American Communities: Congregations and Service Organizations Working Together" [internet]. Hartford Institute for Religion Research, March, 2000 [cited 2001]. Available from http://hirr.hartsem.edu/about/about_orw_cong-report.html.

——, "Connecting Mainline Protestant Congregations with Public Life." In Robert Wuthnow and John Evans, eds., *Quietly Influential: The Public Role of Mainline Protestantism* (Berkeley, CA: University of California Press, 2002).

Becker, Penny Edgell, *Congregations in Conflict: Cultural Models of Local Religious Life* (Cambridge: Cambridge University Press, 1999).

Berger, Peter L., *The Sacred Canopy,* (Garden City, New York: Anchor Doubleday, 1969).

Chaves, Mark, "Religious Congregations and Welfare Reform: Who Will Take Advantage of 'Charitable Choice'?" *American Sociological Review,* 64 (1999): 836–846.

Church World Service, "Fact Sheet – CWS Domestic Terrorism Recovery" [internet]. October 16, 2001 [cited November 20, 2001]. Available from http://www.church-worldservice.org/WTC/factsheet.htm.

Cnaan, Ram A., "Social and Community Involvement" (Unpublished paper, University of Pennsylvania School of Social Work 1997).

Davie, Grace, *Religion in Modern Europe: A Memory Mutates* (Oxford: Oxford University Press, 2000).

Dewan, Shaila K., "Feelings of Loss and the Sound of Silence Greet Families at the Site." *New York Times,* October 29, 2001.

Dunlap, David W., "Near Ground Zero, Unbowed Spires." *New York Times,* September 30, 2001.

Eiesland, Nancy, *A Particular Place: Urban Restructuring and Religious Ecology* (New Brunswick, NJ: Rutgers University Press, 2000).

Furst, Gil, "September 11 Attack: Report" [internet]. Evangelical Lutheran Church in America, November 16, 2001 [cited November 30, 2001]. Available from http://elca.org.dcs/disaster/sept11.html.

"Gallup Poll Topics: Religion" [internet]. The Gallup Organization, 2001 [cited December 1, 2001]. Available from http://www.gallup.com/poll/indicators/indreligion.asp.

Gillespie, Joanna B., "Gender and Generations in Congregations." In Catherine Prelinger, ed., *Episcopal Women*. (New York: Oxford University Press, 1993) 167–221.

Grider, Sylvia, "Preliminary Observations Regarding the Spontaneous Shrines Following the Terrorist Attacks of September 11, 2001" [internet]. *New Directions in Folklore*, October 5, 2001 [cited November 20, 2001]. Available from http://www.temple.edu/isllc/newfolk/shrines.html.

Gross, Jane, "Stretching a Jewish Vigil for the Sept. 11 Dead." *New York Times*, November 6, 2001.

"Harnessing the Spirit of Sept. 11." *New York Times*, November 5, 2001.

Hartford Institute for Religion Research, "How Common Are Interfaith Ties among US Congregations?" [internet]. 2001 [cited November 29, 2001]. Available from http://www.hirr.hartsem.edu/research/quick_question14.html.

Marty, Martin E., "America at Prayer." *Christian Century*, 118 (26), 2001: 47.

McFadden, Robert D., "In a Stadium of Heroes, Prayers for the Fallen and Solace for Those Left Behind." *New York Times*, September 24, 2001.

McRoberts, Omar M., "Saving Four Corners." (Unpublished dissertation, Harvard University, 2000).

Niebuhr, Gustav, "After the Attacks: A Day of Worship; Excerpts from Sermons across the Nation." *New York Times*, September 17, 2001.

——, "At Houses of Worship, Feelings Are Shared and Comfort Is Sought in Greater Numbers." *New York Times*, September 17, 2001.

——, "Clergy of Many Faiths Answer Tragedy's Call." *New York Times*, September 15, 2001.

——, "Shrines Serve the Need for Healing in Public Spaces." *New York Times*, October 6, 2001.

Orr, John B., Donald E. Miller, Wade Clark Roof, and J. Gordon Melton, *Politics of the Spirit: Religion and Multiethnicity in Los Angeles* (Los Angeles: University of Southern California, 1994).

Putnam, Robert D., "Bowling Alone: America's Declining Social Capital." *Journal of Democracy*, 6 (1), 1995: 65–78.

——, Bowling Alone: The Collapse and Revival of American Community (New York: Simon & Schuster, 2000).

Roof, Wade Clark, *Spiritual Marketplace: Baby Boomers and the Remaking of American Religion*. (Princeton, New Jersey: Princeton University Press, 1999).

Soman, Kathryn. "St. Paul's Chapel in Wake of WTC Disaster: 'An Organic New Ministry Finds Us'" [internet]. St. Paul's Chapel News, 2001 [cited November 25, 2001]. Available from http://www.saintpaulschapel.org/news/alert_91.html.

The Salvation Army, "The State of the Relief Effort" [internet]. November 7, 2001 [cited November 30, 2001]. Available from http://www.salvationarmy-usaeast.org/disaster.

Stevens, Mark, "Modern Ruins: How the Spontaneous Outpourings of 'Art' since the Disaster Have Brought a New (Old) Look to the City" (November 12, 2001 issue of *New York Magazine*) [internet]. Newyorkmetro.com, 11/20/01 [cited November 20, 2001]. Available from http://www.nymag.com.

Turner, Victor, *The Ritual Process*. (Ithaca, New York: Cornell University Press, 1977).

Van Veen, Dan, "'How Can I Help?' Christ in Action Ministry Explains What Is Needed" [internet]. Assemblies of God News Service, September 21, 2001 [cited November 26, 2001]. Available from http://ag.org/top/news.

Wakin, Daniel J., "Attacks Spur a Surge of Interest in Religion: As Attendance at Services Rises, Clerics Hope for a General Moral Uplift." *New York Times*, September 30, 2001.

——, "Bronx Mosque Provides a Place for Prayer, and More" [internet]. The New York Times on the Web, November 16, 2001 [cited November 20, 2001]. Available from http://www.nytimes.com/2001/11/16/nyregion.

——, "Seeking Guideposts to Help in No-Man's Land." *New York Times*, November 18, 2001.

Warner, R. Stephen, "Changes in the Civic Role of Religion." In Neil J. Smelser and Jeffrey C. Alexander, eds., *Diversity and Its Discontents: Cultural Conflict and Common Ground in Contemporary American Society* (Princeton: Princeton University Press, 1999), 229–243.

——, "The Place of the Congregation in the Contemporary American Religious Configuration." In James Wind and James Lewis, eds., *American Congregations: New Perspectives in the Study of Congregations* (Chicago: University of Chicago Press, 1994).

World Vision International, "World Vision Response: Making an Impact," November 20, 2001 [cited November 20, 2001]. Available from http://www.wvi.org/home.shtml.

Wuthnow, Robert, *Acts of Compassion: Caring for Others and Helping Ourselves*. (Princeton: Princeton University Press, 1991).

——, *After Heaven: Spirituality in America since the 1950s*. (Berkeley: University of California Press, 1998).

——, *Loose Connections: Joining Together in America's Fragmented Communities* (Cambridge, Mass.: Harvard University Press, 1998).

——, "Mobilizing Civic Engagement: The Changing Impact of Religious Involvement." In Theda Skocpol and Morris P. Fiorina, eds., *Civic Engagement in American Democracy* (Washington, DC: Brookings Institution Press, 1999).

——, *The Restructuring of American Religion* (Princeton, N.J.: Princeton University Press, 1988).

CHAPTER FOUR

"Congregations and Social Services: What They Do, How They Do it, and with Whom," *Nonprofit and Voluntary Sector Quarterly*, 30, December, 2001.

Claman, Victor N., and David E. Butler, *Acting On Your Faith: Congregations Making a Difference* (Boston: Insights, 1994).

Cnann, Ram A. and Stephanie C. Boddie, "Black Church Outreach: Comparing How Black and Other Congregations Serve Their Needy Neighbors" (University of Pennsylvania, CRRUCS Report 2001–1).

Dudley, Carl S. and David A. Roozen (eds.), *Faith Communities Today (FACT) A Report On Religion in the United States Today* (Hartford CT: Hartford Institute for Religion Research, Hartford Seminary, 2001).

Dudley, Carl S., *Next Steps Toward Community Ministry* (Bethesda, Md: Alban Institute, 1996).

Dudley, Carl S., *Basic Steps in Community Ministries* (Bethesda, Md: Alban Institute, 1991).

Dudley, Carl, and Sally A. Johnson, *Energizing the Congregation: Images that Shape Your Church's Ministry* (Westminster/John Knox, 1993).

Dudley, Carl S., *Welfare, Faith-Based Ministries and Charitable Choice* (Hartford Institute for Religion Research, Hartford, CT, March, 2001).

Dudley, Carl, *Community Ministries: Proven Steps and New Challenges in Faith Based Initiatives* (Bethesda, Md: Alban Institute, 2002).

Green, Clifford J., *Churches, Cities, and Human Community: Urban Ministry in the United States 1945–1985* (Grand Rapids, MN: William B. Eerdmans, 1996).

Gunderson, Gary, *Deeply Woven Roots: Improving the Quality of Life in Your Community* (Minneapolis: Fortress Press, 1997).

Harrison, Bennett and Marcus Weiss, *Networking Across Boundaries: New Directions in Community Based Job Training and Economic Development* (Boston: Economic Development Assistance Consortium, 1998).

Horwitz, Claudia, *A Stone's Throw: Living the Act of Faith: Social Transformation through Faith and Spiritual Practice* (Durham, N.C.: Stone Circles, 1999).

Jeavons, Thomas, *When the Bottom Line is Faithfulness* (Indiana: Indiana University Press, 1993).

Loeb, Paul Rogat, *Soul of a Citizen: Living with Conviction in a Cynical Time* (New York: St. Martin's Griffin, 1999).

Perkins, John, *Beyond Charity* (Grand Rapids: Baker, 1993).

Said, Carolyn, "Foundations launch campaign to support safety net charities," *San Francisco Chronicle*, December 5, 2001.

Sherman, Amy, *Reinvigorating Faith in Communities* (Indianapolis, IN: Hudson Institute, 2002).

Sider, Ronald J, Philip N. Olson and Heidi Rolland Unruh, *Churches that Make a Difference: Reaching Your Community with Good News and Good Works* (Grand Rapids: Baker Books, 2001).

Streeter, Ryan, *Transforming Charity: Toward a Results-Oriented Social Sector* (Indianapolis, IN: Hudson Institute, 2001).

Trulear, Harold Dean, "Faith-Based Institutions and High-Risk Youth" (Philadelphia: Public/Private Ventures, Field Report Series, Spring, 2000).

Warren, Mark R. and Richard L. Wood, *Faith Based Community Organizing: The State of the Field*. Jericho, NY: Interfaith Funders, 2001.

Wineberg, Bob, "The Spirit of Charitable Choice" (Greensboro, NC: School of Social Work, University of North Carolina Greensboro, 1999).

Wuthnow, Robert, *The Crisis in the Churches: Spiritual Malaise, Fiscal Woe* (Oxford: OUP 1997).

Wuthnow, Robert, *Poor Richard's Principle* (Princeton: Princeton University Press, 1996).

CHAPTER FIVE

Crane, Robert, "A Wake-up call for America and Muslims World-Wide," in September 2001 issue of *Islam21* on-line magazine, http://www.islam21.net/pages/keyissues/key7–2.htm.

Drew, Benjamin, *The Refugee* or *the Narratives of Fugitive Slaves in Canada related by Themselves with An Account of the History and Condition of the Colored Population of Upper Canada* (Toronto: Prospero, 2000).

El Fadl Khaled Abou, "Islam and the Theology of Power," *Middle East Report*, 221, Winter 2001.

Siddiqi, 'Abdul Hamid, translator and editor *Sahih Muslim: being traditions of the sayings and doings of the Prophet Muhammad as narrated by his companions and compiled under the title* al-Jami'-us-Sahih, 4 vols. (Beirut: Dar al-Arabia, n.d.), 4, 1367.

UASR, *Renaissance Man: Dato Seri Anwar Ibrahim, Former Deputy Prime-Minister of Malaysia*, UASR Regional Report Series, 3 (Springfield, VA: UASR Publishing Group Inc., 2001).

Watt, W. Montgomery, *Muhammad at Medina* (Oxford: Oxford University Press, 1956).

CHAPTER SIX

Aquino, Maria Pilar and Elisabeth Schussler Fiorenza, eds., *In the Power of Wisdom: Feminist Spiritualities of Struggle* (London: SCM, 2000).

Barton, Stephen C., *The Spirituality of the Gospels* (Peabody, Massachusetts: Hendrickson, 1992).

Berry, Thomas, *The Great Work: Our Way into the Future* (New York: Bell Tower, 1999).

Bingen, Hildegard of, *Liber divinorum operum*: Patrologia Latina, vol. 197, 1098–1179.

Bohm, David, *Quantum Theory* (London: Constable, 1951).

Borg, Marcus and Ross MacKenzie (eds.), *God at 2000* (Harrison, Pennsylvania: Morehouse, 2000).

Borg, Marcus, *The God We Never Knew: Beyond Dogmatic Religion to a More Authentic Contemporary Faith* (San Francisco: Harper and Row, 1997).

Borysenko, Joan, *A Woman's Book of Life: The Biology, Psychology, and Spirituality of the Feminine Life Cycle* (New York: Riverhead Books, 1996).

Brown, Joseph Epes, *The Spiritual Legacy of the American Indian* (New York: Crossroad, 1991).

Brown, Robert McAfee, *Spirituality and Liberation: Overcoming the Great Fallacy* (Louisville: Westminster, 1988).

Callen, Barry L., *Authentic Spirituality: Moving Beyond Mere Religion* (Grand Rapids: Baker Academic, 2001).

Campbell, Joseph, *The Masks of God: Creative Mythology* (New York: Viking Press, 1968).

Campbell, Joseph, *The Power of Myth* (New York: Doubleday, 1988).

Carter, Stephen L., *The Culture of Disbelief: How American Law and Politics Trivialize Religious Devotion* (BasicBooks/HarperCollins, 1993).

Chittester, Joan, *Heart of Flesh: A Feminist Spirituality for Women and Men* (Grand Rapids: Eerdmans, 1998).

Collins, Kenneth J., (ed.), *Exploring Spirituality: An Ecumenical Reader* (Grand Rapids: Baker, 2000).

Collins, Sheila D., "The Personal is Political", in Charlene Spretnak, ed., *The Politics of Women's Spirituality: Essays on the Rise of Spiritual Power within the Feminist Movement* (Doubleday: Anchor Books, 1982).

Conde-Frazier, Elizabeth, *Crossing the Wilderness and Desert Toward Community: The Spirituality of Research and Scholarship* (Princeton: Princeton University Press, 2000).

Conlon, James, *The Sacred Impulse: A Planetary Spirituality of Heart and Fire* (New York: Crossroad, 2000).

Conn, Joann Wolski, (ed.), *Women's Spirituality: Resources for Christian Development, second edition* (New York: Paulist, 1996).

Cunningham, Lawrence S. and Keith J. Egan, *Christian Spirituality: Themes from the Tradition* (New York: Paulist, 1996).

Davies, Paul, (ed.), *The New Physics* (Cambridge: Cambridge University Press, 1989).

Dorr, Donald, *Divine Energy: God Beyond Us, Within Us, Among Us* (Liguori, Missouri: Triumph Books, 1996).

Ebert, John David, *Twilight of the Clockwork God: Conversations on Science and Spirituality at the End of an Age* (Tulsa, OK: Council Oak Books, 1999).

Eisler, Riane, *The Chalice and the Blade: Our History, Our Future* (New York: Harper and Row, 1987).

Eliade, Mircea, *Myth and Reality* (New York: Harper and Row, 1963).

——, *The Myth of the Eternal Return: Or, Cosmos and History* (Princeton: Princeton University Press, 1954).

——, *The Sacred and the Profane: The Nature of Religion* (New York: Harcourt, Brace & World, 1959).

Ellwood, Robert S., (ed.), *Eastern Spirituality in America: Selected Writings* (New York: Paulist, 1987).

Ford, Michael Thomas, *Paths of Faith: Conversations About Religion and Spirituality* (New York: Simon and Schuster, 2000).

Fox, Matthew, *Creation Spirituality: Liberating Gifts for the Peoples of the Earth* (San Francisco: Harper and Row, 1991).

Gimbutas, Marija, *The Language of the Goddess* (San Francisco: Harper and Row, 1989).

Glynn, Patrick, *God: the Evidence: The Reconciliation of Faith and Reason in a Postsecular World* (Rocklin, California: Prima, 1997).

Herbert, Nick, *Quantum Reality* (London: Rider & Co., 1985).

Hey, Tony, and Patrick Walters, *The Quantum Universe* (Cambridge: Cambridge University Press, 1998).

Holmes, Urban T., *Spirituality for Ministry* (San Francisco: Harper and Row, 1982).

Hyde, Lewis, *The Gift: Imagination and the Erotic Life of Property* (New York: Vintage Books, 1979).

Johnson, Elizabeth A., *She Who Is: The Mystery of God in Feminist Discourse* (New York: Crossroad, 1992).

Jones, Cheslyn, Geoffrey Wainwright, Edward Yarnold, eds., *The Study of Spirituality* (New York: Oxford University Press, 1986).

Kushner, Rabbi Lawrence, *Jewish Spirituality: A Brief introduction for Christians* (Woodstock, Vermont: Jewish Lights Publishing, 2001).

Land, Steven J., *Pentecostal Spirituality: A Passion for the Kingdom* (Sheffield, England: Sheffield Academic Press, 1993).

Lerner, Michael, *The Politics of Meaning: Restoring Hope and Possibility in an Age of Cynicism* (Addison-Wesley, 1996).

Lonergan, Anne, and Caroline Richards, eds., *Thomas Berry and the New Cosmology: In Dialogue with Gregory Baum, James Farris, Stephen Dunn, Margaret Brennan, Caroline Richards, Donald Senior, and Brian Swimme* (Mystic, CN: Twenty-Third Publications, 1987).

Lorimer, David, (ed.), *The Spirit of Science: From Experiment to Experience* (New York: Continuum, 1999).

Lovelock, James, *The Ages of Gaia: A Biography of Our Living Earth* (New York: Bantam, 1988).

Margenau, Henry and Roy Abraham Varghese, eds., *Cosmos, Bios, Theos: Scientists Reflect on Science, God, and the Origins of the Universe, Life, and Homo sapiens* (Chicago: Open Court, 1992).

Markham, Ian, *Spirituality and the World Faiths in The Spiritual Challenge of Health Care*, edited by Mark Cobb and Vanessa Robshaw (Churchill Livingstone, 1998).

McEvoy J.P., and Oscar Zarate, *Introducing Quantum Theory* (Totem Books USA, 1996).

McFague, Sallie, *Models of God: Theology for an Ecological, Nuclear Age* (Philadelphia: Fortress, 1987).

———, *The Body of God: An Ecological Theology* (Minneapolis: Fortress, 1993).

Meehan, Francis X., *A Contemporary Social Spirituality* (Maryknoll, New York: Orbis, 1982).

Mollenkott, Virginia Ramey, *Sensuous Spirituality: Out From Fundamentalism* (New York: Crossroad, 1993).

Nasr, Seyyid Hossein, ed., *Islamic Spirituality, Volume I: Foundations* (New York: Crossroad, 1987).

———, ed., *Islamic Spirituality, Volume II: Manifestations* (New York: Crossroad, 1991).

Newberg, Andrew, M.D., Eugene D'Aquili, M.D. and Vince Rause, *Why God Won't Go Away: Brain Science and the Biology of Belief* (New York: Ballantine Books, 2001).

Nyssa, Gregory of, (c. 330–c. 395), *The Great Catechism of Gregory of Nyssa*.

O'Murchu, Diarmuid, *Quantum Theology: Spiritual Implications of the New Physics* (New York: Crossroad, 1997).

———, *Reclaiming Spirituality: A New Spiritual Framework for Today's World* (New York: Crossroad, 1998).

Palmer, Parker J., *The Active Life: A Spirituality of Work, Creativity, and Caring* (San Francisco: Harper and Row, 1990).

Paris, Peter J., *The Spirituality of African Peoples: The Search for a Common Moral Discourse* (Minneapolis: Fortress Press, 1995).

Puls, Joan, *Spirituality of Compassion* (Mystic, Connecticut: Twenty-Third Publications, 1988).

Rolheiser, Ronald, *Spirituality for a Restless Culture* (Mystic, Connecticut: Twenty-Third Publications, 1991).

———, *The Holy Longing: The Search for a Christian Spirituality* (New York: Doubleday, 1999).

Roof, Wade Clark, *A Generation of Seekers: The Spiritual Journeys of the Baby Boom Generation* (San Francisco: Harper and Row, 1993).

Snyder, Mary Hembrow, ed., *Spiritual Questions for the Twenty-First Century: Essays in Honor of Joan Chittester* (Maryknoll, New York: Orbis, 2001).

Stewart, Carlyle Fielding, III, *Soul Survivors: An African American Spirituality* (Louisville: Westminster, 1997).

Stone, Merlin, *When God Was a Woman* (New York: Harcourt, Brace, Jovanovich, 1976).

Swimme, Brian, and Thomas Berry, *The Universe Story: From the Primordial Flaring Earth to the Ecozoic Era: A Celebration of the Unfolding of the Cosmos* (San Francisco: Harper and Row, 1992).

Swimme, Brian, *The Hidden Heart of the Cosmos: Humanity and the New Story* (Maryknoll, NY: Orbis, 1996).

Teasdale, Wayne, *The Mystic Heart: Discovering a Universal Spirituality in the World's Religions* (Novato, California: New World Library, 1999).

Tickle, Phyllis A., *Re-Discovering the Sacred: Spirituality in America* (New York: Crossroad, 1995).

Toolan, David, *At Home in the Cosmos* (Maryknoll, NY: Orbis, 2001).

Tyson, John R., *Invitation to Christian Spirituality: An Ecumenical Anthology* (New York: Oxford University Press, 1999).

Vandergrift, Nicki Verploegen, *Organic Spirituality: A Sixfold Path for Contemplative Living* (Maryknoll, New York: Orbis, 2000).

Welwood, John, ed., *Ordinary Magic: Everyday Life as Spiritual Path* (Boston: Shambhala, 1992).

Wheatley, Margaret J. *Leadership and the New Science: Learning About Organization from an Orderly Universe* (San Francisco: Berrett-Koehler, 1992).

Winter, Miriam Therese, Adair Lummis, Allison Stokes, *Defecting in Place: Women Claiming Responsibility for Their Own Spiritual Lives* (New York: Crossroad, 1994).

Winter, Miriam Therese, *Songlines: Hymns, Songs, Rounds and Refrains for Prayer and Praise* (New York: Crossroad, 1996).

———, *The Singer and the Song: An Autobiography of the Spirit* (New York: Crossroad, 1999).

Wuthnow, Robert, *After Heaven: Spirituality in America Since the 1950s* (Berkeley: University of California Press, 1998).

Yoshinori, Takeuchi, ed., *Buddhist Spirituality: Indian, Southeast Asian, Tibetan, and Early Chinese* (New York: Crossroad, 1993).

Zohar, Danah, *The Quantum Self: Human Nature and Consciousness Defined by the New Physics* (New York: Quill/William Morrow, 1990).

Zohar, Danah and Ian Marshall, *The Quantum Society: Mind, Physics, and a New Social Vision* (New York: Quill/William Morrow, 1994).

CHAPTER SEVEN

Appleby, R. Scott, (ed.), *Spokesmen for the Despised: Fundamentalist Leaders of the Middle East* (Chicago: University of Chicago Press, 1997).

Armstrong, Karen, *Holy War: The Crusades and Their Impact on Today's World* (New York: Anchor Doubleday Books, 1991).

——, *Muhammad: A Biography of the Prophet* (San Francisco: Harper Collins Publishers, 1992).

Azzam, Sheik Abdullah, *Join the Caravan* (Azzam Publications, 1987).

The Bible, New Revised Standard Version.

Bragg, Rick, *Shaping Young Islamic Hearts and Hatreds* (*New York Times*, October 14, 2001), sec. A, p. 1.

Cantarow, Ellen, "Gush Emunim: The Twilight of Zionism?" *Media Monitors Network* February 27, 2001. http://www.mediamonitors.net/cantarow1.html>. Cited December 18, 2001).

Chapman, Colin, *Whose Promised Land?* (Oxford: Lion Publishing, 1989).

Faraj, Abd al-Salam, *The Neglected Duty*. Translated by Johannes J.G. Jansen, in *The Neglected Duty: The Creed of Sadat's Assassins and the Islamic Resurgence in the Middle East* (New York: MacMillan, 1986).

Full Text of Notes Found After Hijackings (*New York Times*. 29 September 2001. <http://www.nytimes.com/2001/09/29/national/29SFULL-TEXT.html>. Cited December 20, 2001).

Al-Gamei'a, Muhammad, Interview dated October 4, 2001, translated from Arabic by the IMRA (Independent Media Review Analysis) <http://www.imra.org.il/story.php3> (cited December 15, 2001).

Garaudy, Roger, *The Founding Myths of Israeli Politics* (London: Studies Forum, International, 1997).

Girard, René, *I See Satan Fall Like Lightning*. Translated by James G. Williams (Maryknoll, N.Y.: Orbis Books, 2001).

——. *Violence and the Sacred*. Translated by Patrick Gregory (Baltimore: Johns Hopkins University Press, 1977).

Gottwald, Norman K., *The Tribes of Yahweh: A Sociology of the Religion of Liberated Israel, 1250–1050 B.C.E.* (Maryknoll, N.Y.: Orbis Books, 1979).

Guillaume, A., *The Life of Muhammad: A Translation of Ishaq's Sirat Rasul Allah* (London: Oxford University Press, 1955).

Haykal, Muhammad Husayn, *The Life of Muhammad*. Translated by Isma'il Razi A. al-Faruqi. <http://www.witness-pioneer.org/vil/books/MH_LM>. Cited January 3, 2002.

Herzl, Theodor, "The Jewish State". In *The Zionist Idea*, ed., Arthur Hertzberg (New York: Atheneum, 1959), 204–226.

Jabotinsky, Vladimir, "Evidence Submitted to the Palestinian Royal Commission". In Arthur Hertzberg, ed., *The Zionist Idea* (New York: Atheneum, 1959), 559–571.

Juergensmeyer, Mark, *Terror in the Mind of God: The Global Rise of Religious Violence* (Berkeley: University of California Press, 2000).

Kolatt, Israel, *The Zionist Movement and the Arabs*: In Jehuda Reinharz and Anita Shapira, eds., *Essential Papers on Zionism* (New York: New York University Press, 1996), 617–647.

bin Laden, Osama, "Declaration of War Against the Americans Occupying the Land of the Two Holy Places" August 1996. <http://www.azzam.com/html/articlesdeclaration.htm>. Cited December 12, 2001.

——, "Interview Osama bin Laden." May 1998. <http://www.pbs.org/wgbh/pages/frontline/shows/binladen/who/interview.html>. Cited January 2, 2002.

Laquer, Walter, *A History of Zionism* (New York: Schocken Books, 1972).

Lewis, Bernard, *Semites and Anti-Semites: An Inquiry into Conflict and Prejudice* (New York: W.W. Norton, 1999).

al-Mubarakpuri, Saifur Rahman, *The Sealed Nectar: Memoirs of the Noble Prophet*. Translated by Issam Diab. <http://www.witness-pioneer.org/vil/Books/SM_tsn>. Cited January 3, 2002.

The Qur'an, Trans. N.J. Dawood (New York: Penguin Books, 1990).

Qutb, Sayyid. *Social Justice in Islam*. Translated by William E. Shepard, in *Sayyid Qutb and Islamic Activism: A Translation and Critical Analysis of Social Justice in Islam* (Leiden: E. J. Brill, 1996).

Stark, Rodney, *One True God: Historical Consequences of Monotheism* (Princeton: Princeton University Press, 2001).

CHAPTER EIGHT

Agosto, Efrain, *Paul's Use of Greco-Roman Conventions of Commendation* (Ph.D. Dissertation, Boston University, 1996).

——, *Commendation in Paul* in J. Paul Sampley, *Paul in His Greco-Roman World: A Handbook* (Valley Forge, PA: Trinity Press International, forthcoming).

——, *Leadership in the New Testament* (St. Louis: Chalice Press, forthcoming).

Beker, J. Christiaan, *Paul the Apostle: The Triumph of God in Life and Thought* (Philadelphia: Fortress Press, 1980).

Bonilla, Plutarco, *Los milagros tambien son parabolas* (Miami: Editorial Caribe, 1978).

Borg, Marcus, *Jesus A New Vision: Spirit, Culture and the Life of Discipleship* (San Francisco/New York: Harper Collins, 1987).

——, *Meeting Jesus Again for the First Time: The Historical Jesus & the Heart of Contemporary Faith* (San Francisco/New York: Harper Collins, 1994).

Crossan, John Dominic, *The Historical Jesus: The Life of a Mediterranean Jewish Peasant* (San Francisco/New York: Harper Collins, 1991).

——, *Jesus: A Revolutionary Biography* (San Francisco/New York: Harper Collins, 1994).

——, *Who Killed Jesus?: Exposing the Roots of Anti-Semitism in the Gospel Story of the Death of Jesus* (San Francisco: Harper Collins, 1996).

Fitzgerald, John T., *Cracks in an Earthen Vessel: An Examination of the Catalogues of Hardships in the Corinthian Correspondence; SBL Dissertation Series 99* (Atlanta: Scholars Press, 1988).

Horsley, Richard A. and John S. Hanson, *Bandits, Prophets and Messiahs: Popular Movements at the Time of Jesus* (Minneapolis: Seabury/Winston, 1985).

Jewett, Robert, "Paul, Phoebe, and the Spanish Mission," in Jacob Neusner, et al., eds., *The Social World of Formative Christianity & Judaism: Essays in Tribute to Howard Clark Kee* (Philadelphia: Fortress Press, 1988), 142–161.

Schüssler Fiorenza, Elisabeth, *In Memory of Her: A Feminist Theological Reconstruction of Christian Origins* (New York: Crossroad, 1983).

Tamez, Elsa, *The Amnesty of Grace: Justification by Faith from a Latin American Perspective*. Trans. Sharon Ringe (Nashville: Abingdon Press, 1993).

Theissen, Gerd, *Sociology of Early Palestinian Christianity*. Trans. John Bowden (Philadelphia: Fortress Press, 1978).

Thiselton, Anthony, *The Two Horizons: New Testament Hermeneutics and Philosophical Description* (Grand Rapids: Wm. B. Eerdmans, 1980).

Walters, James, "'Phoebe' and 'Junia(s)' – Rom. 16:1–2, 7" in Carroll D. Osburn, *Essays on Women in Earliest Christianity*, vol. I (Joplin, MO: College Press, 1993), 167–190.

CHAPTER NINE

Bakhtin, M. M., *Art and Answerability: Early Philosophical Essays by M. M. Bakhtin*, ed. Michael Holquist and Vadim Liapunov. Trans. Vadim Liapunov (Austin: University of Texas Press, 1990).

Driver, Samuel R., *Notes on the Hebrew Text of the Books of Samuel* (Oxford: Clarendon Press, 1913).

Gunn, David, *The Fate of King Saul* (Sheffield: JSOT Press, 1980).

Fishbane, Michel, *Biblical Text and Texture* (Oxford, England: Oneworld Publications, 1998).

McCarter, P. Kyle, *Samuel*, The Anchor Bible Series, vol. 8 (New York: Doubleday, 1980).

Miscall, Peter, *I Samuel, A Literary Reading* (Bloomington and Indianapolis: Indiana University Press, 1986).

Newsom, Carol, "Bakhtin, the Bible and Dialogic Truth," *Journal of Religion*, 76 (1996).

Noth, Martin, *The Deuteronomistic History* (Sheffield, England: JSOT Press, 1984).

Polzin, Robert, *Samuel and the Deuteronomist* (Bloomington and Indianapolis: Indiana University Press, 1989).

Prickett, Stephen, *Words and the Word* (Cambridge: Cambridge University Press, 1986).

Simon, Uriel, *Reading Prophetic Narrative* (Bloomington and Indianapolis: Indiana University Press, 1997).

Watts, James, *Psalm and Story: Inset Hymns in Hebrew Narrative* (Sheffield, England: JSOT Press, 1992).

Watts, James, *Psalms and Story: Inset Poetry in Hebrew Narrative* (Sheffield: Sheffield Academic Press, 1992).

CHAPTER TEN

Aquinas, Thomas, *Summa Theologiae*. Trans. Thomas Gilby (London: Eyre and Spottiswood, 1975).

Fukuyama, Francis, *The End of History and the Last Man* (New York: Avon Press, 1992).

Gorringe, Timothy J., *Karl Barth. Against Hegemony* (Oxford: Oxford University Press, 1999).

Herzl, Theodor, *The Jewish State* (New York: American Zionist Emergency Council, 1946).

Lochhead, David, *The Dialogical Imperative. A Christian Reflection on Interfaith Encounter* (New York: Orbis Books, 1988).

MacIntyre, Alasdair, *Whose Justice? Which Rationality?* (London: Duckworth, 1988).

Markham, Ian, "World Perspectives and Arguments: Disagreements about Disagreements", *Heythrop Journal*, 30, 1989: 1–12.

——, *Truth and the Reality of God* (Edinburgh: T&T Clark, 1998).

——, 'The Politics of Inclusivity' in *Humanitas. The Journal of the George Bell Institute*, vol. 2, Issue 2, April 2001: 139–156.

——, (ed.), *A World Religions Reader* (Oxford: Blackwell, 2000).

Menand, Louis, *The Metaphysical Club. A Story of Ideas in America* (New York: Farrar, Straus and Giroux, 2001).

Neuhaus, Richard John, *Doing Well Doing Good* (New York: Doubleday, 1991).

Rosen, Jonathan, 'The Uncomfortable Question of Anti-Semitism' in the *New York Times Magazine*, November 4, 2001.

Rousseau, Richard W., (ed.), *Interreligious Dialogue* (Scranton PA: Ridge Row Press, 1981).

Rubenstein, R. L. and John K. Roth (eds.), *Approaches to Auschwitz. The Legacy of the Holocaust* (London: SCM Press, 1987).

Sherbok, Dan Cohn, *The Crucified Jew* (London: Harper Collins, 1992).

Swidler, Leonard, "Ground Rules for Interreligious Dialogue." In Richard W. Rousseau, (ed.), *Interreligious Dialogue* (Scanton, PA: Ridge Row Press, 1981).

CHAPTER ELEVEN

"Images of the Priesthood: An Analysis of Catholic Sermons from the Late Seventeenth Century (Priests and Pastors in Central Europe: 1500–1700)." *Central European History* 33 (1), 2000: 87.

"Library of Congress Documents Reactions to September 11, 2001, Tragedy for Posterity." *News from the Library of Congress*, September 26, 2001.

Documenting the Tragedy: Organizational Documentation Projects. New York State Historical Records Advisory Board, 2001. Accessed November 25, 2001. Web Site. Available from http://www.nyshrab.org/WTC/projects.html.

September 11 Web Archive. webArchivist.org, Internet Archive, and Library of Congress, 2001. Accessed November 25, 2001. Web Site. Available from http://september11.archive.org/.

Nine Eleven History Dot Net. National Museum of American History The Museum of the City of New York, 2001. Accessed November 25, 2001. Web Site. Available from http://www.911history.net/index.htm.

City Lore. City Lore, 2001. Accessed December 11, 2001. Web site. Available from http://www.citylore.org/.

Iowa Department of Cultural Affairs; the American Spirit Project. Iowa Department of Cultural Affairs, 2001. Accessed December 12, 2001. Web site. Available from http://www.culturalaffairs.org/americanspirit.htm.

Ephemeral Studies. Centre for Ephemera Studies, 2001. Accessed December 12, 2001. Web site. Available from http://www.rdg.ac.uk/AcaDepts/lt/main/ephe/centre/stud.html.

Alembi, Ezekiel B., "Telling Tales: The Use of Oral Narratives in Religious Sermons in Kenya," *Folklore*, 13 (2000): 103–110.

Ammerman, Nancy T. "Personal Conversation About Church Attendance." Hartford, December 12, 2001.

Andrew, Donna T., "On Reading Charity Sermons: Eighteenth-Century Anglican Solicitation and Exhortation." *The Journal of Ecclesiastical History*, 43 (4), 1992.

The Association of Theological Schools in the United States and Canada. "Section 4: The Theological Curriculum." In *ATS Accreditation Standards* (Pittsburgh: The Association of Theological Schools in the United States and Canada, 2002).

——. "Standard 5: Library and Information Resources." In *ATS Accreditation Standards* (Pittsburgh: The Association of Theological Schools in the United States and Canada, 2002).

Black, Barbara, "Noah Adams Interviews Barbara Black, Curator of the Somerset County Historical Society." In *All Things Considered;* December 11 (Washington, DC, 2001).

Carlyle, Thomas, "The Hero as Divinity." In *On Heroes, Hero Worship, and the Heroic in History* (London: J. Fraser, 1841).

Cox, Ana Marie, "Paper Trail." *Mother Jones*, 24 (4), 1999.

Dugan, Eileen T., "The Funeral Sermon as a Key to Familial Values in Early Modern Nordlingen." *The Sixteenth Century Journal*, 20 (4), 1989: 631.

Ellis, Bill, "A Model for Collecting and Interpreting World Trade Center Jokes" *New Directions in Folklore*, 5 (1) 2001.

Fentress-Williams, Judy, "The Bible and Dialogue." See chap. 9 in this vol.

Fineberg, Gail, "Panel Chair Briefs Staff on NAS Report" In *Bicentennial Conference on Bibliographic Control for the New Millennium; Confronting the Challenges of Networked Resources and the Web* (Library of Congress Cataloging Directorate, 2000).

Foges, Chris, "Far from Ephemeral (Study of Graphic Ephemera by the Centre for Ephemera Studies, University of Reading)." *Print*, 53 (2), 1999: 164–168.

Graham, M. Patrick, "The Printed Sermon." In Margret Tacke Collins, ed., *Fifty-Fifth Annual Conference of the American Theological Library Association* (Durham, North Carolina: American Theological Library Association, 2001).

Grider, Sylvia, "Preliminary Observations Regarding the Spontaneous Shrines Following the Terrorist Attacks of September 11, 2001." *New Directions in Folklore*, 5 (2001).

Lappin, Todd, "Preserving the Voices of the Twin Towers" *New York Times*, October 11, 2001, 9.

McKinstry, E. Richard, *Ephemera and the Academic Community*. The Ephemera Society of America, 2001. Accessed December 13, 2001. Web page. Available from http://www.ephemerasociety.org/news-academic.html.

Mirapaul, Matthew, "Arts Online; How the Net Is Documenting a Watershed Moment." *New York Times*, October 15, 2001, 2.

O'Donnell, James J., ed., "Library of Congress Staff Briefing." (Washington, D.C.: Library of Congress, 2000).

Organization, Gallup. *Gallup Poll: Religion Indicators*. The Gallup Organization, 2001. Accessed December 2, 2001. Web site. Available from http://www.gallup.com/poll/indicators/indreligion.asp.

Rainie, Lee, and Bente Kalsnes, *The Commons of the Tragedy. How the Internet Was Used by Millions after the Terror Attacks to Grieve, Console, Share News, and Debate the Country's Response*. Pew Internet & American Life Project, October 10, 2001. Accessed November 25, 2001. PDF Document. Available from http://www.pewinternet.org/reports/pdfs/PIP_Tragedy_Report.pdf.

School, Rare Book. *R B S History Course Offerings*. University of Virginia, 2001. Accessed December 13, 2001. Web Site. Available from http://www.virginia.edu/oldbooks/bulletin/history.html#ephemera.

Silva, Alan J., "Increase Mather's 1693 Election Sermon." *Early American Literature*, 34 (1), 1999: 48.

Stone, Richard, "Junk Mail: Printed Ephemera and Preservation of the Everyday." *Journal of Australian Studies*, 99, September 1998.

Weiner, James, "For an Anthropological History of Indigenous Discourse." *Paideusis-JICS/Journal for Interdisciplinary and Cross-Cultural Studies*, 1, 1998.

CHAPTER TWELVE

Lewis, Neil A., "A Nation Challenged: The Senate Hearing; *New York Times*, December 6, 2001.

Niebuhr, Reinhold, *An Interpretation of Christian Ethics* (New York: Meridian Books, 1956).

——, *The Ironies of American History* (New York: Charles Scribner and Sons, 1952).

——, *The Nature and Destiny of Man*, vol. 2 (New York: Charles Scribner and Sons, 1964).

Purdum, Todd S., "Ashcroft's About-Face on the Detainees," *New York Times*, Nov. 26, 2001.

Tillich, Paul, "Yes and No." In Paul Tillich, *The New Being* (New York: Charles Scribner and Sons, 1955).

——, *Love, Power, Justice* (Oxford: Oxford University Press, 1955).

——, *Political Expectation* (Harper and Row, 1971).

INDEX